OUTDOOR LIFE

ARAM VON BENEDIKT
AND THE EDITORS OF *OUTDOOR LIFE*

THE ULTIMATE
BACKCOUNTRY
SURVIVAL MANUAL

weldon**owen**

CONTENTS

001 Get Out There
002 Do Your Homework
003 Know Your Mind
004 Face Your Fear
005 Get Fit for the Challenge
006 Know Your Options

⊘ GEAR

007 Start with the Pack
008 Pick Your Perfect Pack
009 Compare Your Options
010 Get Framed
011 Pack Your Bag
012 Fine-Tune the Fit
013 Pack a Backcountry Med Kit
014 Prepare for Trouble
015 Pack It Right
016 Go It Alone
017 Make It a Party
018 Kid Around
019 Take Shelter
020 Protect Yourself
021 Choose the Right Sleeping Bag
022 Pad Your (S)lumbar
023 Eat Well
024 Supplement Your Snacks
025 (Back)pack Your Meals
026 Horse Pack It
027 Make a Mess
028 BACKCOUNTRY TOOLKIT:
STEEL CANTEEN
029 Cook Over a Campfire
030 Purify Water
031 Savor a Warm Drink

032 Pick Your Ultimate Backcountry Blade
033 Sharpen a Knife
034 Make It a Machete
035 Keep a Headlamp Handy
036 Choose Your Fire Starter
037 Tie It Together
038 Tie a Clove Hitch
039 Follow These GPS Tips
040 Map It Out
041 Carry a Compass
042 *Aram's Adventures* :
PACKTRAIN WRECK!
043 **TRUE** *Story*: Be Sure of Your Horse
044 Get the Right Clothing
045 Live in Long Johns
046 Dress for the Season
047 Cover Your Head
048 Glove Up
049 Wear the Best Hat
050 BACKCOUNTRY TOOLKIT:
TRASH BAG
051 Break In Your Boots
052 Find the Right Footwear
053 Layer in Luxury
054 BACKCOUNTRY TOOLKIT: **WILD RAG**
055 Keep in Touch
056 Consider a Camera
057 Keep a Charge
058 Take Notes
059 Go Minimalist
060 BACKCOUNTRY TOOLKIT:
MULTI-TOOL
061 Pack like a Caveman
062 Pack in on Horseback

063 Send Yourself (Horse)packing

064 Meet Your Mount

065 Get the Gear

066 Hang a Rifle Scabbard on Your Horse

067 Make a Wool Blanket Gun Case

068 Set Up Your Saddle Horse

069 Pack Your Horse

070 Bring Your Best Friend (or Not)

071 Bring Your Bear Wear

072 Load Up for Bear

073 Avoid this Northern Exposure

074 Hunt Up the Right Gear

075 Go Backcountry Bowhunting

076 Go Bird Hunting

077 Go Old School

078 Know Why You Should Hunt the Backcountry

079 Gear Up to Make Meat

080 Be Gun Safe

081 Go Fish

082 Pack the Ideal Backcountry Fishing Kit

083 Look for Bait

084 BACKCOUNTRY TOOLKIT: **FISHING LINE**

085 **TRUE** *Story*: Carry a Compass

086 Build a Rifle Scabbard

087 Pack a Backcountry Repair Kit

088 Repair Wear and Tear

089 Stash It for Later

CONTENTS

🔥 SKILLS

090	Rig Your Vehicle
091	Always Be Courteous
092	Pocket the Essentials
093	Plan Your Route
094	Estimate Travel Speed
095	Bushwhack a New Trail
096	Read a Topo Map
097	Line Up
098	Comprehend the Colors
099	Measure the Distance
100	Read the Landscape
101	Cross a Creek
102	Watch Your Backtrail
103	Scout with Google Earth
104	Watch Out for Big Storms
105	Weather the Weather
106	Handle Horse Fear
107	Know Your Horse
108	*Aram's Adventures* : **CAUGHT IN LIGHTNING**
109	Gear Up
110	Saddle a Packhorse
111	Hobble Your Horse
112	Use a Halter for Control
113	Give Your Horse a Bridle
114	Learn the Rules of Horsepacking
115	Throw a Diamond Hitch
116	Get Loaded
117	Play Follow the Leader
118	Lead a Pack
119	Loop Your Leadrope
120	Give Your Horse a Stake for Dinner
121	Ride a Horse Right
122	Stay Safe in the Saddle
123	Spur 'Em On
124	Carry a Rifle on Horseback

125 Shoot from Horseback
126 Bring Your Bow
127 Let Your Horse "Blow"
128 Ride an Obstacle Horse
129 Know Where You're Going
130 Cut a Walking Stick
131 Fix Your Feet
132 Tough Out the Trail
133 Pack Some Iron
134 Keep Your Barrel Clean and Dry
135 Make a Bivy Camp
136 Save Your Strength
137 Bring the Bivy Basics
138 Build a Base Camp
139 Tie the Knot
140 Twirl Up a Bowline
141 Tie a Butterfly Knot
142 Make a Rope Tackle
143 Whip Finish a Rope End
144 Start a Tough Fire
145 Carve a Feather Stick
146 Collect Pitch Pine
147 Start a Bowdrill Fire
148 Try Using Your Hands
149 Find the Perfect Site
150 Rig a Tarp Shelter
151 Build an Emergency Shelter
152 Make a Rock Grommet
153 Find Water in the Wilderness
154 Drink Deep
155 Dispose of Waste
156 Avoid Bad-Water Bugs
157 Catch Fish by Hand
158 Build a Fish Trap

159 Set a Trotline
160 Sneak and Peek for Spooky Trout
161 Clean Your Catch
162 Cook Caveman Style
163 Find Camp in the Dark
164 Don't Trash the Backcountry
165 Care for Your Horses
166 Beware Bears
167 Steer Clear of Snakes
168 Be Wolf Wary
169 Watch Out for Bugs
170 Avoid Rut Rage
171 Fight Off a Lion
172 Beware Careless Companions
173 **TRUE** *Story*: Escape a Big Cat's Reach
174 Master Shooting Positions
175 Shoot with Your Pack On
176 Train with Your Rifle
177 Fix a Bow on the Fly
178 Repair a Dropped Rifle
179 Use Your Senses
180 Find a Good Vantage Point
181 Hunt a Midday Nap
182 Cape Your Trophy
183 Bring Weed-Free Feed
184 Skin and Quarter Game
185 Be a Backcountry Meat Packer
186 Horsepack Your Meat
187 Try These Tricks
188 Backpack Your Meat
189 Care for Your Cape
190 Get Some All-American Ivory
191 Choose Your Trophy Style
192 Try Tenderloin

CONTENTS

⏏ SURVIVAL

193 | Be a Field Medic
194 | Care for a Cut
195 | Handle Severe Bleeding
196 | Clean a Wound Right
197 | Know When to Go
198 | Treat a Burn
199 | Prevent Mountain Sickness
200 | Avoid Altitude Sickness
201 | Handle HACE
202 | Save Your Lungs
203 | Be Vigilant
204 | Reset a Dislocation
205 | Take Care of a Break
206 | Make a Break for It
207 | Survive Food Poisoning
208 | Quit Bellyaching
209 | Evaluate and Evacuate

210 | Address Internal Injury
211 | Tame an Earache
212 | Don't Be an Eyesore
213 | Evade the Tooth Fairy
214 | Assist a Choking Victim
215 | Treat Serious Male Trauma
216 | Don't Mix Bears and Blood
217 | Deal with Female Issues
218 | Become a Horse Mechanic
219 | Be a Medic to Your Mount
220 | Sew Your Horse Up
221 | Spot the Signs of Hypothermia
222 | Come In from the Cold
223 | Care for Frostbite
224 | Escape the Trenches
225 | **TRUE** *Story*: Avoid Hypothermia
226 | Dismount in an Emergency
227 | Live Through a Flash Flood
228 | Don't Get Thunderstruck
229 | Prevent Heat Illness
230 | Handle Heat
231 | Treat the Trick Killer
232 | *Aram's Adventures* : MOOSE CONFRONTATION
233 | Doctor an Animal Bite
234 | Handle Scorpion Stings
235 | Avoid Eight-Legged Enemies
236 | **TRUE** *Story*: Chewed On By a Bear
237 | Get Your Bearings
238 | Signal for Help
239 | Stay Put or Hike Out
240 | Build a Crutch
241 | Find a Lost Buddy
242 | Pull Through Panic

243   Survive an Avalanche

244   Build a Duff Bed

245   Sleep Inside a Fresh Hide

246   Crawl into a Carcass

247   Sleep Like a Hobo

248   Be a Backcountry Pharmacist

249   Use Some Yarrow

250   Pick a Plantain

251   Make Use of Mullein

252   Wield a Willow

253   Try Stinging Nettle

254   Eat Bear Root

255   Pick These Plants (to Eat)

256   Bark Up the Right Tree

257   Eat Some Insects

258   Eat Your Horse

259   Pray for Help

260   Carve a Fish Hook

261   Knap a Stone Knife

262   Make Wilderness Jerky

263   Unhook a Fish (You)

264   Tie It All Together

265   Tie a Slipknot

266   Make a Blood Knot

267   Learn the Prusik Knot

268   Tie the Sheet Bend

GO FORTH AND CONQUER!

FINALLY, A PROPER GUIDE TO THE WILDERNESS . . .

It might be said of modern humans that we like the idea of wilderness better than we like the reality of it.

Our literature swells with praises singing the benefits of wild places—as a restorative for the psychically bruised, as a quiet balm for the sensorily overloaded, and as a place of reconnection and meaning for the morally bankrupt.

But plop a backcountry poet down in Montana's Bob Marshall Wilderness, or Utah's high and craggy Uinta Mountains, or almost anywhere north of Edmonton, Alberta, or in rural Africa, and their praises of the wild turn into wide-eyed fear and worry. Wilderness sounds grand on paper (and in lower-case letters), but real Wilderness (in caps) is a place that bites. It is, by definition, remote, hard, and lonesome. There are few resources at your disposal, or comforts that you don't pack on your own back.

You need a guide to experience its larger lessons, but also to get you out of it healthy and alive so that you can continue to extol its virtues.

Your guide to these wild places is Aram von Benedikt, the author of this useful, practical, and occasionally transcendent primer on backcountry survival.

You are in capable hands. Aram is one of the most experienced and authentic backcounty wanderers I know. He accumulated his knowledge the right and hard way: by spending time in places that reward self-sufficiency and punish the unprepared. He is a receptive and good student, and a wonderfully patient and expressive teacher. It speaks volumes about Aram's mettle and his priorities that he still lives very close to the backcountry, in remote southern Utah.

It's there where he is raising a family and horses, where he hikes and hunts and hones the skills that he dispenses in this book. If I were to enter the backcountry with anyone, it would be with Aram, knowing that has the right perspectives, skills, and gear to allow me to enjoy the experience, and come out the other side with a renewed sense of vigor and appreciation for wild places.

Who knows, I might even pen a poem about the restorative powers of the wilderness. That's sort of what Aram has done here, only it's disguised in very practical and understandable lessons for anyone who enters, and exits, the wild and wonderful backcountry of North America.

Come along with him, and you'll emerge from the backcountry happy, healthy, and wiser for the lessons that Aram, and the wilderness he loves, have taught you.

ANDREW MCKEAN
Editor-in-Cheif, *Outdoor Life*

EVERY PERSON, BEFORE THEY DIE, SHOULD HEAR THE BUGLE OF A BULL ELK, LISTEN TO THE HAUNTING BAY OF A LION HOUND, AND THRILL TO THE SOUND OF WILD GEESE.

You haven't truly lived until you have slept beneath the stars, eaten fresh meat roasted over an open backcountry fire, or had a brush with death.

I still remember the first time my brother and I headed into the "backcountry" to camp. We hiked all of three-quarters of a mile out behind our house, set up a little spring-bar tent, ate some ramen noodles, and bedded down for the night. Then, a few minutes later, an angus bull began growling in the distance, letting all the world know that he was the biggest, baddest thing in the woods, and very willing to prove it. Chills ran up and down our preteen spines, and we thought of home. And then another bull tuned in; the pair made a duet of bone-chilling growls which echoed through the black night. We packed our bags and scampered home.

Nearly three decades have passed since that first excursion. I've spent a good number of those years in backcountry settings; I'm much more comfortable in the wilderness than I am in a city—I find heavy traffic and fancy suits far more fearful than bears or bad trails.

I have my father to thank for instilling basic skills in me, as well as a great desire for self-sufficiency. He encouraged me to learn woodsmanship, horsemanship, farming, and blacksmithing. He arranged for me to study saddlemaking, horsepacking, cowboying, and bootmaking. I got to hold a lasso-rope, traditional bow, and rifle in my hands before I was knee-high to a short frog. I worked in the garden, kept honeybees, and drove a team of Belgian draft horses.

When I was 14, I helped an old lady pack for a move to another town. When I dragged several water-stained boxes from the musty crawlspace under her singlewide I discovered pure gold: years' worth of old *Outdoor Life* magazines. She directed me to throw them out; somehow I stammered my way through a request to keep them. It was granted, and I spent many winter hours poring over those old issues, the fire inside me fueled by every story. Thus began my infatuation with one of the greatest magazines ever printed. When Editor-in-Chief Andrew McKean asked me to write this book, I was purely honored.

This book contains the most important tips and techniques on gear choice, backcountry skills, and wilderness survival that I personally know. It's just the tip of the iceberg, which is enchanting and dismaying at the same time. There are scenarios and environments that we simply didn't have the room for. Furthermore, there are skills that I don't know, experiences I haven't had. I'm far from perfect, or expert, or perfectly expert. The wilderness is a capable teacher, and I strive to be an apt student—and so should you.

My hope is that you will benefit from the ramblings of my pen, and perhaps catch a little of the backcountry fire, too. In this age of smartphones, the internet, and instant gratification, we've gotten separated from the heartstrings of the earth—the smell of wood smoke, meat sizzling over an open fire, thirst and hunger, dried blood on our hands, and hard work. We need to return, every so often, and reconnect. To the feel of the wind on our faces, a horse between our knees, the pain of pack straps biting into our shoulders. To the earth. To the wilderness. To God.

May you load your gear, shrug into your pack or swing aboard your horse, and turn your face to the wind. Luck willing, you and I will meet each other someday, out there in the backcountry.

ARAM VON BENEDIKT
Author

001 GET OUT THERE

What is the backcountry? This question needs asking—especially if you're thinking of venturing there. I've lived my life there, and I'm more comfortable in the wilderness than I would be in downtown New York City. That might be the toughest "backcountry" experience for me: I'd be as nervous as the average city dweller is camped at 10,000 feet (3,000 m), listening to trout splashing and thinking about bears as a bull elk screams his eerie bugle into the darkness.

To some, the backcountry is incredibly remote, reached by bush plane. To others, it's anywhere they can't take their car. Most folks fall somewhere in between. The backcountry is a place that requires effort and dedication to reach—weary hikes, placing one tired foot after the other, or hours on end rubbing sores on your backside while sitting on a horse. It's a place mostly unchanged by mankind, where nature and wildlife still follow their natural cycles. It's where we go to regain balance and recover from the unnatural stresses that society places upon us. When we emerge again, we're exhausted by our efforts, especially if we've packed loads of savory meat—high country treasure—out on our backs. But we're refreshed by all that we've seen and done.

Wilderness is another term I loosely throughout this book. U.S. government agencies designate wilderness areas—protected places where any motorized item (even a chainsaw) is prohibited. To me, wilderness means much more; it's a place without cell phone coverage, modern amenities, or vehicular access. It's where you must depend on your own strength, wits, and resourcefulness, instead of smartphones or tech skills, to survive. It's a place synonymous with backcountry, wild living, and wild lands.

This book is full of tips, tactics, and techniques to help stay comfortable and safe in the backcountry, from alpine territory in the far north to the deserts of the southwest. They'll make you a better woodsman even if you never venture deeper than your own backyard. Most of all, I hope that this volume will motivate those of you who still have a little kid inside dreaming of exploring new, exciting, and even dangerous places. Maybe you're a veteran whitetail hunter dreaming of forging into the Rocky Mountains in pursuit of bugling bull elk. Perhaps you just love to see what is around the next bend in the trail, or over the crest of the next ridge. Maybe you fantasize about catching high-country trout from a stream so remote that only bears fish there. To those—you know who you are—this book is for you. May you find what you are searching for.

002 DO YOUR HOMEWORK

A good level of skill in certain areas will serve you well in any backcountry—or front country—setting. Wilderness first aid, navigation, and horse handling are examples of skills that you should invest the time and commitment to master.

PRACTICE MEDICINE Take a course such as Wilderness First Responder (WFR) training from an institution such as NOLS (National Outdoor Leadership School). This is a ten-day intensive class on backcountry first aid. You'll learn how to deal with almost anything that you would encounter in a backcountry

setting, ranging from altitude sickness to tick bites.

BECOME A NAVIGATOR Siri is going to have to take a back seat on this adventure. Excellent courses on map, compass, and navigation are available from schools such as BOSS (Boulder Outdoor Survival School). You'll learn to get from point A to point B, without asking your smartphone.

GET ON HORSEBACK Suppose your guide gets hurt when you are deep on a backcountry excursion. What then?

Can you handle the horse string, load the packhorses, and get everyone to safety? Find a good local school that teaches horse handling (preferably western style) and study up. The skills you gain will serve you well, even if nothing ever goes wrong.

003 KNOW YOUR MIND

In a survival situation, what is your most valuable asset or tool? Your wits. No matter how tough, savvy, or skilled you are, if your mind quits working and panic sets in, you will die. But keep your wits standing firm on the front line of battle, and you can survive almost anything.

STAY IN CONTROL The best way to survive in the backcountry—or better yet, thrive—is to stay in control of your situation. Having the mental strength, physical skills, and wilderness knowledge to keep your self in a good situation and out of trouble is key.

GET THE KNOW-HOW Learn how to be comfortable in the backcountry. Study tips, tactics, and techniques for wilderness living. Learn about edible plants, study how to deal with unruly weather, memorize navigation techniques. When the chips are down the only manual you will have will be in your mind.

PRACTICE SKILLS Reading books is great. But can you build a bowdrill fire, find drinkable water, or tie an important knot when you are cold, hungry, and scared? You need to practice: Build that fire, boil that water, and tie that knot until the skills are firmly ingrained in mind and muscle.

TRAIN YOURSELF The best way to prepare your wits for the wilderness is to immerse yourself a little at a time in the backcountry. Begin in your backyard. Master the skills. Then

camp out, gradually getting more and more remote. Train your mind to stay strong and meet every challenge with confidence.

ADAPT TO EVENTS Sometimes dire circumstances are unavoidable. Altitude sickness, vicious weather, and angry bears can strike without warning. Study this book, practice the skills, and train your mind. When catastrophe does strike, you'll be prepared to survive.

004 FACE YOUR FEAR

It's a great idea to practice before going alone into the backcountry. Being alone, miles from the nearest road, can be intimidating and even scary. Here's how to prepare for the challenge.

STEP 1 Organize your gear. Learn how everything you're bringing works and where it lives in your pack.

STEP 2 Bivvy in your backyard. Pitch your tent, lay out your sleeping bag and your pad, cook a meal on your pocket rocket stove, and spend the night getting used to your gear.

STEP 3 Bivvy out for a weekend. Hike a mile or two from the nearest road and spend a couple nights. Turn your phone off—it won't work in most backcountry settings anyway. Enjoy the solitude.

STEP 4 If you've managed the previous steps, congratulations; you're ready for the backcountry.

005 GET FIT FOR THE CHALLENGE

The backcountry demands fitness. You don't have to be young, or be a marathon runner or body builder. You do, however, need to be able to hike long distance with a full-size pack on your shoulders.

PREPARE EARLY Begin preparing physically months before your trip. Walk, run, or ride a bicycle. Progress to carrying a pack while you walk or run. If your trip includes horseback travel spend regular time in the saddle.

TEST YOURSELF Honestly evaluate your performance: Do you feel healthy and strong? Do you have any joint or tendon problems that might affect your performance? If necessary, modify your adventure to suit your ability.

ENDURE ALTITUDE Many times I've told people who dwell at low elevations that, if they can run a mile (1.6 km) there, they can walk the same distance at 10,000 feet (3,000 m). It's a fact. The air is thin way up yonder; just walking can put a whuppin' on a fit flatlander. Plan to arrive early at your jump-off destination, and spend several days acclimating to the elevation. The body has an amazing ability to adjust, and three days will make a huge difference. As a bonus, you'll be less susceptible to altitude illness.

006 KNOW YOUR OPTIONS

Whether you have your backcountry adventure handled by an outfitter, set up a camp, or do it all yourself, your experience will be very different based on each choice. Let's break down the options.

	WHAT TO EXPECT	PROS	CONS	BOTTOM LINE
Do It Yourself	The ultimate backcountry experience. You'll have to research, plan, and execute the adventure yourself entirely. You'll need strength, skill, and mental fortitude to pull this off. When you're done you will feel like you've won a battle.	Satisfaction, education, and experience come during a DIY adventure. Solitude will be yours. Hunt, fish, and hike as you choose. When you harvest an elk or land a trout you can honestly say "I got this myself, in the backcountry."	The work—and there is a lot—is all yours. You'll have pack, plan, and prepare yourself. If you're lucky enough to harvest an animal, you'll have to pack it out yourself. Safety is a concern, especially solo.	If you truly want to experience backcountry you should earn its rewards, rather than purchasing them. But it'll be tough. You'll have to meet challenges that you've never faced.
Drop Camp	An outfitter will pack you, your gear, and a comfortable camp to a pre-determined area, and back out when you leave. Occasionally the outfitter will provide a camp cook or horse wrangler.	Outfitted camps usually have amenities like wall tents, a wood stove, and basic camp kitchen to help you be comfy. You won't have carry 300 pounds (136 kg) of elk meat out on your back after a successful hunt.	Once they drop you off, you're on your own, and you're tied to one area. You can't pick up and move to a more game- or fish-rich area.	If you've got a couple grand to spend and limited tolerance for roughing it, (but still want some DIY in the experience) this might be your best option.
Full-Service Outfitter	From arrival to departure, your basic needs will be met. An outfitter will pack you and your gear into a backcountry camp, provide a guide, prepare your meals, and care for any meat harvested.	Comfy camp, and good food and company, are common. The outfitter and guide are likely experienced and capable at backcountry living. Hunting or fishing success is likely—your guide will do most of the hard work for you.	The comforts are great, but you lose out on the backcountry experience. Strength, self-reliance, or resourcefulness can't be bought. A good outfitter can become a lifelong friend. The wrong one can be a nightmare.	If you like being pampered, have money to spare, and are limited physically, an outfitter is a great option. Research potential outfitters thoroughly before booking.

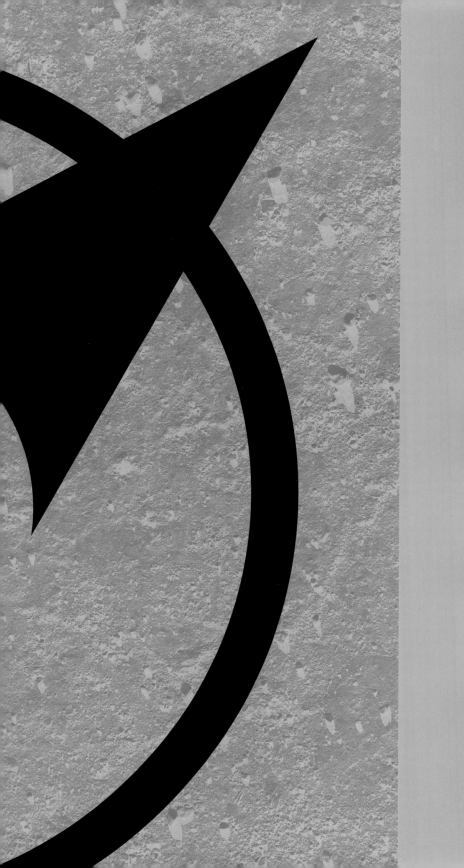

GEAR

SOMETIMES I PAUSE ON A MOUNTAINSIDE

with hundreds of strenuous feet below me, and hundreds more to climb. At those times, I contemplate the contents of my pack, and marvel that I can actually carry such a lightweight home on my back, and even hunt with it strapped to my shoulders all day long.

The equipment available to modern adventurers is nothing short of marvelous. Think about it; a bed that weighs less than a chihuahua yet will keep you warm in the snow. A tent that folds to almost nothing but is strong enough to withstand heavy wind. And so on.

This first chapter details the equipment you'll need to stay warm, dry, and healthy in the wilderness. Read it, study it, and then get the best gear you can afford. When you go shopping, take your time, try on everything from boots to backpack, figure out what you like, and then lay your hard-earned money down. Good equipment lasts for years, and won't fail you when the chips are down.

007 START WITH THE PACK

Packs come in two main styles, top-loading, and back or panel loading. Both are good; follow your preferences when choosing a specific model. You will also have to choose between internal and external frames (see item 010). Every serious pack has certain features in common—here's how to get the most out of them.

TOP (OR LID) This caps the opening of a top-loading pack, and usually has several small pockets to stow small or valuable items. Some top lids can be removed and used as a lumbar pack.

LOAD-LIFTER STRAPS These help balance your load. Adjust them so that the angle between the top of the shoulder strap and its attachment point on the pack is roughly 45 degrees.

DRAWSTRING(S) Used to close up the top of your pack before buckling the top back into place.

LOOPS Also called brackets or daisy chains, attach small objects to the outside of your pack with these.

POCKETS Varying sizes and locations can make for easy storage while on backcountry trips.

SHOULDER STRAPS Adjust to fit comfortably around the tops of your shoulders.

CHEST (OR STERNUM) STRAP Adjust in or out for comfort.

COMPRESSION STRAPS Use these to shape and compress your load.

LOWER STABILIZER STRAPS Tighten to balance your load.

SLEEPING BAG COMPARTMENT The place to put your backcountry bedding.

WAIST (OR HIP) BELT Should comfortably cradle your iliac crest (hip bones). The belt's top edge should sit about 1.5 inches (3.8 cm) above the top of the iliac crest.

GEAR

008 PICK YOUR PERFECT PACK

Carefully consider every element of the trip when choosing a pack. Will you spend a quick night in the woods, or are you going out for an extended backcountry stay? Any chance you'll be called on to pack heavy loads, such as elk or moose quarters? Is the terrain rugged or gentle? Are you going afoot or on horseback? What about weather?

SIZE IT Pack size or capacity is most often noted in cubic inches (C.I.) or liters. Get a pack that will carry what you need for your trip and no more.

Human nature dictates that if there is extra room in your pack you will find something to fill it. Funny thing—that tends to make your pack heavy.

GO BIG If you expect to be carrying a big, bulky, or heavy load, check out an external frame pack. Remove the pack from the frame to strap on a big load.

GET A HORSE Carrying any pack at all while riding a horse is a bad idea—it'll upset your balance and if you get into a situation where agility is needed, you'll

be clumsy. Instead, put your gear on the pack horse and let him carry it. If you absolutely have to wear something on your back while riding, make it a small daypack that doesn't hinder you.

MIND THE WEATHER Backpacks aren't affected by hypothermia or heatstroke. The only real effect that weather should have on your pack choice is the need to carry extra gear for cold or wet conditions. Get slightly more capacity if you expect inclement weather during your adventure.

009 COMPARE YOUR OPTIONS

Choose a pack based on the size you need and the nature of your excursion. Compare them all with this chart and see what your best options will be.

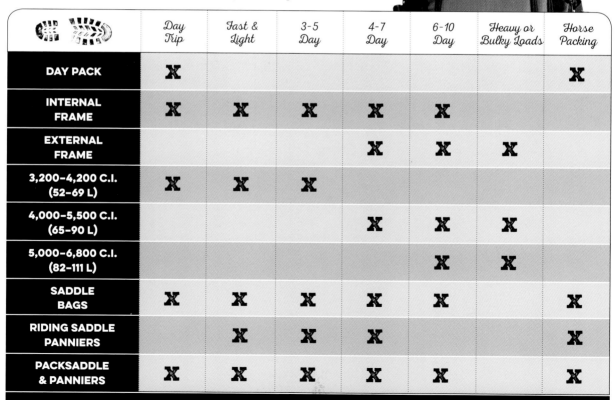

	Day Trip	Fast & Light	3-5 Day	4-7 Day	6-10 Day	Heavy or Bulky Loads	Horse Packing
DAY PACK	X						X
INTERNAL FRAME	X	X	X	X	X		
EXTERNAL FRAME				X	X	X	
3,200–4,200 C.I. (52–69 L)	X	X	X				
4,000–5,500 C.I. (65–90 L)				X	X	X	
5,000–6,800 C.I. (82–111 L)					X	X	
SADDLE BAGS	X	X	X	X	X		X
RIDING SADDLE PANNIERS		X	X	X			X
PACKSADDLE & PANNIERS	X	X	X	X	X		X

010 GET FRAMED

There are two main pack designs. One is suited for the fast, light mountain hunter, backcountry camper, or climber. The other is ideal for a hard core wilderness packer who carries big, heavy, or awkward loads (think moose quarters).

GO INTERNAL Popular among the majority of backcountry adventurers, an internal frame pack does every job great except carrying huge or heavy loads— think over 100 pounds (45 kg)—and some can do a fair backcountry job of that too. This design has a pack, stays, panels, and suspension system integrated together to form an internal frame pack. For most backcountry adventures, this pack is the way to go.

KEEP IT OUTSIDE You'll find external frame packs adorning the broad shoulders of hunting and mountaineering guides who routinely have to carry big heavy loads. The suspension system, pack, pockets, and everything else attaches to an external frame. Typically, when they're carrying very heavy or bulky loads, the pack is removed and the frame alone is used. External frame packs are usually very comfortable, though they are also somewhat noisier than an internal frame pack. If you anticipate packing elk or moose quarters on a fairly regular basis, shrug your shoulders into an external frame pack. Hopefully they're broad—if not, they will be by the time you're finished hauling that huge feast home.

011 PACK YOUR BAG

At the heart of every backcountry setup are ten basic items. These create a foundation to keep you safe, comfortable, and oriented while you are in the wilderness. Keep in mind these items should be high quality. Your life may depend on them.

1 TENT An ultra-light three- or four-season tent.

2 BACKPACK This is where it all starts—the right pack makes all the difference. Look for a comfortable, lightweight internal-frame pack.

3 SLEEPING PAD Ultra compact inflatable pads make sleeping much more comfortable.

4 MAP & COMPASS Electronics can fail. Be sure you have a compass and topo map of your area, and know how to use them.

5 COOKSET All you need to pack are a compact stove with fuel, titanium pot, and titanium spork.

6 WATER PURIFICATION This might be tablets, drops, or a small mechanical purifier.

7 CANTEEN Use a stainless Klean Kanteen; boil water in it to purify.

8 FIRE STARTER Both a weatherproof lighter and waterproof matches.

9 HEADLAMP Bring a compact LED light & extra batteries.

10 SLEEPING BAG You'll want a zero-degree down bag with watertight shell.

012 FINE-TUNE THE FIT

Correctly adjusting your backpack is essential to having a comfortable trip. Here are four steps to getting it right.

STEP 1 Remove the panel or stay(s) from your pack (if it is an internal frame pack) and adjust them to fit the contour of your back—have a buddy help you and stand in a normal posture. Replace.

STEP 2 Adjust the distance between shoulder straps and hip belt. Shoulder straps should curve comfortably around your shoulders and the hip belt should nestle comfortably over your iliac crest, better known as your hip bone.

STEP 3 Buckle your chest strap snugly, adjusting throughout the day for optimum comfort.

STEP 4 Balance the load using your load distribution and load lifter straps. Adjust as necessary during your trek.

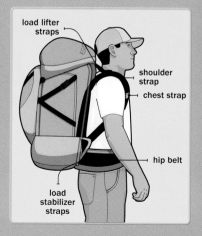

load lifter straps

shoulder strap

chest strap

hip belt

load stabilizer straps

013 PACK A BACKCOUNTRY MED KIT

Backcountry medicine at its finest is, of course, prevention. Good judgment and common sense have circumvented many a disaster before it occurred. But occasionally bad stuff happens, so you'd better carry the basic tools necessary to deal with a wilderness disaster. Here's what you should have in your kit. Keep it small and lightweight.

1 IBUPROFEN "Vitamin I" is likely the most used of all backcountry meds. Treat soreness, injuries, colds, fever, inflammation, and so on.

2 DUCT TAPE Number two in the "most used" column. Treat blisters, create bandages, fix splints, and more. Good for performing first aid on ailing equipment as well.

3 PARACORD This will probably live elsewhere in your pack, but is great first aid material. Sling an arm, build a splint, or fashion a tourniquet.

4 BANDAGES If you're clumsy with your knife or you have an unfortunate encounter with a stick, rock, bear, or other thing, you'll need bandages.

5 COLD MEDS Stock up on some decongestants, cough drops, Nyquil, or the nondrowsy Dayquil.

6 ANTIBIOTICS Meet with your doctor and request a broad-spectrum oral antibiotic to have on hand should you develop an infection.

7 NEOSPORIN Works wonders on sores, boils, scratches, and more.

8 NEEDLES A good tool for draining bad blisters, extracting slivers, and warding off grizzlies.

9 STERI-STRIPS Keep these handy along with some Benzoin ointment; they're especially great for closing small wounds.

10 PERSONAL MEDS This is a big one. Have all personal meds (blood pressure, heart, diabetes, and so on) in the medical kit. Have a spare set in your truck or base camp.

11 HIGH-ALTITUDE MEDS If you're a flatlander headed for altitudes above 8,000 feet, consider meeting with your doctor and requesting prophylactic and/or treatment meds for altitude illness.

12 TWEEZERS Good for pulling splinters and plucking eyebrows.

13 MEDICAL TAPE This fabric tape is great for bandaging, splinting, supporting sprained joints, protecting injuries, and so on.

015 PACK IT RIGHT

A well-loaded pack carries your things comfortably and balances well. A poorly loaded pack will turn you into an uncomfortable and off-balance grouch. Here are your rules for packing right.

Keep heavy items high and/or forward in the pack. Load bulky, lightweight items low or rearward. Pack tiny items in top, side, back, or hip pockets. This will keep them organized and readily accessible. If you have small stuff to put into the main pack organize it into gallon Ziploc bags and then load it.

An example of the above rules: Stuff your sleeping bag (A) (light and bulky) into the very bottom of your pack. Fill your hydration bladder (B) (heavy) and insert into its pocket in your pack (located high and forward). Add your tent and poles (C), cooking kit (D), and food (E) (medium-heavy) forward in the pack, holding them in place with sleeping pad (F), clothing (G), or freeze-dried food (H) (medium-light). Next, load your Klean Kanteen (I) into your pack, held forward by your jacket (J) (medium-light). Finish up with whatever smaller items (K), clothing (L), and medical supplies (M) that you want readily accessible, on top of the load. Tighten the drawstring. Fold the top over and secure it down.

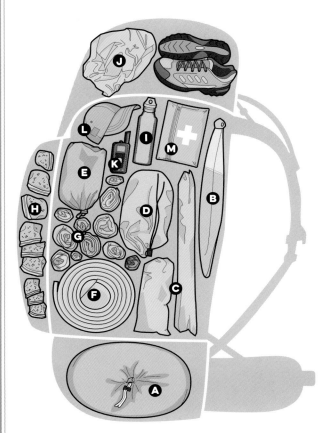

014 PREPARE FOR TROUBLE

Until a few years ago, disaster in the backcountry had to be dealt with in the backcountry. A broken leg was bad; a head injury or heart attack meant desperate evacuation efforts. Solo adventurers who met with misfortune often simply died. Not so any more.

CALL FOR HELP Satellite phones connect via, well, satellite, enabling full communication from the most remote settings. As long as you have a clear view of the sky, you can talk and text all you want (and spoil that backcountry feeling); if disaster strikes, an urgent call to rescue personnel (including injury information and GPS coordinates) will have a helicopter on its way in minutes. Sat-phones can be rented on a daily or weekly basis. They aren't cheap, but they're worth every penny.

GET SPOTTED Satellite Personal Trackers (SPOTs) don't offer the talk-and-text capabilities of a sat-phone, but their greatest feature is an S.O.S. button: once activated, it alerts the nearest rescue facility that you have a life-threatening emergency and need immediate evacuation. Even if you're injured and barely functioning, you just remove the cover and push the S.O.S. button.

SPOTs also allow you to send preprogrammed messages, letting people know that you're okay or need help with a non-emergency situation. They can also send your location to pre-chosen individuals on a regular basis. Someone will always know where you are and you can see your route after a trip. The units are not terribly expensive, require a yearly subscription, are lightweight, and provide substantial peace of mind.

To experience the backcountry at its finest, you should go solo. It's the most challenging thing many of us will ever do. It's dangerous. It's lonely. It's spectacular.

BEWARE OF DANGER The backcountry is not particularly dangerous so long as you respect it. You're far more likely to be in a car accident three miles from your house than to get hurt while soloing in the wilderness. But if you suffer injury, help is a long way off. Break a leg and you're in real trouble. In the best-case scenario you will have a satellite phone or a SPOT beacon (see item 014), and you'll have a great aerial view of the country as a helicopter lifts you to safety. At the worst, you'll have to splint your leg, stay healthy, and forage enough food to keep you alive until you can walk (which could take three to five weeks) or till help finds you.

HANDLE SOLITUDE Being alone is an amazing feeling. But it can also be incredibly frightening. That's why it is very important to practice being alone in the backcountry; introduce yourself to solitude a little at a time. Start small, then go big. Learn to relish it and you'll love being on your own out in the backcountry.

PLAN SMART There's a big difference between challenging yourself and simply endangering your life. Don't be afraid to push your limits—but don't be a fool about it, either. Have judgment good enough to end your trip early if dangerous weather, illness, or other problems develop. Have a route planned and give your itinerary to a responsible person. Should you end up late emerging from the backcountry, help will know where to look for you.

017 MAKE IT A PARTY

Heading into the backcountry with your buddies can be a fine way to enjoy a wilderness experience. But your friends can also ruin the trip—or worse, endanger a life.

CONSIDER YOUR RESOURCES When I'm thinking of a potential backcountry buddy, my first concern is, "If things go wrong and I get hurt, will they be able and willing to do what it takes to get me to help?" It sounds selfish, but they'll depend on me for the same thing.

KEEP GOOD COMPANY A bad attitude causes more trouble than bad weather, bad trails, or bad cooking. It's important to pick friends who will remain cheerful through whatever difficulties your adventure throws at you. Laughter is good medicine, and you need plenty on a backcountry trip. Choose friends you know well and can depend on to stay upbeat. Don't venture into the backcountry with someone careless or foolish.

STAY COMPATIBLE Everyone on a backcountry trip should be able to perform at similar levels. For instance, you don't want to invite someone on a strenuous hiking trip who is in poor physical condition any more than you'd want to invite a marathon runner who wants to race the entire group across the mountains. There are exceptions to this rule, should you want to enjoy your aging parent's company during a leisurely trip through the wilderness or introduce your child to the serene magic of the backcountry. Just be sure to tailor the trip to suit all members of your adventuring party.

WATCH THE NUMBERS Be wary of large group trips. Not only is it more difficult to keep everyone healthy and happy, but larger groups can have an unfavorable impact on the wilderness territory they travel through. And lastly, big groups can defeat the original purpose of the trip; solitude becomes hard to find.

018 KID AROUND

Introducing a child to the backcountry can literally be a life-changing experience. In this age of social media and digital communication, kids can lose connection with the basics. They've never been hungry, tired, cold, or scared. They've never pulled a trout triumphantly from a mountain stream or kindled a fire. They need to learn hardship, victory, and accomplishment, and the wilderness is the perfect teacher.

GAUGE THE RIGHT AGE In my opinion, a child is never too young to soak in the wonders of the backcountry. But don't take children into the wilderness unless you are fully able to meet all their needs. Once a kid is six or eight years old and can carry some—eventually all—of their own gear, they are ready for more distance and bigger adventures. If you've done your part, by the time they are 12 to 14, they should be fully able to pull their own weight on almost any trip.

TAILOR THE TRIP Don't take a child or youth on a trip where they will get cold and miserable. You should design the adventure to provide an experience where they will have a wonderful time playing, camping, creating stuff, fishing, and cooking over a fire. Help them to reconnect with the elements. They will never forget the experience, and they may just turn into your best backcountry companion.

STAY SAFE Kids, because of their smaller bodies, get cold more easily than adults. Choose mild weather for a backcountry excursion. Also, be prepared to deal with sunburn, scrapes, bumps, and bruises. Most of all, be vigilant. Children don't have caution born of experience—you need to provide that. Keep them out of trouble, prevent disaster before it happens, and have a fast exit strategy should something happen.

TEACH THEM Create a learning environment while in the backcountry. Teach your kids how to find food, build fire, and make shelter. Have fun with them while they learn to respect the land, the water, and the wildlife and fish that they hunt, catch, and eat.

019 TAKE SHELTER

Choose your primary shelter carefully. Do you want to have the lightest shelter available? Or would you prefer some space to move around, store your gear out of the weather, and brew up your morning batch of instant oatmeal without rain or snow seeping under your collar? Your options range from a roof (of sorts) over your head to a minimal-footprint sleep sack.

TENTS A wilderness tent should be lightweight with sturdy, easy-to-use zippers and a good rain fly that reaches almost to the ground. It should be rated for "three season" or "four season" weather. The best things a tent offers are comfort and space—which can be critical when waiting out a nasty storm. The downside is having to carry it with you.

TARPS A "fly-only" or "pitch light" tarp can be a great fast and light option. A tarp or fly-tent simply keeps rain and wind from beating you about the head and shoulders. The entire setup involves just the tent/tarp, some cordage, and maybe a few stakes. It's compact and easy to pitch, but won't save you from insects or awful weather.

BIVY SACKS The bivy sack is simply a waterproof shell that houses your sleeping bag with you in it, protecting you from harsh weather. You can't sit up or cook inside it, and your gear is left outside to fend for itself. Nonetheless, it can be a good lightweight, high-performance option.

020 PROTECT YOURSELF

Snuggling deeper in my sleeping bag, I pulled my beanie over my ears and settled in for the night. When I awoke in the morning it was brutally cold, but I slept warm and well. Several days later, I took my best backcountry bull elk ever.

Your sleeping gear is your last line of defense against ferocious weather and hypothermia. It can also help you recover from accidental dunkings. Buy the best quality gear

possible. A cheap tent that leaks, a pad that goes flat, or a sleeping bag that's rated for Arctic conditions but won't keep you warm on a slightly chilly evening can be a fatal combination when you're in the backcountry.

Great gear that fits will give you years of reliable use. You will sleep well, stay dry in bad weather, and feel at home no matter how far away from home you wander.

021 CHOOSE THE RIGHT SLEEPING BAG

Three main considerations apply when choosing a backcountry sleeping bag: Temperature, moisture, and weight. Here are the factors to weigh when choosing the right bag for your trip.

TEMPERATURE Sleeping bags are rated in "degrees." For example, a bag might be rated at 20˚F (-6˚C), thus indicating that you should be fairly comfortably warm sleeping in temps down to 20˚F (-6˚C). It's better to have too much bag than not enough, so choose a bag that can deal with the coldest weather that you are likely to encounter. Unfortunately, there is no industry standard on how bags are rated, meaning that manufacturers can label their bags however they want. The take-away message? Get a quality bag from a reputable manufacturer.

MOISTURE The finest insulation or "fill" for a sleeping bag is goose down. It's super warm, incredibly light, and very compactible. But down has an Achilles heel: If it becomes wet it will cease to insulate, which can become a deadly problem. Manufacturers are now sheathing down bags in water-resistant or waterproof shells, making them more reliable in wet weather. Your alternative to down is synthetic fill. It's heavier and less compactible but continues to do its job even when moisture invades its shell.

WEIGHT When you are planning to carry your camp on your back, shaving off ounces should be a priority. Down should be your material of choice. Carry a mummy bag (B) as opposed to the roomier (and weightier) rectangular bag (A). However, if horses are taking care of your home on hooves or you are traveling in a canoe or raft and weight is not as much of a priority, you may choose a synthetic bag, especially if conditions are likely to be humid or rainy.

022 PAD YOUR (S)LUMBAR

Sleeping directly on cold or rocky ground will keep you uncomfortable and chilly during the night, leaving you stiff, sore, and grumpy. The one good reason to not use a pad is . . . hmm . . . well . . . can't think of one. The only choice is not whether to use one, but what kind.

Sleeping pads can be lumped into two categories: inflatable and foam. Inflatable (or self inflating) pads give the best blend of light weight, comfort, and packability. Foam pads are inexpensive and lightweight, but tend to be bulky and less comfortable.

Modern advances in design have created inflating pads that roll into a 3 inch x 8 inch (7.5 cm x 20 cm) package, weigh in under 1.5 pounds (0.7 kg), and still inflate to offer up some seriously cushy padding. I see no reason to settle for less.

ARAM SAYS "Carry a patch kit for your inflatable pad. The pads are durable, but sooner or later an unfriendly stick or thorn will find a way in—leaving you (ahem) deflated."

023 EAT WELL

Dining in the wilderness should be a magnificent experience. After all, where else do you get to eat instant oatmeal for breakfast five days in a row? All kidding aside, sitting by a campfire, gazing at the far-reaching mountains, and listening to the sounds of the wilderness turns almost any meal into a fine culinary experience. Add in a few fresh-caught trout fingerlings or venison tenderloin sizzling over your fire and your meal just reached perfection.

Backcountry menus need to be carefully planned. Every single meal must contain the calories and nutrients necessary to maintain energy and health, yet be lightweight, compact, and easy to prepare.

024 SUPPLEMENT YOUR SNACKS

Nothing beats a pan full of trout fingerlings or a fat grouse to help supplement your meager meal. Teach yourself how to gather and prepare foods like watercress, stinging nettle, and raspberries, and your backcountry menu becomes fit for a king. Always carry salt and pepper, know and abide by local regulations, and keep a lookout for tasty backcountry tidbits to add to your meals.

025 (BACK)PACK YOUR MEALS

The key to a good backpack menu is to figure out exactly how many calories you need in order to keep your body type performing well. Carry that much and no more in some lightweight and compact foods. Never eat more than your daily allotment, or you'll be going hungry toward the end of your trip.

BREAKFAST Instant oatmeal (three packages per day), energy bar or granola bar, pop-tart, trail mix

LUNCH Hard salami, cheese, energy bar or granola bar

DINNER Mountain House Pro-Pack (freeze-dried but delicious meals; just add hot water and wait 15 minutes)

SNACKS Jerky, trail mix, hard candy

026 HORSE PACK IT

As you might imagine, your menu options expand when your four-footed buddy carries the grub. Still, you should try to keep the whole load as light as possible. Avoid loading up on heavy canned food or drinks.

BREAKFAST Eggs, bacon, oatmeal, toast or bagel, pop-tart, energy or granola bar

LUNCH Sandwiches (meat and cheese or PB&J)

DINNER Spaghetti, meat and potatoes, Mountain House Pro-Pack, ramen noodles, baked beans, biscuits

SNACKS Jerky, trail mix, hard candy, energy bar or granola bar

027 MAKE A MESS

Consider three things when assembling your backcountry mess kit. Weight, because you (or your horse) have to carry it; efficiency (i.e. a can pack stove and fuel canister inside your pot); and reliability, 'cause if it don't work you don't eat.

Backpack

- Superlight cook stove. Tiny, aggressive, and bulletproof, these little stoves will do the job.

- A sturdy, lightweight stainless steel or titanium pot complete with lid. Ideally you'll be able to pack a fuel canister and/or your stove inside of it.

- A superlight titanium or plastic spork (a spoon fork combination) will help complete your kit.

Horsepack

- Enameled metal frying pan, suited to the size of your party

- Enameled metal cooking pot sized to your party

- Small coffee pot with percolator

- Spatula

- Enameled plate, bowl (or deep-dish plate), fork, and spoon for each member of your group

- Dutch oven (for the group that has room on their pack horses and wants the total outdoor culinary experience.)

028

BACKCOUNTRY TOOLKIT
STEEL CANTEEN

While on the trail or camping, people often carry plastic bottles for their water. They look cool, but I prefer the classic steel canteen. I like the ones from Klean Kanteen and I keep one with me all the time, in my truck, backpack, or saddlebags.

TAKE A BEATING A plastic bottle works okay, but it definitely can't stand up to the punishment steel canteens can endure—and water stored in them still tastes great.

HEAT UP Everyone knows that, in a pinch, you can boil water to purify it. A plastic container will melt (and smell terrible), but with a steel canteen you don't even need a pot. Just open the lid, fill it with water

(add tea or coffee grounds, too), and set it over a fire. The steel will easily withstand repeat exposure to flames.

COOL OFF If you need a cool drink, a steel canteen can also help, even miles from a fridge or cooler. Fill it up, wrap it in a layer or two of cloth, and dunk in a stream; the evaporation cools its contents as you hike on.

029 COOK OVER A CAMPFIRE

Cooking over a campfire can be a tricky proposition and there's nothing quite as discouraging as gazing into a pot of badly burnt food, knowing that it's all you have to eat that day. Here are a few hints that will help you be a master backcountry chef.

USE ENAMEL The best cookware for open-fire work is cast iron, but it's heavy! A good second best is metal enamel cookware. Throw the essentials like a pot, frying pan, and coffeepot on the pack horse and you're good to go.

WAIT FOR COALS Hot flame is almost never good to cook on, unless you are simply trying to boil water quickly. Wait until your fire burns down to coals before putting your grub in its grasp and making dinner.

BOIL WATER After your fire burns down a little, create a spot for your pot inside the fire. You should have a thin layer of glowing coals to set your pot on, then surround the pot with some more hot coals and burning wood. Your water will be boiling in a backcountry jiffy.

FRY BACON Face it: Nice, flat, even strips of bacon ain't gonna happen in the backcountry. Cut your bacon strips in half and throw 'em in the pan. Set your pan on a nice bed of coals and stir frequently. You'll end up with a scrambled mess of bacon goulash. Yum!

COVER YOUR VITTLES Campfires toss tiny hot coals and ash around like confetti at a birthday party. Unless you like your soup crunchy, cover it up.

030 PURIFY WATER

Drinking tainted water anytime is a bad idea; in the backcountry it can be disastrous. In some cases water can be identified as potable, but in all other cases it should be purified. Here are proven tools that will clean your drink.

ARAM SAYS "Boiling or adding iodine or chlorine won't remove heavy metals or certain toxins. Fortunately, they're rarely found in backcountry water."

BOIL IT Five minutes at a rolling boil and 99.9% of evil water buggies are annihilated. So long as you have fire and a container, you can make potable water this way.

ADD IODINE It tastes kinda bad, but then again, vomit is much worse. Iodine purification kits (such as Potable-Aqua) usually have two tiny bottles: one with the iodine tabs inside; the other full of neutralizing tablets. Drop in the directed amount of iodine, wait 30 minutes, and then follow with some neutralizing tabs for three minutes. Drink up.

CLEAN WITH CHLORINE Similar to iodine, chlorine purifying kits (such as Aquamira water treatment drops) can quickly kill bacteria and other nasty stuff in 20–30 minutes. It doesn't taste quite as unpleasant and most folks are somewhat used to the flavor from their home water filtration systems.

PUMP AND PURIFY Perhaps the most effective method for entirely cleaning up your water (including removing heavy metals and other contaminants) is a dedicated water purifier. These contraptions function by pumping dirty water through a ceramic or similar filter where it emerges sparkling clean. I have only one complaint when it comes to purifying pumps: They're heavier and bulkier than drops or tablets.

031 SAVOR A WARM DRINK

We were cold. We were wet. It was snowing and the bull elk that we'd worked so hard to close the distance on had vanished. So we crawled under the branches of a friendly pine tree and dug out our stoves. Five minutes later, we were sipping warm tea and regaining a positive attitude.

HAVE SOME TEA Even if you're not a tea drinker, consider drinking some while in the backcountry. Green tea gives a healthy boost when you're struggling to rise and shine in the wee hours before dawn. Herbal teas are great for relaxing and hydrating you before a night's sleep. And either type of tea will warm and cheer you if you get cold or wet during the day.

DRINK UP YOUR VITAMINS Fizzy vitamin drink mixes will mask the taste of iodine, chlorine, or brackish water. They'll also energize you and give your immune system a preventative boost (they're loaded with vitamin C). Use a couple of packets per day in your water.

AVOID ALCOHOL I personally believe alcohol does not need to be part of the backcountry. In an environment where a stupid choice or action could put you or your party in real danger, it's simply foolish to imbibe and take that risk.

032 PICK YOUR ULTIMATE BACKCOUNTRY BLADE

If you'll be climbing onto a horse and riding gallantly off into the sunset, by all means buckle a nice fixed-blade "hunting" knife to your belt, and stow a hatchet in the pack. But if you plan to carry everything on your back, leave the hatchet at home and consider whether a full-size blade is worth its additional weight. If you'll be traveling fast and light, opt for a superlight knife. Carry a spare too—it's pretty tough to quarter an elk without a knife. Stow a spare lightweight blade deep in your pack. If you (or a buddy) ever lose your knife, it'll be there.

1 FIXED-BLADE BUCK "FISHING" KNIFE Buck's model #121 is great for any hunt involving elk or moose.

2 CUSTOM FIXED-BLADE HUNTING KNIFE Slightly heavy, but superbly balanced.

3 LIGHTWEIGHT MORA KNIFE Easy to sharpen, durable. Fantastic knife for the price.

4 SUPERLIGHT BUCK SKELETON KNIFE (#135) This knife may leave a blister, but it's incredibly lightweight, and can—with a little extra effort—take apart any North American game.

5 SUPERLIGHT FOLDER BY BUCK Similar to number four, in a folding model.

6 HATCHET (WOODSMAN BY GRANSFORS BRUKS) OR SMALL CAMP AXE Great for horsepack trips.

7 SMALL SHARPENING STONE I like a small, aggressive diamond stone by Eze-Lap or Montec.

8 MULTI-TOOL A good light to medium weight multi-tool is indispensable on any backcountry trip.

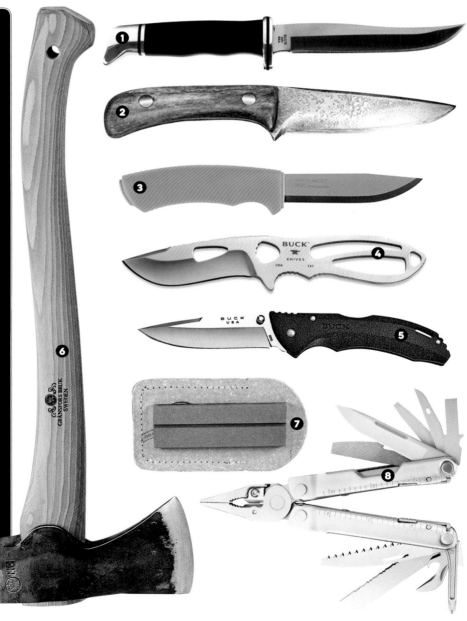

033 SHARPEN A KNIFE

A razor-sharp knife marks a skilled woodsman. Don't be that guy who shows up in camp and asks, "Can I borrow your knife? Mine's kinda dull."

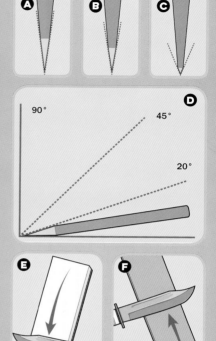

STEP 1 Understand angles. The more acute your edge's angle (A), then the sharper it is, but severely acute edges don't hold up when abused. A more obtuse edge (B) isn't as sharp, but holds longer. Too obtuse (C) will never be sharp. Try to find a happy medium for your backcountry knives. About 20–25 degrees (D) is ideal.

STEP 2 Grind the angle. Use a medium or coarse stone (I prefer large diamond stones by Eze-Lap), alternating on both sides of your edge to get a long, smooth, even grind. When a small burr shows up along the edge, it's a sign your grinds have met. An even burr along the entire edge means it's time to use a fine stone.

STEP 3 Using smooth, steady strokes, draw your blade across a fine stone.

Hone across the stone as though you were trying to shave hair from it (E). Give it about six strokes on each side. Make sure you stroke the entire length of your edge evenly. Now do five strokes per side, then four, till you are down to one stroke per side. Exercise extreme care to maintain the same angle as you did in step 2.

STEP 4 Take about three more gentle strokes on each side, alternating sides between each stroke, and maintaining your angle. The burr should be gone, and your edge should be sharp enough to shave any rogue hair.

STEP 5 Strop your blade by drawing its edge backward across a flat piece of leather that's permeated with fine buffing compound (F). Alternate sides each time, and keep the angle very low, so the blade is lying almost flat on the leather. Stropping will align any microscopic variations in the edge to an incredible sharpness.

034 MAKE IT A MACHETE

Backcountry takes on a whole new meaning when you think "Jungle" or "Rainforest." Some of the biggest wilderness expanses left are made up of huge trees, humidity, hanging vines, and big snakes that like to give you hugs. In these environments one tool reigns supreme—the machete. Jungle dwellers use them to cut their way through vines and tangled undergrowth, build shelters, fashion tools from wood or bamboo, hack their way out of hugs, and myriad other tasks. I've had my share of experience with machetes, trying to hack my way into my overgrown, weed infested garden to get a tomato. They work. And besides—it's an excuse to wear an almost-sword.

035
KEEP A HEADLAMP HANDY

A good headlamp will be your best friend when darkness settles over the backcountry. Gone are the days of chipping your teeth while you grimly clamp your flashlight in your mouth. Whether you need to saddle a horse, cook breakfast, or skin an elk, your headlamp is your huckleberry. Here are four points to choosing a good one.

GET THE LED(S) OUT A good LED headlamp will shine for days. Traditional lights last only hours, meaning you have to carry lots of extra batteries.

ADJUST IT Choose a headlamp with multiple brightness settings; use a dim setting (and help conserve battery life) when performing simple chores. Use your bright setting when looking for a lost buddy or investigating a bump in the night.

SAVE POWER "Hey, your pocket's glowing." This is a common problem when someone shows up with a fancy new headlamp including cool settings and easy-to-activate buttons. I've been a victim to it myself: Let me tell you, nothing makes me want to throw a temper tantrum quite like reaching into my pocket for my light (which I recently put new batteries in) and finding it dead. Easily activated buttons are a bad idea, as they are too quickly switched on in your pack or pocket. Look for a headlamp with well-protected buttons that won't accidentally activate and drain your battery.

AVOID A HEADACHE Get a comfortable, compact headlamp. It's that simple—it should feel good on your head and fit nicely in your pocket.

036
CHOOSE YOUR FIRE STARTER

Matches. Ferrocerium and magnesium. Weatherproof lighters. Primitive friction techniques. How's a backcountry beginner to know what's best?

GET A MATCH Tried and true, matches are still the easiest flame to strike. Carry quality waterproof matches along with a bit of long-burning pitch pine.

LIGHT UP Compact and reliable, a common lighter lives in your pocket, is more durable than matches, and is simple to use. But they can fail, so spend the $1.80 for a good one.

GO WEATHERPROOF Tough and impervious to wind, rain, and snow, a weatherproof lighter blows flame like a mini-blowtorch. Typically refillable, a good one will last many years of hard use. They're expensive, but worth the money.

GET FIRED UP A modern approach to flint and steel, ferrocerium-magnesium fire starters are impervious to, well, everything. Leave it out in the weather for a century and it will still work. But they do have a downside. They are hard to use, especially if you are cold. If you choose a kit as your go-to fire starting method for emergencies, be very sure that you are adept at kindling a blaze with it.

KEEP EXTRAS I carry a kit including waterproof matches, a common lighter, and some pitch pine stashed in my pack or saddlebags. In my pocket I keep a weatherproof lighter. In any circumstances—even if I lose my pack—I can start a fire.

037 TIE IT TOGETHER

Cordage or rope quite literally holds everything together when you're in the backcountry. You can set up a table, hang a meat pole, or pitch an awning with this stuff. If you're on the trail, fishing, or hunting, you can replace a bootlace, catch fish, and hang elk quarters. You can fashion a snare, or start a fire. In short, cordage is—right after your knife—your most versatile wilderness tool.

CARRY CORDAGE Paracord is the most versatile cordage for backcountry living and exploring. Seven inner strands housed in an abrasion-resistant shell create a strong, durable cord (550 pound [249 kg] test is typical). Use full strength to lash firewood to your pack frame or suspend an elk quarter from your meat pole. Need thread to sew your ripped shirt? Want to go fishing or make a small-game snare? Just remove the inner strands and get to work. Every backcountry explorer should have about 25 to 50 feet (7.5 to 15 m) of paracord in his pack or saddlebags.

GET A ROPE An indispensable tool of the horse packers' trade, you'll need rope to truss up bundles, throw a diamond hitch, and tie up your horses at night. Various kinds of ropes are ideal for certain jobs. Five-eighths cotton

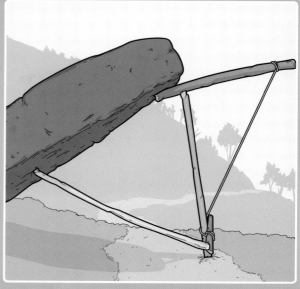

rope is perfect for lead-ropes and for staking horses out to graze. Half-inch manila rope is preferred by many packers for securing a load to a horse with a "diamond" or other hitch. Cheap quarter or three-eighths stuff (or paracord) is used to put together a comfy camp or bind an elk hide into an easily transportable package.

038 TIE A CLOVE HITCH

The clove hitch is a versatile knot that should be in every backcountry hiker, hunter, fisher, or horsepacker's bag of tricks. Both ends of your rope will support weight— together or independently— when you use the clove hitch.

STEP 1 Wrap the working end of your rope around a tree, rail, or sawbucks—

whatever you're tying to. Lay your working end across the standing end.

STEP 2 Make a second wrap and tuck your working end under itself where it crosses the standing end.

STEP 3 Pull everything snug, making sure to work both wraps together till they are tight against each other.

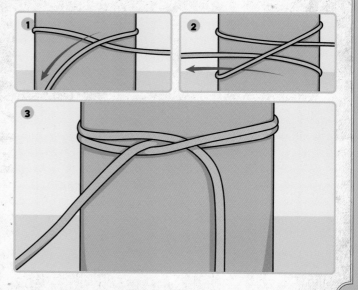

039 FOLLOW THESE GPS TIPS

A GPS unit can save your life. You can mark a waypoint, store a route, or remember a track. It can also get you in deep trouble. I always carry one—but I rarely use it to navigate.

MAKE MARKS The most valuable thing a GPS does is mark waypoints. I like to mark the trailhead or where I leave my truck, my base camp, and where I tie my horse when I dismount to hunt. I love to mark a deep-woods elk wallow or fresh-water spring. Most importantly, I can mark the location of my harvest if it's in a difficult place to relocate. Frantically searching for your elk quarters hanging in 10,000 acres of timber amid heat and hornets is a terrible situation. Mark your kill's location so you can readily return to it.

STORE A ROUTE Storing your track saves you a heap of trouble trying to return to camp in unfamiliar territory.

SEARCH A GRID Finding something or someone can be daunting, especially in rough, broken terrain. A GPS enables you to track and control your movements. Lay out a grid, circle, or pattern that will leave no stone unturned.

DON'T CRIPPLE YOURSELF I believe many—and indeed most—folks today use their GPS as a substitute for good woodsmanship. They monkey with it so much that they don't pay enough attention to their surroundings, instead letting the GPS show them where they are and where they are going. If the unit fails, they're out of luck.

KEEP A SENSE OF DIRECTION Most of us are born with a natural sense of direction. Don't replace it. Cultivate it. Pay attention to your surroundings and learn to navigate using just your God-given ability. Save your compass or GPS as backup for times (overcast, stormy, or dark) when your senses are at a disadvantage.

DON'T TRUST IT ENTIRELY Your GPS can't see everything, and that can be a big deal. It could lead you off a cliff in the dark or tell you to cross a deadly boulder field. Furthermore, it's electronic, so it can fail at any given time. It probably won't, but if it does, you'll have to be able to function without it.

040 MAP IT OUT

Let's face it: Fear of finding their way around in unfamiliar territory is the number one reason that people stay out of the backcountry. Topographical maps are the best tool that will help you turn that fear into confidence.

Does "USGS 1:24,000" look like some kind of code? It is. United States Geological Survey one-in-twenty-four-thousand series maps are the ultimate in go-to maps for backcountry travel. They are lightweight, fold into a compact package, and open large enough to give a true sense of the terrain and topography. Learn how to read a topo map and you'll navigate far better than you ever could using that screen on your GPS.

USGS topo maps are readily available online, in various sporting goods stores, and at many U.S. Forest Service and BLM offices. Research your area, pinpoint whichever drainage, peak, or river you'll travel near, and purchase the map(s) featuring that particular terrain.

If I could choose only one tool to help me navigate through the wilderness, it would be a topo map. GPS can fail, Google Earth stays home, and I get along without a compass by reading the sun, stars, and signs in nature.

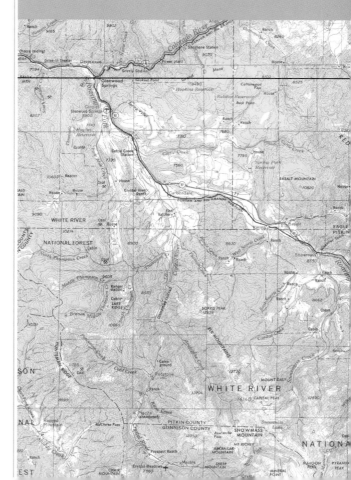

041 CARRY A COMPASS

Even if it's overcast, dark, and the middle of a blinding snowstorm, your compass can still point you in the right direction. Years ago, while guiding elk hunters through such a snowstorm deep in Montana's backcountry, my compass prevented me from making a navigational error that would have put our lives in serious danger.

GO LOW TECH One real advantage a compass has over your GPS unit is that it's free of electronics—meaning it's not as prone to failure. In fact, a good compass is bulletproof (or at least, pretty close). The only way it'll stop working is if you lose it.

GET THE KNOW-HOW Learn how to use your compass. Even with just a rudimentary understanding, your compass will tell you what direction is north, and help you orient your map. Learn how to use it right and you can take bearings, triangulate, and compensate for declination. People navigated with compasses for centuries before GPS units were invented.

TEAM UP WITH A TOPO A compass works best when used in conjunction with a topographical map. Take a reading with your compass, orient your map, and make precise navigational calculations.

042 **PACKTRAIN WRECK!**

The weather was unusually hot—water holes were drying up and our livestock were struggling to get enough to drink.

I was cowboying on one of the most remote cattle ranges anywhere, a full day and a half ride from the nearest road.

When I arrived at the wash, I stopped my saddle horse, dropped the tired pack string's leadrope and stepped off my horse. A tall embankment separated us from the seep below.

I thought the wore out horses would stand quietly while I tied my saddle horse and then took them one a time to water.

I tied my horse and ran to the edge of the wash expecting to see a tangled wreck of horses, packs, ropes, and (my biggest fear) broken legs or necks.

To my surprise and delight, the horses were all crowded around the seep, sucking noisily. Not one was hurt. I spent the next 20 minutes unraveling a cobweb of horse's pack ropes and tamarack brush.

We started our cattle herd up the trail toward the summer range. After a few miles I loaded the pack horses and tallied them and our spare saddle horses into a string six horses long.

The horses were really thirsty, so I headed for the last water I knew of: an alkali wash with some tamarack brush and a little seep in the bottom.

To my horror, the lead horse—desperate for water—turned and dove right off the sheer embankment dragging the entire string of horses off the dirt cliff after him.

Once the horses had all they wanted to drink, I trailed 'em back together and headed up the country to rejoin the cattle herd thankful that the horses were all safe and sound.

043 BE SURE OF YOUR HORSE

In September 2004, I packed into the Eagle Cap wilderness in northeast Oregon with my friends Paul and Ron and my brother Joseph to bow hunt for elk. We got to the trailhead late, but were eager to get going. All of us were on solid, experienced horses except for my brother, who'd gotten a young, less experienced mount.

While climbing along a narrow trail a mile into the backcountry, we ran into trouble.

"Better mount up," I said. "She's not going to relax until she has to carry your weight."

Short seconds later, I listened in horror as Joseph's horse—with him on it—fell into the recesses of a dark canyon, repeatedly flipping end over end on its way down to the bottom. I flung myself from my own horse and scrabbled to the edge, frantically calling my brother's name into the darkness below. The chances of surviving such a wreck without being crushed and broken are perhaps one in a hundred.

"I'm okay," his voice quavered up from the murky dimness below. "God protected me."

Paul, Ron, and I helped Joseph scramble his way back up to the trail. Quick thinking and fast reflexes born of years in the saddle had enabled him to abandon ship as his horse performed its backflip over the canyon edge. He had been thrown violently against a downed log, severely bruising his right leg, and leaving him slightly addled from a knock on the head—but he was alive.

Paul and I followed a scattered trail of camping gear, freeze-dried food, and ramen noodles toward the bottom of the dark canyon. Working by headlamp, I spliced together various lengths of ropes before we reached the bottom of the almost vertical gorge. If the horse was still alive, I doubted that it could climb back up to the trail.

We found Joseph's horse virtually unhurt, but stuck in deadfall timber. I tied the rope to its halter and Paul and I removed the packs and saddle. As I pulled the saddle free, the horse erupted in a mad scramble out of the deadfall and straight up the side of the gorge. Scattering like quail, Paul and I tried to get out from underneath her as she charged the canyon wall, throwing a trail of sparks from her steel shoes. I knew that if she lost her footing and tumbled back into the canyon we were directly in her path. It happened: An eerie half second of silence followed by crashing told me that she was tumbling toward us in the inky darkness.

Suddenly, her fall was arrested: My quick-thinking buddy Ron, on the trail above, had snubbed the rope to a tree. Stretching as taut as a fiddle string, it held. Unbelievably, after three more attempts the horse climbed with shaky legs back onto the trail.

Post Assessment

This was a terrifying experience that miraculously ended well. It could have been much, much worse. Here's what we learned.

👍 DONE RIGHT

- Good equipment (headlamps, ropes) helped to minimize damage and get the horse back to safety.

- Ron's quick thinking when he snubbed the rope to a tree saved Paul and me from almost certain injury. The rope also supported the horse each time it lost its footing, ultimately helping it to regain the trail.

👎 DONE WRONG

- Arriving late at the trailhead, our eagerness to get into the backcountry almost cost Joseph his life. Rather than trying to travel sketchy mountain trails in the dark, we should have camped at the trailhead and packed into the wilderness at first light.

- Taking a green or inexperienced horse on a wilderness trip is usually a bad idea. Only a very savvy horse person should attempt it—and then only with a buddy along to help if something goes wrong.

- I made the biggest mistake: I should never have told Joseph to mount a horse that was primed to blow up while on a narrow mountain trail. He'd made it that far already, leading his horse. He should have waited for a flat open meadow before mounting.

044 GET THE RIGHT CLOTHING

Volumes could be penned about clothing for the backcountry and what makes great clothing for a specific environment along with its accompanying climate. Your wilderness clothing should be efficient, durable, and packable (the opposite of bulky). To super-simplify, here are some basic approaches that will help keep you covered.

TRY TRADITIONAL Wilderness travelers have survived and even thrived in traditional clothing—think wool—for a very long time. Wool excels when in snowy, cold conditions, and it also performs satisfactorily in rainy weather. It's even tolerable during fair weather, since it provides some insulation against heat.

MAKE IT MODERN Some recent advancements in technology and design have created clothing that meets and exceeds every need that you could possibly have while roaming the backcountry. Flexible, weather-resistant, flame-retardant, and bogeyman-proof shirts and pants will keep you warm and protected at all times. All kidding aside, modern wilderness clothing is fantastic stuff. Companies such as Kuiu, Sitka Gear, and Under Armour make gear that will take care of you when the chips are down.

BUY ON A BUDGET Shop at thrift, army surplus, and online stores to turn up some great wool clothing at affordable prices. Look for Pendleton shirts, military pants, Filson vests and jackets, gloves, and whatever else you need. You can get yourself set up for a fraction of what you'd pay for brand new gear.

045 LIVE IN LONG JOHNS

I'd sooner leave my rifle or bow behind than my long johns. Well, almost. Long underwear, long johns, longhandles—whatever you call them, these are indispensable in the backcountry.

USE THEM RIGHT First, grasp the waistband with both hands. Insert right foot into right leg of long johns. Pull. Okay, okay; tongue out of cheek. I depend on my long johns to keep me warm when I'm sleeping, or sitting over an elk wallow and the temps plummet, or I'm making that drowsy midnight dash to answer a call of nature. They provide a warm next-to-skin insulation that makes a difference in cold conditions. Just slip them off and stow them in your pack when the weather turns warm, or when you need to make a brutal uphill dash to get to a big muley buck before darkness sets in.

WEAR WOOL Wool long johns are lightweight, comfortable, and continue to insulate even when damp. Wool will even absorb scent molecules, aiding in scent control. And it's also a natural flame retardant, should you need protection from fire. Companies like Woolpower and Red Dog offer some quality wool long johns in a variety of weights—and heavier is warmer—for every single backcountry occasion. Of course, red ones are best, because that's what John Wayne wore.

046 DRESS FOR THE SEASON

From summer heat to winter storms, there are basic lists of clothing to suit the season. Research the climate, conditions, and forecasts before your trip, and pack accordingly. Don't overpack, but don't limit yourself to these lists. Prepare for the worst that nature is likely to show. If you need to go super fast and light, cut down clothing to one outfit, but take two sets of long johns. In an emergency, strip off the wet outfit, put on dry long johns, and burrow into your sleeping bag.

Summer	☐ 1 "Wild Rag" (See #054) ☐ 1 pair medium-weight gloves ☐ 1 change of undergarments	☐ 2 T-shirts ☐ 1 long-sleeve shirt ☐ 2 pair lightweight pants ☐ 3 pair socks (1 medium wool, 2 light)	☐ 1 lightweight jacket ☐ 1 pair lightweight long johns ☐ 1 pair lightweight boots
Winter	☐ 1 "Wild Rag" ☐ 1 pair medium-weight gloves ☐ 1 change of undergarments ☐ 3 pair socks (one lightweight, two heavy)	☐ 2 pair pants (one medium, one heavy) ☐ 2 long-sleeve shirts (one medium, one heavy) ☐ 2 pair long johns (one medium, one heavy) ☐ 1 down vest and warm coat	☐ 1 warm hat (beanie or bomber style) ☐ 1 pair heavy gloves or mittens ☐ 1 pair warm medium-weight waterproof or leather boots
Spring / Fall	☐ 1 "Wild Rag" ☐ 1 pair medium weight gloves ☐ 1 change of undergarments ☐ 3 pair socks (two medium-weight, one heavy-weight)	☐ 2 pair long johns (one lightweight, one medium) ☐ 2 pair medium-weight pants ☐ 2 long-sleeve shirts, medium weight	☐ 1 beanie hat ☐ 1 light vest 1 warm jacket ☐ 1 T-shirt or lightweight long-sleeve shirt ☐ 1 pair medium-weight boots

047

COVER YOUR HEAD

A lot of heat can be lost through your head, so keeping your noggin warm and happy should be pretty high on your list of priorities.

TRY A BEANIE
The best backcountry buddy for your bean is a beanie. Seriously, though, a beanie is both warm and comfortable, as well as lightweight and compact, and easy to wear while you sleep. The only time that they can fall short is in extremely cold conditions.

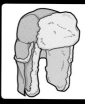

WARM UP IN A BOMBER
When the mercury falls below a certain point, a fur bomber hat will make sure your head is warm and comfortable. Besides, they look just as awesome as the Memphis Belle coming in to land.

PUT ON A BALACLAVA
Yeah, how is that word even rightly pronounced? At any rate, a balaclava pulls over your head like a sock with eye and mouth holes and it will keep your face and neck warm when it's well and truly cold outside. It's also super effective when used in combination with a beanie or bomber hat.

048 GLOVE UP

Cold hands can be deadly in a backcountry situation. Starting a fire, building a shelter, or even zipping your coat can become incredibly difficult. Carry protection for your hands and when the mercury starts to fall don't hesitate to put those gloves on.

EARLY SEASON Carry a pair of lightweight gloves for early-season temperatures. Use lightly insulated leather work gloves if you're horsepacking. They're better than wool or synthetic gloves for working with ropes, pack gear, axes, and so on. Waterproofing them before your trip with toilet ring wax is a good idea. (I prefer to use new wax.)

MID SEASON Warm synthetic or wool gloves are great when frost begins to manifest itself on chilly mornings or a bit of snow covers the ground. If temps get really chilly, try out "glommits," a combination of glove and mitten. They feature half-fingers, thus leaving your fingertips free to perform fine work, but feature mitten pull-overs that cover your fingers to keep them toasty when not in use.

LATE SEASON When the mercury plummets, the best hand protection is mittens. They keep fingers together, (while gloves separate fingers to fend for themselves) so your hand stays warmer; when you need to handle fine work you can quickly slip your hand out, do the job, then slip the still-warm mitten on again. If it's -40˚F (-40˚C) below or colder, you might be better off leaving the mittens on and muddling through your work as best you can.

ARAM SAYS "If you expect damp weather, carry two pair of gloves or mittens. Should one pair become wet, you can change into your dry pair and hang the wet ones to dry."

049 WEAR THE BEST HAT

Choosing the right backcountry gear is very important, whether it's footwear, clothing, backpack, gun, or bow. Ultimately your comfort and success depend on your gear. So choose wisely. This top-to-toe outfitting starts at the top, with the right hat. There's a better option than a ball cap when you're spending days on end in the backcountry. My personal favorite is a crushable wool fedora or outback style hat, for the following reasons.

PROTECTION This hat will keep your head warm—it's got some handy-dandy earflaps that pull down to keep your ears warm on a cold and frosty morning. If it rains, the brim will keep rain from running into your ears and down your neck. It will provide shade from a blistering sun. It even makes a good pillow for a mid-day nap.

CONVENIENCE The hat is crushable. Feel free to smash it, stuff it in your pack, and later it'll pop right back into shape.

CLASS Fred Bear's favorite kind of hat was a fedora. He wore it all the time, especially when he was hunting. What more need I say?

---

050 BACKCOUNTRY TOOLKIT
TRASH BAG

One tool can save you a drenching, chill your meat, and even keep you alive. It's easy to find, lightweight, and inexpensive. It's a contractor-grade trash bag (CTB). Roll one—or several—tightly and carry them in your backpack, daypack, or saddlebags. Here are just a few uses.

STAY DRY Cut a hole in the bottom of your CTB. Pull it over your head to keep you, your backpack, and your gun or bow dry.

CHILL During hot weather enclose deer or elk quarters in a CTB and chill them in a cold wilderness spring, creek, or lake.

SNUGGLE Use your CTB as an emergency bivy sack. Stuff with dry leaves, duff, or clothing and climb in. Pull some more insulation in after you. Sweet dreams.

STORE Wrap firewood, gear, or anything else that you want to keep clean, dry, and protected in a CTB.

COLLECT During a rainstorm spread the mouth of your CTB wide to gather potable water. Alternately, cut it open and spread it to funnel water into your canteen.

051 BREAK IN YOUR BOOTS

One of the worst mistakes made by aspiring wilderness hunters is showing up at the trailhead with a brand-new pair of boots. All boots need breaking in, and your feet need time to become accustomed to your boots. Otherwise, you will develop soreness and blisters that will seriously compromise your ability to perform—possibly even ending your trip prematurely.

BREAK 'EM IN Several weeks or months before your trip, begin wearing your new boots for a short time every day. Increase your time wearing the boots gradually. When a sore or hot spot develops, give your feet a couple days' break to toughen up. If the trouble persists, examine the problem area in the boot. Resolve any issues. Keep up the routine until you can hike for hours free of pain or soreness. You (and your boots) will be ready for the backcountry.

CARRY SPARE SOCKS Keep a pair of ultra-thin "blister proof" socks in your pack. If you begin developing hot spots, slip them on under your regular socks. They will keep you in the game.

052 FIND THE RIGHT FOOTWEAR

Footwear is literally the foundation you walk on when in the backcountry. Choose wisely; depending upon weather, terrain, temperature, and hunt style your footwear can make or break your adventure. You might choose rubber-bottomed pack boots for a late-season hunt in the snow, or fast-and-light hunting sneakers for an early-season bowhunt. Or, you may just sneak off in your socks.

ARAM SAYS "I prefer all-leather boots where possible. Seal them against snow and water by rubbing toilet-ring wax (just use new wax) into the warmed leather."

FOOTWEAR	WHEN TO WEAR IT	PROS	CONS
PACK BOOTS	For hunting in super-cold conditions (especially with snow)	Can be worn with a pair or two of wool socks for extra warmth (size up a half step first); can include air-bob soles	Heavy; not very breathable; very stiff—need lots of breaking in
INSULATED HIKING BOOTS	Cold environments or when snow is possible	Aggressive soles; lightweight insulation; great for active hunting in cold conditions	Not the best for extreme cold
HUNTING SNEAKERS	Early season and when stalking game	Lightweight; reduce fatigue significantly; quiet movement	Little ankle support; not much insulation
WOOL SOCKS OR BAREFOOT SHOES	Early season and when stalking game	Extremely lightweight; virtually silent	No ankle support; virtually no protection against cold

053

LAYER IN LUXURY

Learning how to regulate your temperature (while performing various activities in all kinds of weather conditions) is key to performing well while you're in a backcountry setting. A change of just a couple degrees in body temperature can prove fatal if you're far from the nearest road. Layering is a proven method of maintaining body temperature, health, and comfort. Simply add layers to warm up as activity or temperature drops or remove layers to cool off as heat or activity increases.

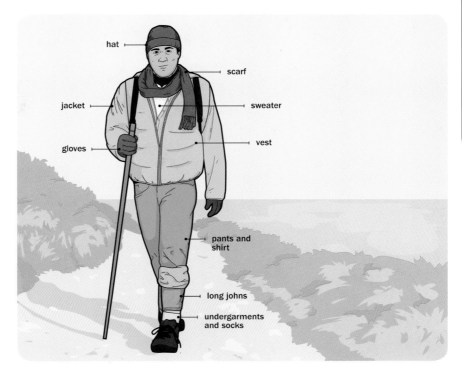

hat
scarf
jacket
sweater
gloves
vest
pants and shirt
long johns
undergarments and socks

---

054 — WILD RAG

One of the most versatile backcountry items (and one of my personal favorites) is a 3 x 3-foot (1 x 1-meter) silk scarf or "wild rag." It's one of the most versatile things you could bring with you.

KEEP WARM Wear cowboy style around your neck (even asleep) to conserve heat.

FILTER WATER It won't purify water, but will get the big nasties out of your drink.

SLING IT Improvise a sling to hold an injured arm stable.

BIND A WOUND Fashion a bandage to cover an injury.

TIE A TOURNIQUET If you've had worse than a

minor injury and risk severe blood loss, use your scarf to make a tourniquet.

CRAFT A CONTAINER A wild rag makes a perfect improvised gathering basket.

BREATHE EASY Wear it over your face in dusty or smoky conditions.(Dampen it first to help filtering.)

DO EVEN MORE This scarf's usefulness is limited only by your own ingenuity.

055 KEEP IN TOUCH

Cell phones rarely have service in backcountry settings, so calling or texting your buddy over the next ridge isn't an option. One thing aside from smoke signals does work, though: a handheld radio.

COMMUNICATE Radios are invaluable any time you're temporarily separated from your buddies. Imagine returning to camp in the dark, expecting to find your hunting partner at the campfire—but he's not there. You look, wait, and shout his name into the wee hours of the night. Then he comes stumbling in, a silly grin on his face and his pack loaded with meat from an elk that he shot five miles away just at dark. Radios could have prevented the emotional trauma that you've just endured.

GET POWERFUL Cheap walkie-talkies with a one-mile (1.6 km) range won't cut it in the backcountry, especially in rugged terrain. Shop for radios with a powerful signal and extended range of 50 miles (80 km) or more. You're not going to need to call that far—but the signal will penetrate rocky ridges and deep canyons better.

FIND ELEVATION Remember that radio signals don't travel well without a clear line of sight. If you do need to communicate, find a high spot to stand while you make the call.

056 CONSIDER A CAMERA

Photos from backcountry trips can become treasures. Remember that spectacular rainbow over Don Juan peak? Or that terrible storm? We all looked like drowned rats; man, I'm glad I shot that photo. Record the highs and lows with a camera.

SKIP THE SMARTPHONE
Smartphones these days take great everyday photos. But they also tend to lose their charge fast, so unless you have a compatible solar charger and a sunny forecast, consider taking an actual camera with you.

POINT AND SHOOT The best photo opportunities occur spontaneously, and are over in a moment. A compact camera stowed in your shirt pocket will give you a fast-draw chance at getting that photo. Plus having your camera readily available will inspire you to take more photos.

PACK A DSLR If you love spectacular photographs, are a journalist, or simply enjoy photography, consider packing the extra weight of a DSLR camera. It will enable you to take incredible photos of incredible places.

STAY TOUGH When you're in the backcountry your camera is likely to be exposed to heat, cold, humidity, downright bad weather, dust, and other things that cameras don't generally approve of. Get a tough (preferably weather-resistant) camera. Keep it stowed in a padded case and, if dusty or wet conditions threaten, store the device in a zip-lock bag.

057 KEEP A CHARGE

Gazing mournfully at my dead camera—with a spectacular photo opportunity in front of me—is not an experience I wish to repeat. Here's how to stay powered.

REDUCE JUICE Set your devices to their power saving mode unless you need them. In some cases (such as a satellite phone that you will only use in an emergency), remove the battery entirely and stow it out of contact with anything that could waste its charge.

CARRY A SPARE Bring spare batteries for each electronic device that you take with you. Don't forget batteries for your headlamp, GPS, and so on.

HARNESS THE SUN Carry a superlight solar charger to hang on your pack or tent. Get adapters to charge as many of your devices as possible.

058 TAKE NOTES

Jotting down notes—thoughts, weather conditions, how to find that great elk wallow again—is a good way to collect valuable info for future trips and keep memories to share. Check out Fred Bears' *Field Notes* for a great example of recording backcountry adventures.

GRAB A PEN To keep notes, you need a writing implement. A compact pen is great, and is more legible than pencil. In a pinch, get creative—I've written notes with the lead tip of a bullet.

WRITE ON THE BACK The best notebooks for backcountry record keeping are made of water-resistant paper, but are a bit heavy; great for horsepacking, but less desirable to a fast-and-light backcountry traveler.

Try writing on the back of your topo maps. It won't add an ounce to your load, and there's plenty of space.

KEEP IT HANDY Stuff your pen and paper in a gallon freezer bag and stow somewhere accessible. You'll be more

likely to pull out your paper and jot down a thought if it's easy to retrieve.

WRAP WITH TAPE Who can get along without duct tape? Wrap a foot or two around the midsection of your pen. It'll come in handy.

059 GO MINIMALIST

Who needs high-tech gear? Why not just pick up a good knife and walk into the wild? There are people who do just that, but you need tremendous skill to survive in the backcountry with next to nothing. You need strength, health, and skill to manufacture or find tools and shelter, and stay alive long enough to hunt or gather food.

GO NATIVE I live in the same area as Matt Graham (host of *Dual Survivor* and *Dude, You're Screwed*). When I was consumed with learning everything I could about hunting big game, packing horses, and shooting bows and guns of every description, Matt was walking alone into the desert and living—not just surviving—for a month and a half at a time. He only carried the very basic essentials, preferring to make everything else he needed from materials that he gathered from the land.

DON'T TAKE IT, MAKE IT If you have the knowledge a skill (and are in the right place) you don't need to bring anything to survive. Break a sharp blade from a chunk o chert. Make a hand-drill and build a fire. Gather plant f twist up cordage, and build small-game traps. Find an overhang or build a shelter, and stuff it with leaves and to keep warm. Wade into a creek and hand-fish for din gather watercress or nettle for a veggie dish. Fashion a l from clay. Boil water to purify it. Knap out a better ston blade and build a good bow and arrows. Kill a deer, bra tan the skin, and make clothing.

MAKE A DECISION Should you try it? Probably not. Y need a lot of skill, and you'd be mighty cold and hungr things went awry. Primitive survival is still fascinating should jump at a chance to learn. You might need it son

060 MULTI-TOOL

The tool I use most in a backcountry (or other) setting is my Leatherman multi-tool. Perhaps the only place I don't carry it is to church—and I've even wished I had it there.

SIZE IT RIGHT Don't carry something huge that changes choke tubes or head gaskets. A mini model won't do the job either. Get a mid-size model with the tools you need.

CUT IT OUT Every multi-tool should have one good blade.

PLY YOUR WAY Another mainstay, pliers are great for untying tight knots, twisting wire, and pulling slivers.

OPEN IT UP A can opener is never an unwelcome tool.

BE A GUNSMITH With the screwdriver, I've fixed many a gun in the backcountry, even using it as a makeshift punch to drift iron sights that are knocked out of alignment.

061 PACK LIKE A CAVEMAN

Picture yourself headed into the wilderness; you're allowed to take only five items with you. What would they be?

I recently had this debate with several of my survival instructor buddies; here's what we settled on.

1 KNIFE Big enough to perform small chopping chores, but small and handy enough for everyday use.

2 STAINLESS STEEL CANTEEN This can function as a cooking pot, a water boiling utensil, and, of course, as a water carrier.

3 FIRE STARTER Lighter, matches, magnesium/striker set, flint and steel, bow drill, or hand drill.

4 CORDAGE Paracord, to be more precise. It's good stuff—strong, versatile, and lightweight. Its possible uses are near endless.

5 SPACE BLANKET A high-quality reflective survival blanket (or tarp, or rubber poncho, or buffalo robe) won fifth place. Shelter is paramount to survival. A good space blanket can give shelter from the elements (rain, sun, wind), will reflect body heat, and can serve as a water catchment device.

062 PACK IN ON HORSEBACK

Wheels may have come along and spoiled the idea, but the fact remains: Mankind belongs on horseback.

PACK A HORSE The main reason to use pack horses is transporting gear—lots of it. You can be safer and more comfortable (think wall tent with cozy wood stove during a high-country blizzard) than with just what you can fit on your back. You can also carry enough food to stay in the wilderness for extended periods.

RIDE A HORSE You double your charm simply by standing near a horse, and quadruple it the moment you mount up. But, seriously, riding a horse in the backcountry will leave you fresher once you reach your destination. You'll also get a better view of the beautiful places you pass, because you'll be looking around instead of watching where you put your feet. Your horse can wade easily across rushing high-country creeks. And should you become lost, your horse will likely know its way to camp or the trailhead.

TRANSPORT MEAT You've backpacked a long way into the backcountry to hunt elk in an unseasonably hot September. It's midmorning and already sweltering. You're within easy range of the bull of your dreams—he's bugling and tearing a hapless tree apart, oblivious to your presence. But you've got a problem: If you shoot the bull, you'll never get the meat cool and out of the wilderness before it spoils. Do you let the bull of your dreams walk off . . . or do you shoot, knowing full well that your meat will spoil? You know the right choice. But it'll haunt you forever. If only you had a horse . . .

BE SAFE Pack and saddle horses are a responsibility, and they can be dangerous. Wrecks can happen, good horses can get surprised, ropes can tangle, and horses can tumble down mountainsides. Awareness and a calm attitude are key to staying safe. Learn everything you can about handling horses, and never, ever show off.

063 SEND YOURSELF (HORSE)PACKING

So you want to go on a backcountry horsepack trip or hunt? Here are two ways to make it happen.

GO OUTFITTED The easiest and safest way is to hire an outfitter or cowboy to provide the stock, do the packing, and handle the horses. More pampered and less rewarding, this is nonetheless a great way to experience a backcountry horse trip, especially if you are not an experienced horseman.

BUILD YOUR OWN STRING If you have the resources and time, forming your own string of savvy mountain horses is a rewarding enterprise. Search out well-trained, gentle horses worthy of a backcountry pack string: horses with good minds, good confirmation, and friendly attitudes. This book is about teaching you to be a backcountry animal, not how to train a pack horse—for that, check out a delightful old book titled *Horse Packing in Pictures*.

064 MEET YOUR MOUNT

A horse can be your best friend. It can also try to kill you. The difference between these two steeds may not be obvious, but can be discovered with a discerning eye. Here's how to find a good backcountry saddle or pack horse.

LOOK HIM IN THE EYE A gentle horse with a calm, good-natured attitude will usually have calm, good-natured eyes. They will be large and soft, and show calm interest, or just sleepiness, rather than viciousness. You won't see the white around his eye unless he is nervous or excited.

LISTEN TO THE EAR Your horse can swivel his ear around on its base in order to pick up sounds coming from different directions. (Watch your saddle horse's ears as you ride; he will regularly swivel an ear in your direction to check on you.) A horse's ears will typically point toward whatever he is interested in—unless he is feeling antagonistic. Then he will lay his ears backward or "pin his ears" in horseman vernacular. Watch a horse who does this frequently; he's

likely a troublemaker. If he pins his ears flat against his head, look out: He's about to attack the object of his displeasure. A stern shout can often dissuade him.

A judgment call may be in order, though, as some older, very experienced horses who are just feeling grumpy about going to work (know the feeling?) will pin their ears a bit. They will never pin them hard (unless it's at another horse that's misbehaving) and they won't cause trouble; indeed, these horses are the rock-solid foundation of your equine string. Be alert to this difference.

WATCH OUT FOR THE DANCER Most young horses will fidget, paw the ground, and shuffle around, trying to see everything that's happening. A little of this is okay in a young or green horse, but it's not good at all in an older, experienced, or well-trained horse. It indicates nervousness and a lack of common sense. This horse may cause trouble in the string and, if you get in a "jackpot" as the old timers call it, he's likely to come to pieces and get someone hurt.

065 GET THE GEAR

Every backcountry horsepacking trip needs a basic set of shared horse and camp gear.

A HATCHET Use a small camp axe to pound in stakes, split kindling, and do general tasks around camp.

B SAW One of the most important items on the list. Use it to cut deadfall logs that are blocking your trail and to make firewood for your camp. Fasten it to the top of a load so it's always handy when you're on the trail.

C SCALE A small handheld scale is great for weighing and balancing loaded panniers.

D NOSEBAGS Bring one nosebag per two or three horses. Feed them some grain to supplement the grass that they can forage; that way you can keep their nutrients up.

E WIRE Bring a medium-small roll of tie-wire along. You'll need it to fix and repair tack and gear, make a lantern hook, and solve any number of mishaps.

F CORDAGE My favorite is paracord, but I've used an awful lot of haystring over the years. Stuff some into saddlebags or a pack where you can grab it to fix or secure gear that works loose while on the trail. Use it to stretch tarp shelters or a clothesline and for 101 other purposes around camp.

G EASYBOOTS Throw in a couple of appropriately sized boots as a temporary fix for a horse that's lost a shoe.

H CURRY COMB Use it to curry horses till they're clean and free of dirt, dried sweat, and other gunk before saddling up. Pay special attention to areas where saddle pads, cinches, and bridles will rub the horse.

I TARP Handy anytime, tarps are essential in bad weather. Stretch them into lean-to or A-frame shelters and stow gear, firewood, and such underneath.

J TRASH BAGS If your horses wade in water that reaches up to the panniers, everything inside will get soaked. Stow everything in contractor grade trash bags and it'll stay dry.

066 HANG A RIFLE SCABBARD ON YOUR HORSE

Carrying a rifle on a horse can be tricky. A well-fitting saddle scabbard is often the best answer, especially if your rifle has a slim profile. Here's how to attach your rifle scabbard to your saddle.

STAY UPRIGHT Hang your rifle right side up, otherwise your sights or scope could be damaged.

TAKE A KNEE Hang your scabbard right under the bend of your knee. Slide the scabbard between your fender and the stirrup leather, butt forward. Orient it so, when mounted, your knee bends right around the bulge formed by the rifle.

HANG IN THERE Be sure you attach the scabbard securely to your saddle. It's a bona fide backcountry disaster to have your scabbard break free and end up dropping your rifle down a mountainside or into a pile of rocks. Attach the front scabbard strap through the forks. Don't hang it around the horn; if your horse jumps a big log it could pop off. Attach the rear strap to the rear cinch ring. Hang the butt slightly higher than the muzzle.

067 MAKE A WOOL BLANKET GUN CASE

Take a page from the history of the Old West by making a gun case from a wool blanket. Whether at the range or in a hunting camp, your rifle will have the coolest ride around. (This case is best for iron-sighted firearms: lever guns, long rifles, shotguns, or similar.)

What You Need

- Wool blanket
- T-pins
- Scissors
- Heavy nylon thread
- Sewing machine or semi-large sewing needle
- Embroidery thread
- Leather string

STEP 1 Find a wool blanket at least a foot (30 cm) longer than your gun (eBay and military surplus stores are good places to look). Hand-wash it in warm water or on the gentle cycle in your washer, then air-dry on a clothesline.

STEP 2 Lay the rifle on the blanket and fold the blanket so it covers the gun completely with its open edge facing the gun's underside. Pin the case into shape around the rifle and draw an outline 2 inches (5 cm) around it. At the muzzle, mark a ½-inch (1.25-cm) allowance instead. Extend the case about a foot behind the stock.

STEP 3 Remove the rifle and cleanly cut the outline of the case.

STEP 4 If you're machine-sewing, pin the seam heavily to keep the wool from moving. Leave the last 3 inches (7.5 cm) of the seam on the long side unsewn for a good look; don't sew the end shut, either. If you're hand-sewing, make small stitches—¼ inch (6 mm) or shorter—reinforcing both ends of your seam with extra stitching.

STEP 5 Bind the edges of the case opening with heavy embroidery thread so they don't fray. For a more finished look, turn the case inside out; you can also upgrade it with canvas lining, leather fringing, antler buttons, and so on.

STEP 6 Poke four holes in one side of your case about ½ inch (1.25 cm) apart, 4 inches (10 cm) from the opening. Thread a leather string through the holes, leaving about a foot or two (30–60 cm) of string free at either end. Slip in your rifle, tie the opening shut, and embrace your inner mountain man.

068 SET UP YOUR SADDLE HORSE

Your saddle-horse gear is personal. No one else gets to use it, and no one else is responsible for taking care of it. Here's what you'll need.

BRIDLE Try a heavy leather bridle with a headstall, long split reins, and a well-balanced swivel-shank snaffle bit (most horses respond well to this bit/bridle combination).

SADDLE A quality saddle, preferably western (they're much easier to tie gear onto) that fits you and the horse(s) you ride.

SADDLE SCABBARD Hands-down, this is the best way to carry a rifle on horseback.

SADDLE PAD A good fleece-lined or wool felt pad. If you want something special and have the cash to burn get an authentic Navajo saddle blanket and use over a wool felt pad.

SADDLE BAGS These tie on the back of your saddle, for a place to keep small necessary items. Get medium-sized leather saddlebags (not the big floppy canvas or nylon ones).

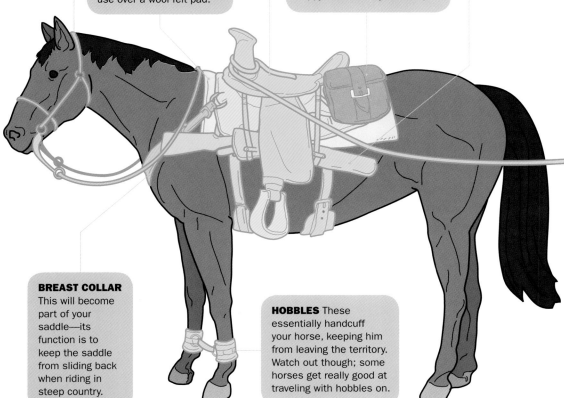

BREAST COLLAR This will become part of your saddle—its function is to keep the saddle from sliding back when riding in steep country.

HOBBLES These essentially handcuff your horse, keeping him from leaving the territory. Watch out though; some horses get really good at traveling with hobbles on.

069 PACK YOUR HORSE

Each pack horse should have its own set of gear, set up and adjusted to fit him and the load he's expected to carry. A good setup will include the following.

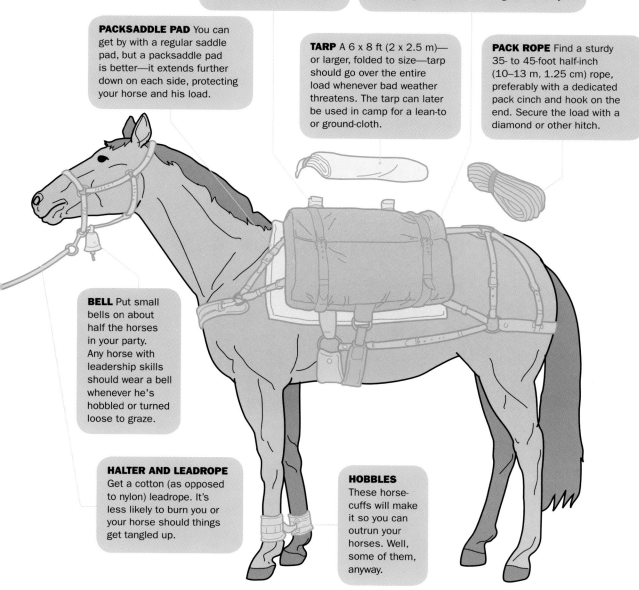

PACKSADDLE I prefer a good Sawbuck packsaddle with "humane" bars. They're easy to use, versatile, and have that classic look.

PANNIERS Pronounced "panyerds" for some long-forgotten reason, these are the containers that carry your load. Each horse needs a set of soft or hard panniers, depending on what he's assigned to carry.

PACKSADDLE PAD You can get by with a regular saddle pad, but a packsaddle pad is better—it extends further down on each side, protecting your horse and his load.

TARP A 6 x 8 ft (2 x 2.5 m)— or larger, folded to size—tarp should go over the entire load whenever bad weather threatens. The tarp can later be used in camp for a lean-to or ground-cloth.

PACK ROPE Find a sturdy 35- to 45-foot half-inch (10–13 m, 1.25 cm) rope, preferably with a dedicated pack cinch and hook on the end. Secure the load with a diamond or other hitch.

BELL Put small bells on about half the horses in your party. Any horse with leadership skills should wear a bell whenever he's hobbled or turned loose to graze.

HALTER AND LEADROPE Get a cotton (as opposed to nylon) leadrope. It's less likely to burn you or your horse should things get tangled up.

HOBBLES These horse-cuffs will make it so you can outrun your horses. Well, some of them, anyway.

070 BRING YOUR BEST FRIEND (OR NOT)

No matter how much you love being in the backcountry, your dog will love it twice as passionately as you do: enticing new smells, little critters to chase, and excitement around every bend in the trail. Your dog can be a great addition to a backcountry trip, but much depends on how well behaved he is—does he "sit," "stay," and "quiet" reliably on command? Or is he likely to chase every elk, jump into every fishing hole, and torment a mama grizzly into an enraged charge?

BRING BRUTUS It's a great idea to take your dog along on any hiking, fishing, or horsepack trip where you are not hunting or scouting for big game—especially if you're going solo. He'll bring some great companionship and security to your experience.

LEAVE HIM AT HOME Don't bring a dog on any big game hunts unless he is superbly trained and will faithfully stay in camp and stand guard. You don't want your dog yapping at the heels of the big buck or bull you were stalking. You should keep him away from grizzly country, too—he'll likely bring more trouble than security.

GIVE HIM HIS LUGGAGE There's no reason for you to carry Brutus's stuff; his "stuff" equals food, and he can sure carry that in his own pack. Get a nice doggy pack that fits him well and get him used to it before your trip. (He's likely in better shape than you, so maybe he should carry your vittles as well.) If you're horsepacking it's a moot point; leave the doggy pack at home and stow his grub on the pack horse.

TAG YOUR BUDDY Rivet a metal nameplate with your name and contact information onto Brutus's collar. Should you become separated, some kind soul will likely find him, see the info on the collar, and help to get you reunited with your best friend.

071 BRING YOUR BEAR WEAR

I believe that fear of bears causes more concern to backcountry adventurers than any other single thing. In some places (such as Kodiak Island) this concern is legitimate. But for the most part hypothermia, poor navigation, and stupidity are much greater backcountry threats than bears will ever be.

PREP FOR BEAR TROUBLE Good judgment and conscientious camping techniques will help prevent bear trouble 99 percent of the time. But if you're heading into an area with a high population of bears, and especially if they have a reputation for starting trouble, you should prepare for the worst.

GRAB SOME IRON The best kind of firearm for the fast and light backcountry hiker, fisherman, or bow hunter (check your state regulations before carrying a firearm while bowhunting), is a compact large-bore handgun. If fast and light is not a concern, opt for a short-barreled pump-action 12-gauge shotgun loaded with heavy slugs. It's critical to know how and when to use your sidearm. Shooting up a mad grizzly is about the worst thing you can do, unless you shoot him very dead, and that's hard to do.

PACK BEAR SPRAY You may opt (for various reasons) to carry bear spray instead of a firearm. Bear repellent can be effective but you have to deploy it right. If you shoot too soon—plenty of folks understandably get excited when a bear charges them—or if the wind is blowing hard, you'll just end up being spicy human rather than standard fare. If you have to spray a bear, wait until he's 15 to 30 feet (4.5–9 m) away. Using two hands (so that the recoil from the blast doesn't flip the can back and shoot you, and not the bear), spray a Z pattern in the air between you and the bear. Back up a couple steps and repeat. Ideally, wind will carry the cloud to the bear and away from you. Wear your spray or weapon where it's readily available at all times. Practice quick drawing and deploying till you're smooth, accurate, and automatic.

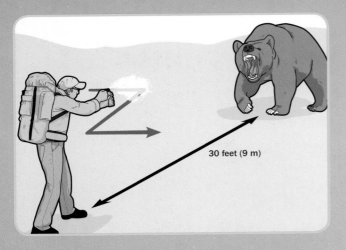

30 feet (9 m)

072 LOAD UP FOR BEAR

Even in the best of circumstances your chances of stopping a charging bear are less than ideal, so try to do everything you can to avoid getting yourself into that situation. If it does happen, choice of caliber and projectile are critical—here's what may work to stop that charge.

PACK A BIG SIX-GUN There's no such thing as a great pistol caliber when it comes to stopping big mad bears. A .44 Magnum round should probably be considered a minimum, with the .500 Smith & Wesson as close to ideal as you can come in a handgun caliber.

PUMP SOME IRON There's a reason that cops like shotguns: They're good at stopping the big mad stuff that's trying to kill you. A pump-action shotgun in experienced hands can disperse an awesome amount of lead in a very short period of time. If you're in big bear (brown or grizzly) territory, sling one muzzle-down over your off-shoulder (faster to deploy).

GO SLUG-HEAVY Lots of energy and deep penetration are essential when you're trying to stop a mad bear. If you're packing a pistol, use a heavy bullet that will hold its shape and drive deep (such as a 300+ grain hard-cast semi-wadcutter). When toting a shotgun, stoke it with heavy, hard-hitting slugs— no "reduced recoil" loads here.

073 AVOID THIS NORTHERN EXPOSURE

Most of us will never be fortunate enough to venture into the great white bear's territory. But for those of you who do go, here's what's different about Nanuq (the Inuit name for polar bear, pronounced "Nanook").

Grizzly bears may attack you in defense of cubs, food, or territory. Black bears might capitalize on an opportunity to eat you. But polar bears will hunt you. Silently padding across his icy homeland, invisible against the snow or ice, he (the hunter) may be upon you (the prey) before you're even aware of his 1,500-pound (700-kg) presence.

The best way to protect yourself from Nanuq? Prayer and respect. It's how the Inuit do it, and I'm not one to argue with that. Take the usual precautionary measures (bear spray, big gun), but rely on tradition.

074 HUNT UP THE RIGHT GEAR

Every experienced hunter forms opinions on what works and what doesn't. In this table, you'll find gear and equipment that's served me well—some through decades of backcountry hunting. There are other great optics, deadly broadheads, or fantastic calibers. But these are old and trusted friends, or the latest and greatest (like Hornady's ELD-X bullet) that have already proven themselves worthy. I'm confident that they will treat you as well as they have me.

ANIMAL	SEASON	RIFLE & CALIBER	AMMO/ BULLET	OPTICS
MULE DEER	October to November	• Bolt-action, semi-lightweight • 6.5 Creedmoor • 6.5X284 • .270 Win • 30-06 Sprg	• 130–180 gr • Hornady ELD-X • Federal Fusion • Sierra Game King • Rem Core-lok	Leupold 2-8X32 or Zeiss 3-15X42 Riflescope with Ballistic Reticle and/or Turret Swarovski 10X42 or 8X32 Binocular Zeiss/Swarovski Spotting scope Rangefinder
ELK	September to November	• Bolt-action, semi-lightweight • .270 Win • 30-06 Sprg • 7mm Rem Mag • .300 Win Mag	• 150–200 gr • Hornady ELD-X • Nosler Partition	Leupold 2-8X32 or Zeiss 3-15X42 Riflescope with Ballistic Reticle and/or Turret Swarovski 10X42 or 8X32 Binocular Rangefinder
PRONGHORN ANTELOPE	August to October	• Bolt-action • 6.5 Creedmoor • 6.5X284 • .270 Win • 30-06 Sprg	• 130–180 gr • Hornady ELD-X • Nosler Ballistic tip • Sierra Game King	Zeiss 3-15X42 or Vortex 4-16X44 Riflescope with Ballistic Reticle and/or Turret Swarovski 10X42 Binocular Zeiss/Swarovski Spotting scope Rangefinder
MOOSE	September to October	• Bolt-action, weatherproof • 7mm Rem Mag • 30-06 Sprg • .300 Win Mag • .338 Win Mag	• 150–250 gr • Hornady ELD-X • Nosler Partition	Leupold 2-8X32 or Zeiss 3-15X42 Riflescope with Ballistic Reticle and/or Turret Swarovski 10X42 or 8X32 Binocular Rangefinder
COUES DEER	October to January	• Bolt-action, lightweight • 6.5 Creedmoor • 6.5X284 • .270 Win • 30-06 Sprg	• 130–180 gr • Hornady ELD-X • Nosler Ballistic tip • Sierra Game King	Zeiss 3-15X42 or Vortex 4-16X44 Riflescope with Ballistic Reticle and/or Turret Zeiss 15X56 Binocular w/ lightweight woodsman tripod Zeiss/Swarovski Spotting scope Rangefinder

BOW TIPS	SPECIAL GEAR	OTHER CONSIDERATIONS
Traditional: 45–60 pound (20–27 kg) draw, Woodsman 250 gr broadhead, Easton Axis arrow; max range 30 yards (27 m) **Compound:** 45–70 pound (20–32 kg) draw, 100 gr G5 Montec broadhead, Gold-tip arrow; max range 60 yards (55 m)	Lightweight footwear for long-distance hiking through rugged terrain 3000–4000 CI (49–66 L) pack—if you harvest a deer "way back" you can bone and haul the entire deer out in one superhuman effort	Be prepared for long shots in windy conditions Plan on spending lots of hours glassing for deer
Traditional: 50–65 pound (23–30 kg) draw, Woodsman 250 gr broadhead, Easton Axis arrow; max range 35 yards (32 m) **Compound:** 50–70 pound (23–32 kg) draw, 100 or 125 gr G5 Montec broadhead, Gold-tip arrow; max range 60 yards (55 m)	Primos bugle and cow-call Medium-weight waterproof hunting boots Pack or daypack with basic gear that helps you stay alive through an unexpected night in the woods	Elk are big and weather is often warm; be sure you can get the meat cool and out of the backcountry before it spoils
Traditional: 45–60 pound (20–27 kg) draw, Woodsman 250 gr broadhead, Easton Axis arrow; max range 25 yards (23 m) **Compound:** 45–70 pound (20–32 kg) draw, 100 gr G5 Montec broadhead, Gold-tip arrow; max range 50 yards (46 m)	If you're bowhunting, you'll want a collapsible decoy and a pop-up ground blind Superlight boots (try Danner's "Tachyons")	Glass 'n go; Speed goats are active throughout the day, so hunt till Mr. Big shows up in your scope Expect long shots in windy conditions
Traditional: 50–70 pound (23–32 kg) draw, Woodsman 250 gr broadhead, Easton Axis arrow; max range 40 yards (37 m) **Compound:** 50–70 pound (23–32 kg) draw, 100–125 gr G5 Montec broadhead, Gold-tip arrow; max range 70 yards (64 m)	Sturdy external-frame pack Top-quality rain gear Moose call	Be prepared to carry huge loads of moose meat on your back Most moose live where the big bears are; exercise caution
Traditional: 40–60 pound (18–27) draw, Woodsman 250 gr broadhead, Easton Axis arrow; max range 20 yards (18 m) **Compound:** 40–70 pound (18–32 kg) draw, 100 gr G5 Montec broadhead, Gold-tip arrow; max range 40 yards (37 m)	Lightweight cushion to sit on while glassing Comfortable leather boots Snake gaiters Sunscreen	Plan to spend 6–8 hours per day glassing Shots will likely exceed 200 yards (183 m) and can easily double that distance Expect lots of cactus

075 GO BACKCOUNTRY BOWHUNTING

Hunting the backcountry with stick and string requires hard work, physical fitness, and dedication. But the rewards can be huge: beautiful fall weather and scenery, bugling bull elk, and bachelor bands of above-timberline bucks, to name a few. If you're really lucky, or really good, you just might bring a high-country trophy home with you.

GET RUGGED GEAR Tough terrain demands tough equipment, including archery gear. You can try to pamper a bow, but it's likely to take a beating. Find the toughest sight, rest, and accessories you can.

STRETCH IT OUT Shot distance can stretch beyond typical whitetail hunting ranges, especially when hunting the open terrain of the west. Whether you shoot traditional or compound, you'll be well served to extend your ethical effective range.

GO TRADITIONAL There are serious drawbacks (such as half the effective range), but traditional archery gear also has real advantages over modern gear. It's far more durable (there are no sights, rest, cables, or cams to damage) and lighter. A takedown longbow or recurve may be an ideal backcountry bow. Your entire set—bow, arrows, armguard, and glove—disassembles into a package that will fit in the side-pocket of your backpack, and takes fast 'n' light to a whole new level.

076 GO BIRD HUNTING

Most of my backcountry bird hunting has been a result of some overwhelming opportunivorous urges. Essentially, I become quite a bit of a hunter-gatherer when I'm out in the wilderness and birds make quite the welcome addition to my menu. (Somebody please pass me the salt.)

GET A GROUSE Upland bird seasons run concurrent with big game hunts across much of the west. Turning a grouse from scenic to succulent in a poof of feathers is great practice during any archery hunt, and if a finer tasting bird exists I'm not aware of it.

GO DUCK HUNTING The same shotgun that you carry for bear protection will function admirably as a short-range duck gun. High-country ponds and lakes often support a small population of resident ducks that can be jump-shot with good success.

STAY LEGAL Even in the wilderness (where likely no one is watching) it's important to obey the law. Before venturing into the field, study up on local seasons and regulations, especially if you hope to supplement your menu by hunting and gathering.

077 GO OLD SCHOOL

Walking into the wilderness with a muzzleloader in hand (especially if it's a traditional muzzleloader) makes you as close as you can get to a modern mountain man.

TAKE THE OPPORTUNITY Some states offer dedicated hunts and seasons to hunters who wish to carry a front-stuffer. Study regulations and guidebooks to identify them. You may find a rut-hunt for elk or an early-season muley hunt, which with a little extra effort and skill (muzzleloaders are short-range weapons) can produce big.

PRACTICE FOR PROFICIENCY It takes dedication to become proficient with your muzzleloader. Practice until you know it inside and out before taking it into the backcountry.

BE MISTER CLEAN Black powder and modern substitutes are both incredibly corrosive. Thoroughly clean your rifle soon after every shooting session, or the bore will rust and accuracy will deteriorate. The rifle's lock or action will also corrode and malfunction; you'll be left sitting there listening to bugling elk while holding a useless rifle.

078 KNOW WHY YOU SHOULD HUNT THE BACKCOUNTRY

Actually, you shouldn't hunt the backcountry. That way I'll still have it all to myself. In all seriousness, wilderness hunting is a great blend of magnificence, brutally hard work, golden opportunity, and desolation. It's not for the faint of heart. It is for those few hardy souls who still yearn for wild country, places, and experiences—and are willing to earn them.

DITCH THE CROWD Opening day on front-country public land looks like a farmer's pumpkin patch after the first frost: orange-clad nimrods perched on every point, meadow, and travel route. Dawn is shattered by rifle fire sounding from every direction, wildlife scattering to the four winds.

ENJOY SOLITUDE Opening day in the backcountry will typically dawn quiet and a bit chilly. You may hear a shot in the distance—some other hardy soul making meat. Wish him well and continue your stalk.

HAVE THE RIGHT MIND-SET The wilderness is not for everyone. In fact, most folks prefer the comfort and security of home and civilization to all the rigors and unknowns of backcountry living and that's okay. But if you don't mind being alone, and you like to hunt in big, untrammeled spaces, you should try hunting way back. You may like it. It may even turn into an addiction.

079 GEAR UP TO MAKE MEAT

Once you have an animal down, processing and caring for your meat becomes paramount. Being in the backcountry (far from ice, cold storage, and butchers) necessitates careful and conscientious handling—you can't just yank the innards out and deliver it to the nearest Hack-n-Pack shack. So here's what you need to carry every time you hunt.

STAY SHARP Carry two knives (A) when you hunt (see items 032 and 033). Should you lose or dull one, you can continue your work without delay. Also, carry a small stone with you (B) for sharpening.

DOUBLE BAG IT Carry two suitably sized, lightweight, durable game bags (C). Flies, hornets, and birds are your meat's biggest enemies in the backcountry (flies will crawl into every cranny and lay huge gobs of ultra-disgusting eggs; hornets and birds will just eat your meat). You will want to have everything—quarters, backstraps, and scrap meat—contained in breathable game bags.

TAKE OUT A CONTRACT Yup, contractor-grade trash bags (CTBs) are good for everything (D). I carry two. Use one to line the inside of your backpack or pack panniers before loading meat for the pack out. It'll keep your gear clean and free of bloodstains. If the weather is warm, load your meat into the CTB and submerge it (except for the mouth of the bag) in a cold creek, spring, or lake. This will chill your meat and prevent it from spoiling until you're ready to go.

080 BE GUN SAFE

Everyone knows how to be safe when using a gun, right? Wrong. Guiding plenty of gun-toting hunters has shown me that many folks either don't know or are too stupid to handle firearms safely. Don't be that person.

Firearms can discharge without warning—even empty ones. Indeed, most experts will tell you that if you handle guns long enough you will eventually experience an accidental discharge. It's imperative that you always keep the muzzle of your rifle pointed in a safe direction. The one biggest safety mistake that hunters make is getting careless and waving their rifle at people. Just remember: Never allow your muzzle to point at anything that you are not willing to destroy or kill.

Keep your rifle's chamber cleared while you are hiking, especially if you are in a group. Require all others in the group to do the same. Only if a shot is imminent, or you are sitting down in ambush, should you chamber a round. If the opportunity doesn't pan out, clear your chamber before moving on.

081 GO FISH

Whoa! Look at that! Among a plethora of average-to-small trout lay a fish that could only be described as a lunker. My son and I had been excitedly craning our necks at a mountain goat above us. Now, not allowing our attention to be distracted by something as mundane as a mountain goat, we focused on the huge brook trout swimming in the creek below.

MAKE IT A TRIP Sparkling backcountry lakes and rushing white-water streams offer some of the most pristine fishing left anywhere. Trout who've never seen an artificial lure in their lives sip flies from the surface of slow serpentine creeks. Legend informs us that an angler need cast only a bare hook and he'll reel in creels full of hard-fighting native trout. The fishing alone makes a wilderness trip worthwhile.

SUPPLEMENT YOUR MENU If you are hiking or hunting in the backcountry, you should carry a basic fishing kit. Freeze-dried food gets tiresome and freshly caught trout dusted with salt and pepper makes for a fishtastic addition to the menu. Besides, what better way to while away the midday hours than stalking a deep hole with line, hook, and hopper?

SAVE YOURSELF Should you find yourself caught in a true survival situation, wilderness waters are a great source of food. Even if you don't have modern fishing gear, you can hand-fish (catch fish from hidey-holes under rocks and banks with your hands), build fish traps, and spear fish.

082

PACK THE IDEAL BACK-COUNTRY FISHING KIT

My ideal wilderness fishing kit would include the items below. This kit would be compact and lightweight enough to carry on all trips except really hard-core fast 'n' light trips. It would be capable of catching fish in most waters. If I were enjoying a trip dedicated to fishing, I'd pack a bit more extravagantly and add a spinning rod/reel. If hunting, I'd probably trim it a little, but I still consider this the best all-around fishing kit.

1. Six or seven-piece collapsible fly rod

2. Fly reel with appropriate line

3. Extra leaders and tippet

4. Spool of standard fishing line

5. Two dozen flies

6. Two dozen assorted hooks

7. Lead sinkers/weights

8. Artificial grubs and worms

9. One half-dozen lures (spoons and spinners)

083 LOOK FOR BAIT

I've personally never tried the bare-hook thing, but I do know from experience that backcountry fish will often hammer almost anything you offer with enthusiasm. Try whatever you find—it'll probably work.

BE A ROCK HOUND Turn over large rocks to find grubs, beetles, and worms.

ROLL A LOG Bears know where to look for termites and grubs. Try the same places: Roll old rotten logs, look underneath, and search in any crevices.

STRIP DOWN Peel off your shirt and use it to catch grasshoppers. If backcountry modesty prevents that, use your hat, a towel, or anything else you can throw over those athletic high-country hoppers. Pin 'em down and reach under to grab them.

084 BACKCOUNTRY TOOLKIT
FISHING LINE

If I had to choose just one item for fishing the backcountry, it would be a spool of fishing line. And it's not just for catching fish, either.

CATCH FISH You can make a fishing pole, carve hooks from wood or bone, rig weights, or find bait in the backcountry, but making cordage that's not highly visible to fish is the tough part.

GO HUNTING With a roll of sturdy fishing line, you can bind a spear point to a stick, or an arrowhead and fletchings to a shaft to craft arrows. With some work, fishing line can even be used to help build a deadfall.

PATCH UP You can sew up tears in clothing—or, if you really need, stitch an injury (the nylon in fishing line is the same used in surgical sutures). You can even floss your teeth with it, if you need to.

085 CARRY A COMPASS

One cold October, I guided two hunters from North Dakota on a backcountry elk hunt in Montana's Bitterroot Mountains. They were familiar with the cold, but not with big timber and wilderness terrain.

One day, we picked up the tracks of two mature bulls. We trailed them for hours through the snow, winding across ridges and through canyons. The weather was cold and a light snow continued to fall, the sky totally overcast. Finally we had to abandon the trail—it was near nightfall and we had miles to hike to camp.

My sense of direction has always been excellent and I was confident that I knew just which way to go to get back to camp. I'd been playing a game with my hunters: We would all guess where north was and then I would pull out my compass. I was typically right on, but we'd all laugh when one or both of them was way off. But this time, when I pulled out my compass, it pointed the wrong way. This was a big deal for me; like I said, I have placed a lot of trust in my sense of direction.

After stomping around in the snow for a few minutes, I decided it was more likely that I was messed up than that the poles had shifted. We decided to follow the compass.

Several hours later we stumbled into camp, weary but happy to warm ourselves by the fire. That night, the mercury fell to -20˚F (-29˚C). If I hadn't trusted my compass, we likely would have frozen to death in some lonely canyon.

Post Assessment

 DONE RIGHT

Swallowing my pride and trusting my compass enabled us to find our way safely back to camp, hot food, and warm sleeping bags. Essentially, we lived to hunt another day.

DONE WRONG

If I'd refused to believe my compass (or worse yet, hadn't carried a compass) and forged off into the woods away from camp and safety, we would have been in real danger of freezing to death.

086 BUILD A RIFLE SCABBARD

A good saddle scabbard will carry and protect your rifle when you're on the trail. Here's how to build your own. Scabbards for iron-sighted rifles are easy; for scoped rifles it's harder.

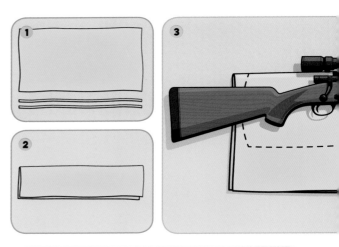

Tools and Materials

- Saddle-skirting leather, about 2 x 3 ½ feet (0.61 m x 1 m), 11–12 ounces (4.4–4.8 mm) thick
- Contact cement
- Two harness needles
- Awl (larger than the needles)
- Heavy waxed nylon sewing thread
- One $^3/_4$-inch (1.91-cm) D-ring
- Two $^5/_8$-inch (1.5-cm) buckles
- Copper #9 rivets w/set (optional)

STEP 1 Cut two leather strips, each $^5/_8$ inch by 3½ feet long (1.5 cm x 1 m), for straps to buckle your scabbard to a saddle.

STEP 2 Dampen your leather evenly, just enough that it's malleable and holds whatever shape you make it. Fold the leather in half along the centerline.

STEP 3 Lay your rifle (wrapped in plastic to prevent rust) on the leather, barrel just below the centerline fold. If the rifle has a scope it will protrude above the centerline fold. Draw a line along the contour of the rifle 3 inches (7.5 cm) out for a slender lever action, 4 inches (10 cm) out for a rifle with a wider profile (such as a bolt action). If it has a scope, make a mark on the fold 2 inches (5 cm) ahead of the objective bell.

STEP 4 Open your folded leather and cut along your line up to the fold. Refold the leather, trace your cut onto the lower leather, open, and cut that side. For a scoped scabbard, cut directly down the center of the fold to the mark that you made two inches in front of your scope. Finish out the end with a teardrop shaped cut.

STEP 5 Cut a $^5/_8$-inch (1.5-cm) strip of leather (from the scrap of one of your fresh cuts), full length from end to fold, to serve as your "welt." Cut another strip from your scrap, 4 inches (10 cm) wide and 1 inch (2.5 cm) longer than your centerline scope cut. Cut one end into a long taper, and round out the tip. We'll call this the scope leather.

STEP 6 If you're building a non-scoped rifle scabbard, skip this step. Otherwise, spread a thin layer of contact cement along both sides of your scope cut and around the teardrop shape at the front end of the cut. Put the glue on the grain

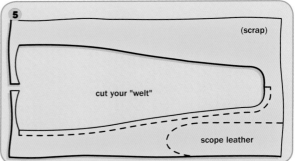

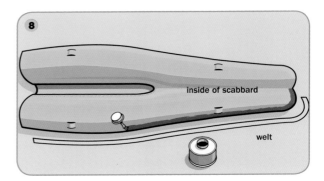

(top) side of the leather. Spread a thin layer of cement along both edges and around the taper of your scope leather, on the flesh (bottom) side. Let the cement dry until it has almost lost its tack, then stick your scope strip firmly into place, overlapping about ½ inch (1.25 cm). Sew into place with a saddle stitch (see step 9).

STEP 7 Make four clean cuts on each side of your scabbard, ¾ inch (2 cm) long and ¾ inch (2 cm) apart, to form bridges of leather that your straps will later slide through. Cut a leather strip ¾ by 4 inches (2 x 10 cm) and fold through your D-ring. Stitch or rivet this into place on the side of your scabbard, about 5 inches (12.5 cm) from the mouth.

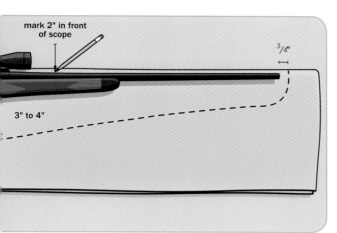

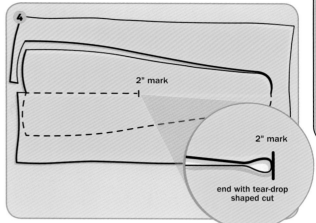

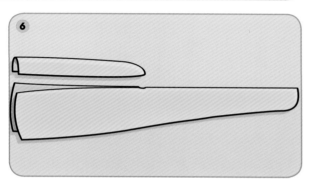

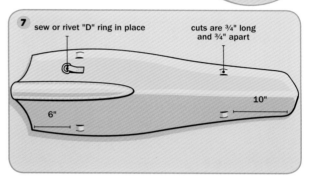

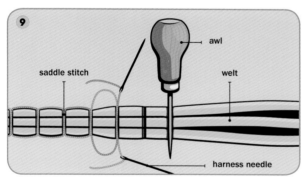

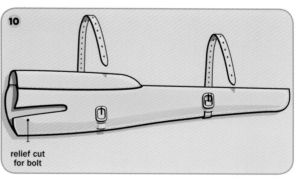

STEP 8 Spread a thin layer of cement on the flesh side of your scabbard along both edges to be sewn, and on both sides of your welt. Let it dry until the tack is almost gone, then stick the welt in place along one edge. Fold your scabbard shut and stick the second edge to the welt, lining up everything perfectly.

STEP 9 Sew along the entire welt with a saddle stitch. Make your seam about ⅜ inch (1 cm) from the edge of the leather, stitches approximately ¼ inch (6 mm) long. Keep the leather damp while you sew. Cut your thread 2½ times longer than your seam and thread a needle onto each end. Pull your stitches nice and tight. End with a square knot, cut your ends

½ inch (1.25 cm) long, and burn off with a match so your knot never comes undone. (Wrap your pinky finger in electrical tape so the thread doesn't cut into your finger when you pull the stitches tight.)

STEP 10 Clean the edges of your leather with an edger or knife, and polish smooth with a damp cloth. Make a relief cut to accommodate a bolt if present. Sew or rivet buckles to one end of your straps, cut a taper to the other end, and punch holes 1 inch (2.5 cm) apart starting below the taper. Thread through your bridge-cuts on your scabbard. Let dry completely (ideally with your plastic-wrapped rifle inside), and apply neatsfoot oil. Saddle up and head for high country.

PACK A BACKCOUNTRY REPAIR KIT

I recall one hard core elk hunt I went on with several friends. My brand-new pack ruptured a buckle before we even left the trailhead. I quickly pulled out my wire and fixed the buckle, and on we went without a hitch.

Buckles break, packs tear, and sleeping pads get punctured. Bridle reins get broken and cookware comes apart. These things are best repaired in the field. Here's what should be in your backcountry repair kit.

GET WIRED A small spool of good 14-gauge wire can work wonders in the backcountry. Fix hardware, sew leather strapping, repair buckles, fashion a hook—I could keep going.

PATCH IT UP It's a real sinking feeling to lie down on a leaky pad. Bring a suitable patch kit for your sleeping pad, 'cause sooner or later it's gonna get punctured.

SEW WHAT Anything that needs it. Pack a couple harness needles and about 10–15 feet (3–4.5 m) of heavy waxed nylon leather sewing thread.

TAPE IT You can repair anything with duct tape, right? Bring a small roll.

088 REPAIR WEAR AND TEAR

The best time to fix worn or broken gear is not when you are on the trail, but during long winter evenings. It'll keep the spark alive and start you dreaming and planning next year's wilderness adventures.

PATCH UP SLEEPING GEAR Check anything you sleep with, such as tents, sleeping bags, and especially sleeping pads, for holes. (Holes in sleeping pads are usually pinholes—to find them, fully inflate the pad and then submerge it in your bathtub. Mark any bubble sources with a sharpie.) Repair as necessary.

FIX PACKS Check your backpack and horsepacks for damage. Repair broken buckles, stitch blown seams, and patch up any holes you might find.

OIL YOUR LEATHER Oil any dried-out leather on your saddles, packsaddles, bridles, hobbles, scabbards, and or other leather item with neatsfoot oil. Warm the oil so it penetrates the leather and repeat applications until the leather becomes supple but not saturated.

CHECK HARDWARE Sharpen knives, axes, and saws. Repair stoves and cookware. Fix headlamps, flashlights, and lanterns, and straighten tent stakes.

089 STASH IT FOR LATER

When the fun is all done, and you return home from your backcountry adventure, it's time to clean and stow your gear away.

DON'T BE LAZY Don't just unload stuff onto the garage floor and head for the shower. Now is the best time to tend to your gear.

SCRUB IT Clean everything that has mud, blood, or other grime on it. Launder and fold meat sacks so they'll be ready for your next hunt. Scrub dishes and cookware. Wash boots. You get the picture.

MARK DAMAGE Inspect your gear as you store it. Mark any needed repairs with tape to quickly find and fix it when you find time.

STOW IT Organize and store everything. Next time you're ready for the backcountry, it'll be waiting.

SKILLS

I STOOD WIDE-EYED, LISTENING

to a modern-day mountain man recount a tale of a wilderness elk hunt.

"We'd run out of food, and I was getting hungry. I always hunt the best when I'm hungry."

I thought about that. It made sense to me.

"I was hunting my way through thick timber when I smelled elk—just a quick sniff, then it was gone. I started zigzagging back and forth across the wind, trying to pick up the scent again."

I mentally filed that away for future reference.

"Catching the scent, I worked my way upwind, following the smell to the elk. The smell grew stronger, and there they were in a little meadow. They busted for the timber, and I shot at the bull, and hit him. He kept running. I shot again, and then again, hitting each time. We built a fire, and roasted fresh elk meat on green sticks. It was sure good."

"How big was he?" I asked.

The mountain man looked at me. "He was a six point."

Skill must be earned. It's not cheap, and can't be gained all at once. This chapter is all about skills to help you flourish in the backcountry, and it's only the tip of the iceberg. But master these techniques and you're ready for a backcountry, caveman kind of adventure. Study up, put these skills to use, and develop some wilderness wisdom of your own. When we meet, I'd love to learn from you—in a way, I'm still a beginner too.

The backcountry is a good teacher. Listen to her.

090 RIG YOUR VEHICLE

Leaving your car or truck at the trailhead is your final step out of civilization and into the wilderness. And when you're ready return to civilization, it's the vehicle (pardon the pun) that will carry you there. Here are some things that will ensure it's ready when you need it.

STASH A KEY Hide a key securely under your vehicle. (I leave one there permanently.) Wire or attach it somewhere that's not hard to access, but where it's hidden from renegades, outlaws, and such.

CARRY CABLES Stow a set of jumper cables in your rig. If something runs the battery down, you'll be able to request help from a friendly soul and jump-start your vehicle.

PREP FOR TIRE TROUBLE It's a sinking feeling (I speak from experience) to return tired and hungry from being in the backcountry to find that your truck or trailer has a flat tire. Carry a good spare, jack, and lug wrench; in addition, carry a small but sturdy air-compressor that plugs into your cigarette lighter. Add a tire plug kit and you'll be set to deal with almost any deflating emergency.

STASH SURVIVAL GEAR I always keep a spare sleeping bag and pad, as well as a set of clothing, some food, and some water in my vehicle when I leave it at the trailhead. Should I or another member of my party find ourselves close to the trailhead and in trouble, there will be warm, dry clothing, food, water, and a place to sleep.

CHAIN UP If you'll be leaving your rig at a remote, high-elevation trailhead, you might want to consider stowing a good set of tire chains inside. Snowplows don't often visit those remote trailheads, and if an unexpected high-country snowstorm buries your vehicle, you'll be able to chain up and bully your way out of trouble.

091 ALWAYS BE COURTEOUS

Trailhead etiquette simply entails being considerate of other hikers, horsepackers, fishing parties, and hunters you meet.

GIVE GROUND Don't crowd people, especially if they're loading or unloading pack animals. Give them room to work.

COMMUNICATE Introduce yourself and share travel plans. This will help avoid potential traffic jams on narrow mountain trails and give everyone an idea of where other people will be—and who knows? You might make some new friends.

PREVENT CROWDS No one goes out into the backcountry hoping to find a crowd of strangers. If you do happen to learn that another party plans to go the same place that you and your folks are headed, think about changing your plans a bit so both parties have some space. If you can't be or aren't willing to be flexible, consider gently informing the other party that you'll be in the same area, and offer them some goodwill such as "Let me know if I can be of service" or "I'll be hunting that area too; perhaps we can communicate or work together?" A little communication goes a long way.

092 POCKET THE ESSENTIALS

From the time that you pass the trailhead sign on your way into the wilderness, until the time you arrive safe and sound back at your vehicle, there are a few items you should always have in your possession. Someday they might even save your life.

HEADLAMP I learned this the hard way one black night, very nearly breaking my leg in a tangled morass of dead and down timber. Make it a habit to keep a good headlamp in your pocket (or on your head).

LIGHTER A cold night away from camp is made bearable—and survivable—by the crackle of a friendly fire. Should you become lost, hurt, or otherwise stranded overnight, you'll always have the means to start a fire.

MULTI-TOOL Whether you need to disassemble a jammed firearm, skin a deer, open a can of tuna, or pull a cactus spine, this little jack-of-all-trades has you covered. Keep one on your person at all times.

093 PLAN YOUR ROUTE

Before embarking on a wilderness trip you should plan out where you will go, how long you will stay there, and when you will return.

CHOOSE YOUR PLEASURE The purpose of your trip will dictate where you go. Are you scouting for a backcountry hunting area? Do you dream of fishing unspoiled waters? Have a goal of hiking a historic trail? You should determine your destination(s) first.

GO POINT TO POINT Study topo maps to find maintained trails that will access your destination lake, high-country basin, or climbing peak. You may get lucky and find a trail that leads directly there. More likely, you will discover a trail that, while perhaps a bit circuitous, can still provide a solid route to your destination. You might find a pair of equally favorable routes, giving you the opportunity to explore one trail on the way in and the other while traveling out.

STAY AWHILE Decide how long you'd like to spend in your backcountry honey-hole. Then calculate how much travel time you'll need on your way in and out, and total it up. Plan a day as a cushion at the end of your trip so, if something unforeseen happens, you'll still have time to make that wedding or clock into work.

NOTIFY SOMEONE Give your family members or friends a detailed itinerary, including dates, travel routes, predicted camp locations, and most importantly, when they should expect you to emerge from the wilderness. That way an efficient search can be organized, should you encounter a problem and need rescuing.

094 ESTIMATE TRAVEL SPEED

To predict a day's travel distance, you'll need to know the weight you're carrying, whether you're backpacking or horsepacking, and the terrain.

A reasonably fit person carrying a load of 35 to 45 pounds (16–20 kg) can hike about 2 miles per hour (3 km/h). If the terrain is gentle and the hiker very fit, they may travel a bit faster. With a heavy load and/or steep or rough terrain, it'll be slower. Eight to 12 miles (13–19 km) is a good long distance for a backpacker to cover in a day, especially if they want energy left over to do a little fishing, hunting, or photo shooting.

Packhorses carrying loads of 125 to 175 pounds (57–80 kg) will average nearly 3 miles per hour (5 km/h). If loads are heavy or terrain is steep, they'll slow down to about 2 miles per hour (4 km/h). Loaded horses will cover 15 to 25 miles (24–40 km) in a day, depending on terrain and altitude. They will need a good ration of grain or pellets, or plenty of time to graze each night, if you want them to maintain that rate of travel for days on end.

Air gets pretty thin way up yonder; even a horse or hiker that lives at 6,000 to 7,000 feet (1,800–2,100 m) will struggle for oxygen at 10,000 to 12,000 feet (3,000–3,600 m). Go easy on yourself or your horse when at high altitudes—especially if you come from the lowlands.

095 BUSHWHACK A NEW TRAIL

Often the best hunting spots and finest fishing waters have no trail leading to them. Make your own route into those places and you'll have your own little hunting or fishing paradise.

ABANDON SECURITY Many folks find it incredibly intimidating to leave the security of maintained trails in favor of bushwhacking their way into the unknown. If this describes you, I urge you to gather up your courage, navigate carefully, and go explore new places. You will be rewarded with the joy of having undisturbed territory all to yourself, like a real adventurer.

RUN THE RIDGES Oftentimes, the best traveling is on the crest of a ridge. Terrain is less steep, brush more open, and visibility better. If you're hunting, though, you'll want to avoid skylining yourself by traveling just off the crest.

SCOUT A ROUTE The best time to learn that a route is impassable is not the night before opening day. Learn the best way in and out of an area before you need to get there in a hurry, or pack a load of meat out.

DON'T TIME YOURSELF You should never set any kind of tight schedule when you're working on bushwhacking your way through new-to-you territory. You might make it to your planned destination in less than a day, or it might take you twice that long.

DON'T HORSE AROUND Exercise great caution when taking horses—especially a string of pack animals—through uncharted territory. Avoid heavy deadfall timber, boulder fields, and cliffy areas. If you're trying to travel through really rough areas it's best to scout a route on foot before trying it with horses.

096 READ A TOPO MAP

Before satellites, Google Earth, or GPS systems, there were topographical maps. Now, by grace of modern technology, all you must do is set your GPS to "Go To" a specific destination and stumble blithely along, staring at your screen and missing all the wonders of the backcountry. Don't let your GPS become a crutch that replaces good woodsmanship.

Topo maps are one of the best tools you can use in the backcountry. Your GPS can lead you around like a blind person on a string, but a topo map will give you a real understanding of your location, route of travel, and your terrain. The best size for backcountry use is the 7.5-Minute, 1:24,000 series USGS map.

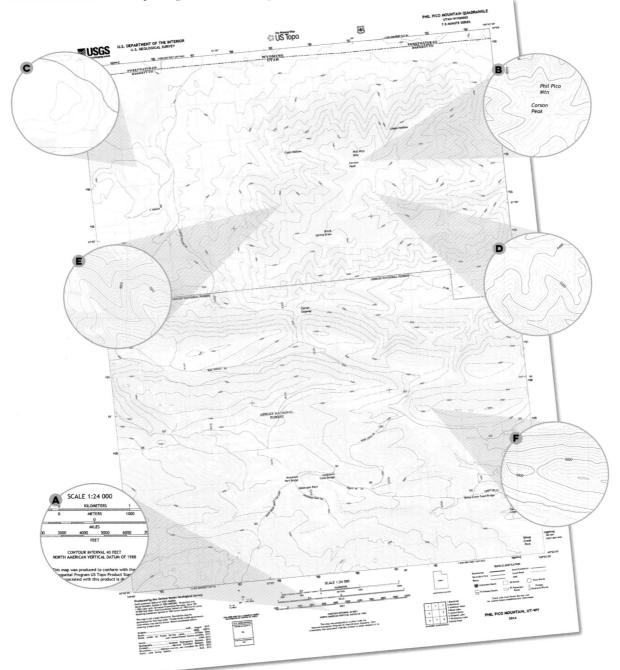

097 LINE UP

Arguably the most important feature on a topo map, contour lines show the shape of the terrain. Ridges, valleys, canyons, saddles, and peaks all stand out in stark relief once you understand contour lines.

Ⓐ CONTOUR INTERVAL You'll find this on the margin of your map. This will tell you how much distance there is between each contour line. A common interval is 40 feet (12 m), meaning that there is 40 feet (12 m) of difference in elevation between lines. (Remember that contour lines maintain the same elevation along their entire path.) Close together lines denote steep terrain, while more distant lines designate gentler terrain. Every bolded fifth line will show the elevation of that specific line.

Ⓑ PEAKS Look for a series of circuitous contour lines (each line follows the hill or peak around to form a whole circle), usually irregularly shaped, that end with a final small circle. This is the top of the peak. A small hill may be shown by a single circuitous contour line.

Ⓒ DEPRESSIONS Similar to peaks, these are represented by a circuitous contour line; the difference is demonstrated by inward facing tic marks.

Ⓓ RIDGES Two series of contour lines roughly parallel each other, coming together at the point or end of the ridge.

Ⓔ DRAINAGES AND VALLEYS These are shown in similar fashion to ridges, with the difference being that the apex of each V points uphill or upstream. Often times, you'll see one or more blue lines designating creeks or streams at the bottom of the drainage.

Ⓕ SADDLES Low places in ridges or between peaks, these often offer an easy path across the ridge. Trails pass through them, utilized by people and wildlife alike. Keep this in mind when scouting for a route or good hunting spot.

098 COMPREHEND THE COLORS

There are six colors used on topo maps to designate landscape, water, terrain, and other features.

BROWN Contour lines are shown in brown. Very gentle terrain, where the lines are far apart, will sometimes have intermediate contour lines (half the distance of standard contour interval) shown in very thin light brown lines (G).

GREEN Timber, trees, or overhead canopy (H). Remember, every tree can't be shown, so green means an area of thick timber. Single trees, or even small clumps of trees, won't be shown at all.

WHITE White denotes open areas—typically grass, meadows, rock fields, or surfaces (I).

BLUE Solid blue lines designate flowing streams or rivers. Dashed or dotted blue lines are a sign for intermittent water. Solid blue areas are lakes; marshes appear similar to lakes, but show little blue grasses or reeds rather than solid blue (J).

BLACK Man-made features—trails, roads, campgrounds, airstrips, and so on—are shown in black (K).

RED Survey marks and information are shown in red, but won't mean much in a backcountry setting.

099 MEASURE THE DISTANCE

The bar-scale (L) shows a scale that demonstrates distance on your map, usually in feet and miles. Cut a small piece of string or jewelry chain to the length shown as a mile (1.6 km). You can measure distance on your map with a fair degree of accuracy by tracing the trail one section at a time with your string or chain. Just remember to keep count of the sections.

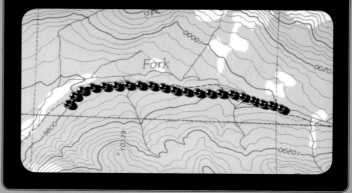

100 READ THE LANDSCAPE

Do you know if you can climb up that ribbon cliff? Is that meadow just tall grass, or is it a bog that you or your horse could become trapped in? Can you cross this roaring creek here, or should you find a better place? Ability to read the landscape comes with time and experience. Here are some tips that will get you started.

CLIMB THROUGH ROCKS Getting up a cliffy mountainside is tricky, especially if you're wearing a pack. Study (this will be a recurring theme) the mountainside for a route before you begin your ascent. Find a route that provides good footing, plenty of handholds, and safe margins from long drops all the way from your position to the top of the ascent.

DON'T GET BOGGED DOWN Mountain meadows and marshes don't pose much threat to a person on foot. But your horses' sharp hooves can cut through the surface turf and find . . . nothing. He'll have to lunge and fight his way back to solid footing, and it'll take everything he's got to do it. An experienced horse will recognize boggy conditions

and try to turn away. You'll have to make a call: Is this spot dangerous, or can your horse wade through the muck with a little courage and effort? If the surface jiggles and quivers like the surface of a waterbed, get out fast.

LOOK AHEAD Study the landscape for the best travel route. Look for gentle ridges, open woods, and low saddles. Learn to recognize good places to travel; avoid problem areas such as deadfall thickets, boulder fields, and any steep brushy mountainsides.

SWITCH BACK The best way for a horse to climb steep terrain is in a switchback pattern. It works great for the backpacker carrying a heavy load, too.

ROCK UP AND DOWN Steep, smooth rock surfaces are dangerous for horses. Don't walk him across any steeply slanted rock surface. Make him go straight up or down. He may slip and slide, but he'll stay on his feet. Take him across and he's almost sure to fall.

101 CROSS A CREEK

I don't know about you, but cold water makes me gasp, and I don't like the idea of being swept away one bit.

ESTIMATE CURRENT Study the water. Rapid water deeper than your knee or thigh is not safe on foot; fast water that reaches midway or higher up your horse's side will rob him of secure footing. Look downstream: if you're swept away, what's out there?

READ FOOTING Check the bottom. A rocky bottom means no quicksand; you won't mire a foot or bog a horse.

CUT A WALKING STICK If you have to cross a rapid creek, use a sturdy stick or two (A). Take one careful step at a time, while keeping your stick(s) securely braced to your downstream side for more stability.

PREPARE TO JETTISON It's a worst-case scenario: If you go down and can't immediately regain your footing, you'll need to get out of your pack and, if you're wearing any, your hip boots or waders (B). If you don't, you'll drown. It's going to leave you in a really tough survival situation—no tent, no dry clothes, no gear—but at least you'll be alive to try.

HORSE CROSSING A horse can cross rough water far better than a person (C). Let him take his time and pick his way. If he gets swept downstream stay with him; he may regain his footing. If he has to swim, then get off and float alongside so that you don't push him under, but maintain a death-grip on the saddle horn. Keep guiding him downstream, in a quartering direction toward a bank he can climb out on.

Stay calm, and keep him calm. If you lose hold of the saddle horn grab his tail. It'll be floating on the surface, and he'll tow you to shore.

102 WATCH YOUR BACKTRAIL

You're not looking for a posse, but still, you should memorize the terrain you've come through. Everything looks different when you look back. Watch your backtrail, and you'll be able to retrace your steps out of the backcountry with greater confidence.

103 SCOUT WITH GOOGLE EARTH

In today's technologically advanced world, information is available at the touch of a keyboard. Wilderness terrain is no different (perhaps unfortunately). Google Earth will give you a bird's-eye view of anywhere.

STUDY TERRAIN Zoom in on meadows or parks to see if they are grass or rock fields. Measure exact distance using the "ruler" feature. Examine ridgelines, saddles, and drainages for good travel routes. Check out high points and buttes in search of good vantage points to hunt from.

LOOK FOR WATER Check and verify water sources with a close-up look. Remember: the image you're viewing is likely not current (they're updated every several years) and a pond that's full in the photo may not be full in real life. Reliable water sources such as springs, creeks, lakes, and marshes show a different shade of green for year-round water.

FIND A BIG GAME HONEY-HOLE Study your target area to find potential elk wallows, feeding and bedding areas, likely travel routes—and heck, even a good tree to hang a stand in.

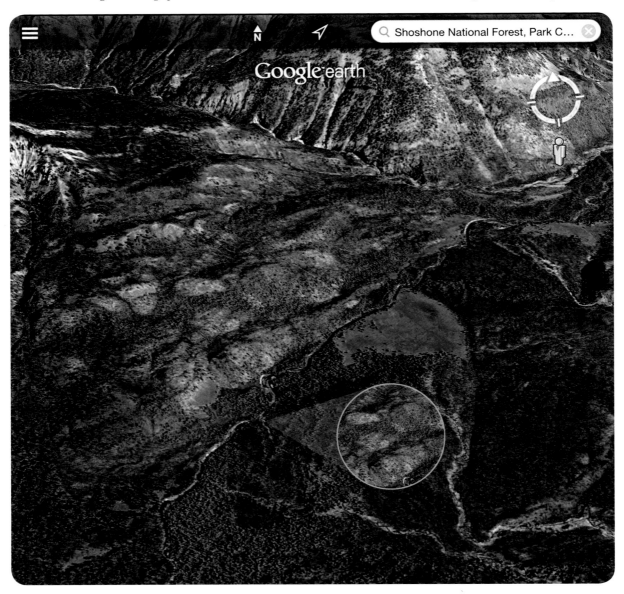

104 WATCH OUT FOR BIG STORMS

In my experience, the most dangerous backcountry storms take place in either high-elevation mountains, or the arid canyon-country of the desert southwest. Rain, snow, high winds, and lightning will buffet you in the high-country, while heavy rains in the desert can cause flash floods of epic proportion.

Study weather forecasts before your trip. It's just a prediction and can't forewarn you completely, but it'll at least give you an idea of what to expect. Then, keep an eye to the sky and a feel to the wind to anticipate weather in your locality.

When you sense a big storm coming (after a few encounters with violent storms you'll feel it in your bones) you should consider hightailing it for the trailhead—especially if you are not prepared for such weather, or if you have children along. If you do decide to stay in the wilderness, aggressively gear up to weather a heavy storm.

105 WEATHER THE WEATHER

Wilderness storms pose a greater threat to the average backcountry hiker than anything else. Other things we can control or manage, but not so with the weather.

AVOID A STORM I've come close to getting struck by lightning several times and have a healthy respect for that much electricity in one place. If a lightning storm is headed your way, you'll want to avoid any exposed ridges and peaks and try to distance yourself from bodies of water and metal objects. Avoid tall trees and big open spaces. Find a semi-large grove of average-sized trees, get in the middle, and hunker down till the storm blows over.

DON'T GET BLOWN AWAY Falling trees are usually the scariest result of high wind. Although, watching your tent cartwheel across a meadow with your gear inside isn't great either. Pick a campsite absent of widow-makers (large standing dead trees). Pay extra attention to securing your tents and tarps so the wind won't carry them away.

STAY HIGH AND DRY Heavy rain can drench you in moments, making you miserable and susceptible to hypothermia. It can also cause flooding, washing under your tent and through your camp, and turn docile creeks to raging rivers. Use a little foresight when choosing a campsite (don't put it in a hollow or ravine) and setting up sturdy shelters for yourself and your gear.

COME IN FROM THE COLD I'd rather deal with snow in the backcountry than rain, but a big snowstorm is still dangerous. If you're caught away from camp in a heavy snowstorm with strong wind—a recipe for some blinding whiteout conditions—it's easy to become disoriented, and your GPS won't work very well. Find shelter and hunker down until the weather clears a bit, and you or your GPS regain a sense of direction. Another scenario in which snow becomes dangerous is heavy accumulation, resulting in 18 to 48 inches (45–120 cm) of snow on the ground. Deep snow is hard to walk through, especially if you are carrying a pack. Trails become hard to follow, and your situation can rapidly become desperate.

106 HANDLE HORSE FEAR

Horses are prey animals. They understand that there's always something somewhere that would like to eat them. This, understandably, keeps them on their toes.

Many people are, unfortunately, scared of horses. The ironic thing is, no horse would ever expect that of us. The idea that a person (semi-predator) would be afraid of them (prey) would be absurd, to their way of thinking. The result of this phenomenon is that when your horse senses that you're afraid he thinks, "Uh-oh; danger lurks nearby." He considers you the leader of the herd, far wiser than himself, and trusts your judgment. If you become nervous, he's got good reason to follow suit.

Even if you are nervous, fake a calm, confident air. Relax your shoulders. Breathe deeply and look at some beautiful scenery. Pat your horse's neck and speak to him in a calm gentle tone. Pretty quickly, he'll become convinced that there's nothing to be afraid of. He'll relax, so will you, and soon you'll be moving cheerfully along together.

107 KNOW YOUR HORSE

Most horses are nice folks. They're predominantly honest, typically willing to work hard, and, if treated right, forgiving in nature.

CARE FOR HOOVES Horses' hooves should be trimmed every couple months, or they will grow long and eventually begin to break off in chunks, potentially laming the horse. When a horse is working regularly, you'll want to keep him shod, replacing shoes every six to ten weeks.

DON'T GO BAREFOOT Backcountry travel is often rough and rocky. Horses need to be well-shod before your trip so they aren't likely to "throw" or lose a shoe. If they do, they will become sore-footed and lame before long. Carry an easy-boot or two on your packhorse to cope with such an eventuality.

JOIN THE HERD Horses are, by instinct, herd-bound. This means that they feel vulnerable anytime they're separated from their buddies. This can be a good thing when you're in the backcountry, keeping your horses together and preventing those turned loose to graze from straying far. It can also be a real problem if you try to ride a single horse away from the main group. Savvy experienced horses will be used to this and won't make a fuss, but my recommendation is to take a second horse along if you want to take a backcountry jaunt. Just don't leave one horse alone at camp, for the same reason. As long as there are two or more horses together they're usually okay.

MAKE FRIENDS Get to know your horse-buddy, what he likes, where to scratch him, his favorite snacks. Pamper him a little, and he'll develop a loyalty to you. He'll work better for you, trust you more, and try a little harder.

DON'T AMBUSH Even the most experienced, trail-savvy horse will jump if he's startled. Young and "green" horses expect danger to pop up from behind every rock; they're especially apt to shy or even lash out with their feet in self-defense when scared. Be aware that horses are wired this way, and take pains to avoid startling them.

Storm clouds loomed ominously above us.

The edge of the plateau was still several miles away when the storm caught us.

Lightning crashed all around us but there was nowhere to hide.

Finally we reached the edge of the plateau, trotting our nervous horses down the rain slippery trail and into the timber.

We sat on our horses and watched the thunderstorm roll on across the mountain and away. Safety never felt so good!

109 GEAR UP

Saddling your horse isn't rocket science, but does need to be done right. Here's how. To unsaddle, just reverse the steps.

STEP 1 Brush or curry your horse. Be sure his withers, back, and cinch area are nice and clean.

STEP 2 Inspect the underside of your saddle pad for stuff like hairballs, dirt, twigs, burrs, and stickers. Once it's all clean, set it on your horse's back, a little forward of right. Pull it gently backward and into place. This will smooth his hair down nice and comfortable.

STEP 3 Always from the left side of your horse, swing the saddle smoothly into place, exercising care to not bang or smack him with any of the loose trappings (stirrups, cinches, breast collar, and so on).

STEP 4 Ensure all the trappings are hanging free, not stuck under the saddle. Set your saddle well centered on your pad. If your cinches are hung on carriers, let them down.

STEP 5 Test the fit of your cinch by holding it in place on the right side of the horse—observe where the center of the cinch falls on the horse's brisket (sternum). Adjust the cinch up or down at the billet till its center sits just a mite short of mid brisket (as you tighten the cinch it'll center up).

STEP 6 On the left side of your horse thread your latigo out through the front cinch ring and then back in through the rigging ring. Go down and out through the cinch ring again, and your wraps are complete. Pull snug and buckle.

STEP 7 If your cinch doesn't have a buckle end, tie a latigo knot as shown.

STEP 8 Buckle your back cinch, if present. You want it not quite snug.

STEP 9 Buckle the breast collar, if present, just short of snug. Congratulations! You're done. Remember to re-tighten the front cinch before mounting.

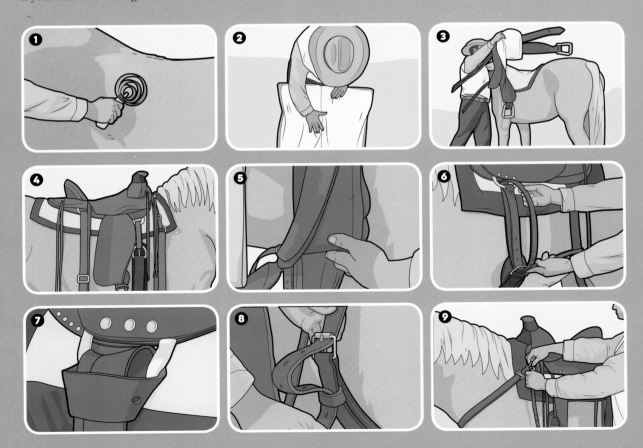

110 SADDLE A PACKHORSE

Follow these directions to unlock the mysteries of saddling a pack animal. Remember to always saddle and unsaddle from the horse's left side. To unsaddle a packhorse, again, just reverse all the steps.

STEP 1 Brush or curry the horse free of all dirt, dried sweat, and debris.

STEP 2 Check the pack pad for nasties. Clean, and smooth it into place on your packhorse's back.

STEP 3 Pile the latigos, cinches, breast collar, and britchen on top of your packsaddle. Set the whole thing on the horse, centered nicely on the pack pad.

STEP 4 Disassemble your big stack of tack from atop the packsaddle till latigos, cinches, and breast collar are

hanging down, and the britchen is piled behind the packsaddle on the horse's rump.

STEP 5 Do up the front cinch first. Follow by doing up the back cinch, which should sit directly behind the front cinch, tightening it in similar fashion. Packsaddles will typically have latigos on each side of the saddle, rather than a billet on the right side as a riding saddle does. The latigos should be fastened with a wrap just like a riding saddle, and be used to adjust the pack cinches till they are even and square on the horse's chest.

STEP 6 Buckle the breast collar almost snug.

STEP 7 Pull the britchen gently down over the horses' hindquarters till it

settles into place. Adjust all the straps just short of snug. The broad horizontal strap at the bottom of the britchen should be adjusted to ride as shown.

STEP 8 Pull the horse's tail gently sideways and out from under the britchen. A tail is personal property, so get his permission and show a little respect during this maneuver.

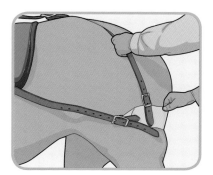

111 HOBBLE YOUR HORSE

Tantamount to handcuffing a ruffian that you want to detain and contain, putting hobbles on your horse will keep him around—or at least slow his escape. If your horse has never worn hobbles before, you should make sure he's in a nice open area with soft ground or grass the first time you put them on. He's likely to lunge around and rear repeatedly, waving his forelegs in the air (don't get struck) while he learns to deal with being hobbled. It's okay; just stay calm and let him work it out. Once your horse learns what it's all about, he'll stand quietly while you put the hobbles on and then go right to grazing.

STEP 1 Once again, work from the horse's left side. Pet his legs a bit to let him know you're there, and if his feet are far apart gently lift the near (left) foot and set it down by the off (right) foot.

STEP 2 Wrap the middle of the hobbles around the offside fetlock (ankle) and thread the end through the first square "ring." Follow up by threading the end through the second square ring.

STEP 3 Buckle the hobbles around the near fetlock. Be quick and gentle, but try to get the hobbles nice and tight so that your horse won't slip out of them. If he doesn't like being hobbled, and gives you a fight, buckle the hobbles between his knee and fetlock. The hobbles will settle down around his fetlocks pretty quick.

STEP 4 Be aware that your horse will need to build calluses before wearing hobbles for long periods of time. So just put them on for an hour or two until he gets used to them and his ankles get tough.

112 USE A HALTER FOR CONTROL

A horse needs to be haltered anytime you want or need control of him. If you're tying him for the night, loading a pack on him, or tailing him in a pack string, he needs a halter. Here's how to put it on—as always, from the left side.

STEP 1 Sidle up to your loose horse, kinda careful-like, give him a treat or a pat, and put your leadrope around his neck just behind his head. This will help you hold him should he decide that he just doesn't want to show up for work today.

STEP 2 Put your right arm over the horse's neck. Grasp the halter with the buckle end in your left hand and the tongue end in your right. Capture his nose inside the halter. (Plenty of horses will politely lower their noses into the halter of their own accord at this point.)

STEP 3 Pull the halter up till it fits almost snug, and then buckle or tie it in place.

STEP 4 Remove the lead-rope from around his neck—you're all done.

113 GIVE YOUR HORSE A BRIDLE

Putting a bridle on your horse is a simple task, but it seems to stymie many beginning rider. Here's how to do it as always, from the horse's left side.

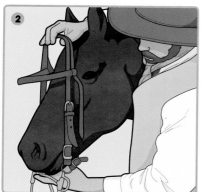

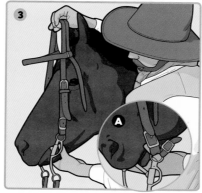

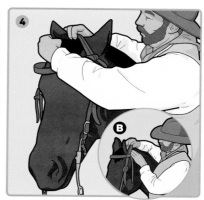

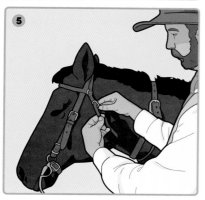

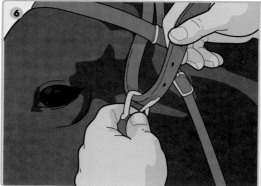

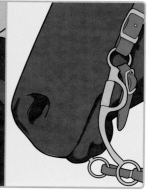

STEP 1 Some riders leave the halter on and put the bridle over it. If you prefer to remove the halter, do so, but buckle it around his neck so he won't wander off while you're bridling him.

STEP 2 Grasp the bridle by the headpiece (which goes behind his ears) with your right hand. Take the bit assembly in your left hand, spreading the bit and chinstrap into position. Gently slide everything over the horse's nose so that he's captive and can't move his head to escape.

STEP 3 Carefully but confidently insert the bit between your horse's teeth. If he clamps his teeth together, stick your left thumb into the corner of his

mouth and tickle his gums (A); he'll open up. (There's a wide gap between his front and rear teeth; don't worry about getting bitten.) Lift the headpiece with your right hand to pull the bit fully into your horse's mouth and hold it there.

STEP 4 Pull the headpiece gently over the horse's right ear, then his left. (Use your left hand to manage the ears so you don't crumple them too badly as you pull the headpiece over.) Adjust his mane and forelock so he'll be comfortable, and fix the brow band so it's nicely in place.

STEP 5 Buckle the throat latch, to hold the bridle in place should anything try to pull it off.

STEP 6 Adjust the cheek-pieces until the bit sits comfortably in the corners of your horse's mouth, with just a tiny wrinkle pulled into the skin. Unbuckle the halter from his neck, and you're ready to go.

> **ARAM SAYS** "In cold temps, you should warm the bit before inserting it (no one likes having their tongue stuck to frozen metal) by holding the bit in your hands, or hanging the bridle over the horse's saddle-horn, with the bit tucked under a corner of the saddle blanket where it's against the horse's warm hide."

114 LEARN THE RULES OF HORSEPACKING

The packer's art is delightfully complex and takes work to master. These tips will simplify things and get you on the path to being a master backcountry horse-packer.

DON'T OVERLOAD One hundred and fifty pounds (68 kg) is a good weight for most packhorses to carry, with 200 pounds (90 kg) as the maximum. Some animals can carry more (I once had a huge mustang who carried 350 pounds [159 kg] with amazing ease), but they're rare and, well, exceptional.

BALANCE THE LOADS Both panniers should weigh the same. Extra care here will pay off on the trail—it's a real drag to have to stop and deal with an unbalanced load that rolls every 15 minutes.

GUARD FRAGILE GEAR Pack anything that's breakable toward the back of your panniers, and the tougher stuff (such as grain or sleeping bags) toward the front. As your horse travels up the trail, cheerfully banging your expensive gear into every available rock or tree, the tougher stuff will take the brunt of the attack, protecting the breakable things.

PROTECT YOUR HORSE Keep hard, sharp, or rigid stuff away from your horse. My worst horsepacking mistake was putting a heavy steel packing stove in the pannier, right against my big mustang's side. He walked sideways up the trail, courageously doing what I asked him to, pain be damned. When I finally figured out what was wrong, his side was bloody from the gouging that stove gave him with every step. I still feel bad about it.

STAY BALANCED Whatever you carry right on top of the packsaddle should stay put almost of its own accord. Otherwise the item, called a top-pack, will slide to one side or other, ultimately rolling your pack. Wall tents, big duffel bags, and such make good top-packs.

115 THROW A DIAMOND HITCH

There are lots of variants on a diamond hitch. If you become serious about horsepacking, you'll be well served to learn them, but the basic tie is really all you need. Here's how to throw one.

STEP 1 Use a 40-foot (13-m) pack-rope with a cinch tied to one end. Start on the left side of your horse. Throw the cinch over your loaded packhorse, catching the cinch as it swings back under the horse toward you. Thread your rope into the hook or through the ring. Toss your rope gently back over the load to the right side.

STEP 2 Thread the end of your rope through the pack-cinch ring on the right side. You should now have two strands of rope over your pack. Pull them good and tight, making sure that your pack-cinch stays centered under the horse (A). From this point on, you'll need to maintain tension on the rope.

STEP 3 Reach to the very top of your load and get hold of your two rope strands. Turn them, one over the other, at least one full turn (B).

STEP 4 Maneuver your pack rope around the front of the right pannier and up to the diamond that you turned into your rope. Thread it through and toss it over to the left side (C).

STEP 5 Pull your rope down and around the front of the left pannier and through the ring, continuing around the back of the pannier and up to the diamond atop your pack. Thread the rope through and toss your remaining slack to the right side.

STEP 6 Run the rope down and around the back of the right pannier and through the pack-cinch ring (D). Pull good and tight and tie off with several half-hitches. All done, pardner!

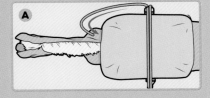

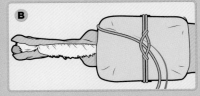

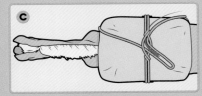

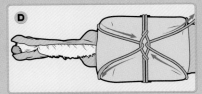

116 GET LOADED

Just throw packsaddle and panniers on your horse, stuff in your gear, and off you go . . . right? Wrong. Here's the right way to load up.

STEP 1 Tighten front and back saddle cinches before hanging the panniers.

STEP 2 Hang the loaded and balanced panniers on the sawbucks. If you're working alone, hang one pannier and then hurry around the other side and hang that one on before the saddle rolls. If you have an assistant, load your panniers simultaneously.

STEP 3 If you plan to load something (such as cots or duffels) on top of your panniers, be sure they weigh about the same. Ensure they fit comfortably atop the pannier and aside the sawbucks.

STEP 4 If your load includes a top-pack, set it on, making sure it's evenly distributed from side to side. Work it down atop the sawbuck until it's firmly in place.

STEP 5 If any inclement weather threatens, cover the load with a tarp so as to keep everything dry.

STEP 6 Tie or "throw" a diamond or other hitch over the entire load. It'll keep everything snugly in place while you're on the trail.

117 PLAY FOLLOW THE LEADER

When one rider has multiple pack animals to lead, the best option is to tie them together in a string, one behind the other, in a single file.

TAIL 'EM In my opinion, the best way to string your horses together is to tail them (A). Tie each horse to the previous horse's tail. Your front or "lead" horse should rank high in the pecking order of your horse band, to avoid trouble in the ranks. Don't tie your leadrope to the actual tail; a good jerk could break it. Tie your rope to the long tail hair just below the actual tail. Never tail horses together when riding on dangerous trails—especially cliff trails. Should one horse fall, he'll pull the entire string over with him.

BREAK AWAY Any time you're riding on dangerous trails, use a breakaway between each horse (B). That way, if a horse takes a fall, he'll break free of the other horses, and won't pull them over the edge with him. Breakaways can be as simple as a loop of haystring that will break, or a split metal ring that will bend open. Tie your breakaway to the rear sawbucks on each packsaddle, and your leadrope to the breakaway.

TURN HIM LOOSE Many experienced packhorses perform fine if just turned loose to make their own way. They'll follow cheerfully along, stopping to grab a bite and then hurrying to catch up. This method can make your job easier, but avoid having loose horses when riding dangerous trails.

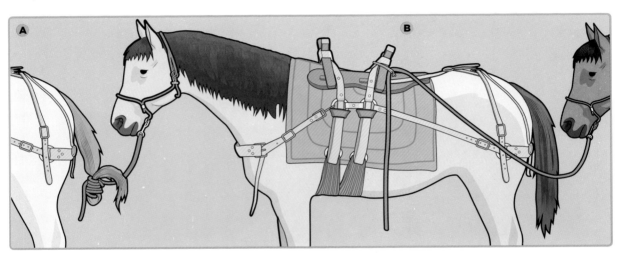

118 LEAD A PACK

Leading a packhorse or pack string is not hard, but you've gotta pay attention or you'll end up in a jackpot.

DON'T TIE OFF Never tie a packhorse's leadrope to your saddlehorn. You never know when the packhorse will fall down, or see a bear in the bushes and try to jump all the way to Jupiter. If you're tied hard and fast, he'll jerk your horse down, or cause a general disaster. Just hold onto the rope, typically in your right hand. If your packhorse starts to drag on your arm, take a dally on your horn, but be ready to pull it up and off should something go awry.

PLAY "CHOO-CHOO" Remember back when you used to pretend to be a locomotive pulling a bunch of train cars

around? When you're leading a pack train, think of you and your saddle horse as the locomotive and the packhorses as the train cars. When you're winding through timber, around rocks, or especially making a U-turn, everything has to follow a serpentine pattern.

DON'T GET TAILED The best way to convince your tried-and-true saddle horse that he's a young bronc full of spit and vinegar is to allow your packhorse's leadrope to get up tight under his tail. He's likely to hump up and then jump around, or maybe demonstrate some good old-fashioned bucking. Avoid letting that happen. Train your horse ahead of time to tolerate a rope under his tail—'cause sooner or later it's going to happen in the backcountry.

119 LOOP YOUR LEADROPE

While you're out riding in the backcountry—especially if you're leading packhorses—you'll regularly need to dismount and tie up your saddle horse so you can fix a pack, clear a deadfall, or shoot a grouse for dinner. Here are two ways to keep your leadrope handy, but out of the way. (Tip: When you cross a creek, you'll need to untie or unhook your leadrope from the horn so your horse can reach his nose down to the water for a drink.)

GET HITCHED My favorite way to tie up my saddle horse's leadrope is with a quick clove hitch around my saddle horn. Leave enough slack between horn and halter that your horse can move naturally, but not so much that your rope will snag and tangle on brush and branches along the way.

LOOP IT Another method I like is to tie a loop in my leadrope which I can then hang over the horn. This method is super fast. You can jump off your horse and grab and toss the rope over a limb or post or toss it to a buddy to hold while you chase that big buck off through the trees.

120 GIVE YOUR HORSE A STAKE FOR DINNER

Sometimes the best way for you to let your horse get a belly full of grass, without turning him loose to graze, is to just stake him out nearby, using a 15- to 20-foot (4.5–6 m) rope.

USE COTTON Use only large diameter (³/₄ inch [2 cm] is ideal) cotton rope. Anything else will rope-burn badly if he gets tangled in it—and he will.

STAKE STRONG Be sure whatever you stake your horse to will withstand a hard jerk, or you may end up chasing a stake that's following your horse to the trailhead.

KEEP TABS Until your horse has experience with a stakeout rope, he'll get tangled. Keep an eye on him; when he needs help, go unravel him. He'll eventually learn to avoid trouble.

121 RIDE A HORSE RIGHT

Horse cultures around the globe train steeds differently. Some techniques are common; some are unique to place and people. Here's how to ride a western saddle horse right.

GO AND WHOA To start your horse, nudge him in the ribs simultaneously with both heels. The harder the nudge, the more urgent the command. To stop your horse, pull back on the reins until he halts. If he doesn't respond, pull harder till he does. Once stopped, ease up and he should stand quietly.

REIGN WITH THE REINS Bridle reins are a kind of steering wheel. A well-trained horse will "neckrein," moving away from rein pressure on his neck. To neckrein, hold both reins in one hand (typically your weak hand, leaving your strong hand free to lead a packhorse, swing a lariat, or shoot bad guys). To turn your horse, move the reins to the side, putting pressure on the side of the horse's neck. He should move away from the pressure. Some horses only direct or "plow" rein. Ride these horses with a rein in each hand, and pull in the direction you wish to go. For example, if you want to turn right, pull on the right rein.

STEER WITH YOUR FEET No one wants to see you steering your car with your feet. Bad idea. By contrast, controlling a horse with your feet is the mark of a good rider. A well-trained horse will move away from foot pressure. To turn your horse's front end, swing your foot a trifle forward of its normal position and nudge with your heel or spur. To move the horse's back end, swing your foot a little to the rear and nudge. Keep nudging as long as you need for the horse to keep moving. A good rider can move a horse sideways to swing a large gate, or perform other technical tasks without dismounting.

BE AN ACTIVE RIDER Don't slump in the saddle or hold on to the horn while riding. Sit up straight and relaxed, move with the horse, and stay balanced. If you're riding uphill keep your torso upright by leaning forward; if going downhill, lean back instead.

ARAM SAYS "The biggest mistake I see beginning riders make is giving mixed signals to their horse, combining heels (telling the horse to go) and reins (telling him to stop). If you want to go forward, leave the reins slightly slack. If you want to stop, don't let your feet squeeze or press the horse's ribs."

122 STAY SAFE IN THE SADDLE

Just like riding in a car or on a bicycle, horseback riding has inherent risks. Read on to help you ride safe.

LOOSEN YOUR LACES Always loosen your shoelaces while riding, unless you're wearing proper riding boots. If you fall off or get thrown, your foot will pop out of your shoe should it get caught in the stirrup.

RIDE LOOSE Whenever you're riding dangerous terrain, especially a steep or cliffy trail, slip your feet mostly out of your stirrups. Stay relaxed, but ready; if your horse goes down or falls, you can emergency dismount without getting tangled up in your horse.

ESCAPE A HANGING Getting a foot caught in a stirrup is seriously dangerous. Your horse is likely to bolt, dragging you behind. You'll be thoroughly beat up or even killed. If you're being dragged by a hard-running horse, you have a few options.

If you're still holding the reins or can grab them, try pulling your horse to a stop and get him to stand still while you get free. If that's not possible, try rolling in his direction. It's counter-intuitive, I know. Your foot is likely to come free if you roll toward him. (I've never done this, but I'm told it works.) As a last resort, draw your sidearm and pump as many rounds into your horse's lungs as you can. It'll be unfortunate and sad, but hopefully he'll die before you do.

123 SPUR 'EM ON

Many well-meaning but poorly informed people believe that spurs are cruel and unnecessary. If anything, the opposite is true; they are simply tools that help a horse and rider communicate with each other. Spurs create a sensitive point of contact that enables precise signals to be given. (Would your prefer to see a horse pedaled down the road by flapping legs and pounding spur-less heels?) A good horseman never hurts his mount with his spurs.

124 CARRY A RIFLE ON HORSEBACK

Carrying a rifle on horseback has always been a challenge. For those of us hunting wilderness territory it still is. Here's what works for me.

PUT IT IN THE SCABBARD The best way to carry your rifle on horseback is under your leg in a leather scabbard (A). The best rifles for this are slim, lever-action, iron-sighted carbines. I love that style of rifle, and I use one when I'm out cowboying or lion hunting. However, I prefer a modern sporting rifle with greater reach when big-game hunting. These rifles, complete with optic and bolt handle, don't fit real well under your leg. You'll need a scabbard tailored to your big game rifle and you may want to hang it vertically from your saddle-forks (B).

SLING IT If you don't have a saddle scabbard, or if you prefer to keep your rifle on your person, you can carry it slung across your back. If you're traveling a long distance, and wish to protect your firearm from brush and weather, you can employ a slim-profile soft case complete with carrying strap. Sling it over your head and shoulder the same way you would a rifle.

KEEP IT IN HAND Anytime that a potential shot is imminent you should carry your rifle in your hand. You'll be ready to slide off of your horse and shoot, without struggling to get your gun out of its scabbard or off your shoulder. Carry it across your saddle forks, or down along your leg, or by resting the butt on your thigh, muzzle pointing skyward (C).

125 SHOOT FROM HORSEBACK

In the movies, guys can shoot the cigarette out of a bad guy's mouth from the back of a running horse. Not so in real life—a horse is in constant motion, so accurate shooting is all but impossible.

DRAW YOUR BOW One notable exception to this rule is instinctive shooting with a traditional bow. I've watched my brother gallop his horse past five old car tires, each about 10 yards (9.1 m) apart, and put an arrow inside each one. You won't be shooting any cigarettes, but it worked on buffalo and is more fun than should be legally allowed.

DON'T REST Again, in the movies, heroes regularly make difficult shots by resting their rifle over a saddled horse. But unless you can teach your steed to hold his breath and not wiggle his ears, that won't work either—I've tried; it's like resting your gun over a waterbed with a kid jumping on it.

GET CLOSE Shooting from horseback can be effective at close range. Your horse needs to be steady enough that you can drop your reins over the saddlehorn and use both hands for a careful shot. Just be sure he won't blow up and toss you into the nearest pine tree when you pull that trigger.

126 BRING YOUR BOW

Some of the most effective armies in history were hosts of horseback archers. It's a simple matter to swing aboard your cayuse with a traditional bow in hand, but not so with modern archery gear.

COMPOUND CARRY Due to their somewhat delicate nature, compound bows need to be treated with great care when carried horseback. My favorite method is with a Primos bow sling across my back. Next is simply in my hand, like I'd carry a rifle. Just make sure you don't drop your bow or bang it on a tree, knocking your rest or sights out of kilter. If you get tossed from your steed, try to land under your bow.

TRY TRADITIONAL TACTICS Longbows and recurves are much easier to carry when riding, due to their light weight and indestructible nature. I like to just carry my bow in my free hand.

PACK A TAKE-DOWN BOW Collapsing to a small bundle with the turn of a couple bolts, take-down recurves and longbows stow readily in your backpack or pannier, making them the ultimate horse-trip bow.

> **ARAM SAYS** "Stow your arrows in a capped PVC tube for safe transport into and out of the backcountry."

127 LET YOUR HORSE "BLOW"

When climbing up steep trails, your horse will need to stop periodically to catch his breath or, in horseman vernacular, "blow." Don't let him get lazy and stop every ten steps, but watch for signs that he's winded; when you see them, give him a short break.

128 RIDE AN OBSTACLE HORSE

The backcountry is full of bumps, lumps, and tricky stuff that your steed will need to navigate through. Here's how to deal with some common ones.

A ROCKS Whenever you encounter rocky terrain, just let your horse to slow down and pick his way. Point him in the right direction, and let him choose his path. He'll find the best route to navigate his hooves through the rough stuff.

B LOGS Most timbered terrain is rife with dead and fallen logs or deadfall. Horses can cross them with surprising ease; the best will crawl over anything they can, jumping only if a log is too high to get over. Keep him slow and deliberate if he's working a deadfall so he won't get impatient and begin jumping everything. Don't cross logs that have "stobbs" — jagged or sharp points — that could stab your horse's belly.

C SMOOTH ROCK Smooth stone faces are slippery under your horse's hooves. Don't gallop on them. If you're on a

steep, smooth face, travel only up or down — if you try to ride across, your steed's feet will fly out from under him quickly.

D WATER Lots of equines take issue with crossing water, be it a quiet puddle or a raging creek. When you approach on a water-shy horse, give him time to take a good look at it, and maybe smell it, before you urge him to cross. If he balks, ask a companion on a steady horse to cross first, inspiring yours to follow. As a last resort, dismount and lead him across, but don't ever let him get away with refusing. If you do, the next battle will be even harder to win.

ARAM SAYS "When riding in rough terrain, your horse can get a hoof stuck. It's rare but it happens; if he suddenly stops, and doesn't want to move, look at his feet. If one is stuck, get off and work it loose."

129 KNOW WHERE YOU'RE GOING

Wilderness is backcountry, but not all backcountry is wilderness. In the U.S., different land designations demand different types of gear, mobility, and even behavior. What these various types of designations have in common is that they are almost all public, which means you own some of the most handsome country on earth.

FEDERAL WILDERNESS AREAS Designated by Congress, these are typically large blocks of uninhabited land. Some, like mountain ranges in the West, are high and alpine. Others, like canyon country in the Southwest, are dry and rugged. They all share a prohibition on wheeled travel, including bicycles. Most restrict motorized power of any sort, even chain saws. Horses and hiking boots are the way to get around.

FEDERAL WILDLIFE REFUGES Some of the larger refuges, such as Artic National Wildlife Refuge in Alaska or Montana's Charles M. Russell National Wildlife Refuge, have extensive backcountry. Behavior is often restricted by the season, and while camping, hunting, and fishing are often allowed, be sure to check with refuge managers on property-specific regulations.

FOREST SERVICE AND BLM LAND By far the largest landowner in the American West is the federal government, which manages most of its holdings under these two agencies. Theses have the fewest restrictions; you can drive on most roads, and camp, hike, and ride where you want, with a two-week limit on camping in any single spot.

NATIONAL MONUMENTS Some large chunks of federal land are designated as monuments, with access restrictions that generally fall somewhere between that of BLM and designated wilderness.

NATIONAL PARKS Some of the nation's best-known and most-visited backcountry areas are managed by the National Park Service. Think Yellowstone, Grand Canyon, and Great Smoky Mountains. Access to national parks is relatively restrictive; camping is in designated areas and backcountry exploration often requires a permit.

130 CUT A WALKING STICK

Ever tried to traverse a steep talus slope while carrying a heavy pack, or cross a rushing thigh-deep creek? Hard to keep your feet under yourself, isn't it? Cutting a pole—or a pair of poles—as temporary walking sticks can save your day.

CLIMB HARDER Hardcore hikers understand the benefit of a pair of trekking poles. Use one in each hand to give added thrust as you climb. You'll climb faster and tire less.

DESCEND SAFER I recently returned from a backcountry Coues deer hunt in some of the most rugged and dangerous terrain I've ever encountered. My brother and I killed deer two days apart, both high on a near-vertical ridge during the last moments of daylight. The moonless nights were black as

the inside of a coal mine as we carried our heavy-laden packs through talus slopes and across cactus fields, making this treacherous descent by the light of our headlamps. Just before beginning the trek, we each cut two yucca stalks to use as walking sticks. We'd brace the sticks against the slope below as we precariously made our way off the ridge. I'm fully convinced those poles prevented numerous slips, falls, and potential injuries.

CROSS CONFIDENTLY One of the best ways to make a rough-water crossing safer is to use a walking stick (or two). Brace them firmly downstream of yourself to help keep your footing. Edge your way slowly across, moving only one of your four points (two feet, two poles) at a time.

131 FIX YOUR FEET

Feet in the backcountry are like tires on the road. Flat tire or blistered foot, you've gotta stop and fix it before moving on.

BREAK IN YOUR BOOTS Prevention is the key to, well, preventing blisters. Try wearing your backcountry footwear frequently ahead of time, till they are well broken in, and your feet are thoroughly accustomed to them.

STOP WHEN IT'S HOT So-called "hot spots" are your foot's way of sending you a message that a blister is on the horizon. When a hot spot shows up, stop and fix it. Fresh socks, a spot of duct tape or moleskin, or a quick change of shoes can save you from endless hours of misery later.

PROTECT A BLISTER If a blister forms (if you disregarded the advice above), you'll need to protect it so that it doesn't become worse. Make a thin bandage with medical or duct tape, patching the center with gauze. Build up the area around the center patch slightly (like a donut) in order to provide some relief from pressure to the blister. Change your footwear if you can.

DRAIN THE FLUID If a blister becomes swollen to the point that it prohibits use or movement, you'll have to drain it. You want to keep the skin covering the blister intact, so don't just stick a knife point or needle in the blister. Instead, insert the point of a sharp needle into the skin ⅛ inch (3 cm) from the edge of the blister. Push the needle point over into the blister (the key is to keep the needle point between layers of skin) then withdraw and gently squeeze the fluid out of the blister. When you're done the hole will re-seal, preventing bacteria from entering the wound.

> **ARAM SAYS** "Carry a pair of ultra-thin, high-tech 'blister proof' socks. If you feel a hot spot, stop and put the new socks on under your regular socks."

132 TOUGH OUT THE TRAIL

You're five hours into your backcountry adventure. Your pack feels like it weighs a ton, your shoulders are on fire, and both heels have developed hot spots. You're grumpy as an old grizzly with a sore tooth and the last leg of the trip to your destination seems insurmountable.

FUEL THE ENGINE As you travel, make a point of drinking and snacking regularly. Staying hydrated along with keeping adequate calories in your belly are essential to maintaining the high level of performance demanded by the backcountry.

FIX WHAT HURTS Persistent pain can spoil the fun of your wilderness experience, so if something hurts, stop and fix the problem. Hot spots on your feet, a badly loaded pack, or your knife gouging under your hip belt every step are quick and easy things to fix. Go ahead and take the time—it'll speed you up in the long run.

ADJUST YOUR PACK Unless you're a total animal, a pack that is heavily loaded will make you hurt. Keep discomfort to a minimum by making regular adjustments to the suspension system on your pack. Hike with your hip belt tight and your shoulder straps slightly loose, so your waist carries most of the weight. When your hips grow tired, or you have to hike uphill, tighten your shoulder straps and loosen your hip belt. Adjust your sternum strap to change pressure. Mix things up and you'll stay more comfortable.

SHOW TRUE GRIT There eventually comes a time when the backcountry will separate the men and women from the boys and girls. Toughness and good attitude will show through. Don't be the person who whines, complains, and allows others to pull his share. Do be the one who pushes through the tough moments, helps those who struggle, and maintains a cheerful attitude.

133 PACK SOME IRON

Several good methods of carrying your rifle or bow in the backcountry exist; you should learn to use them all.

SLING IT The most popular carry method for hunters around the world, a good sling carries its own weight and more (I know, bad pun) in the backcountry. You can carry your rifle on either shoulder or across your back, keeping it readily accessible at all times. The same goes for a bow. In the latter case, give Primo's bow sling a try—you'll be impressed.

CARRY IN HAND Anytime that a shot seems imminent, you should have your weapon ready and in your hands. Should a big bull or tasty cow elk suddenly present, you'll be ready to shoot in an instant. But there's another good reason to pack your rifle or bow in-hand. When terrain gets steep and the footing gets sketchy, your weapon will be safest when it is handheld (except of course for when it's stowed on your pack, where it will be all but inaccessible). Here's the key: When you traverse rough and steep terrain, keep your rifle or bow in your downslope hand. If your feet do go out from under you, you'll land under your rifle or bow, rather than slamming it into the rocks and then landing atop it.

STRAP IT ON Carrying your trusty rifle or bow strapped firmly to your backpack has one fairly serious downside: It makes your weapon of choice hard to access easily. But the method is still gaining favor among backcountry hunters and for a good reason. It's hands-down the most comfortable way to carry a weapon, and offers good protection against unexpected violent encounters with rocks and hard places. Many packs offer hidden or detachable "boots" specifically designed to carry your rifle or bow. While on a recent backcountry Coues deer hunt in incredibly rugged Arizona terrain I had a big "Aha!" moment: I strapped my lightweight foam sitting-pad (every seasoned Coues hunter carries one) firmly against the exposed side of my rifle and scope, padding it against damage should I end up taking a bad fall. It worked like a charm, safeguarding my shootin' iron through several nasty crashes.

134 KEEP YOUR BARREL CLEAN AND DRY

Want to keep your barrel safe? Cover your rifle's muzzle in electrical tape. It'll keep moisture from rain and snow, fragments of twigs and brush, and dust and dirt out of your barrel.

Don't worry about removing the tape before shooting; the blast will blow it free ahead of the bullet. Wind some tape around your barrel so you'll have extra, should you need it.

135
MAKE A BIVY CAMP

Bivying out is an incredible way to reach remote big-game honey-holes. A great bivy's location is sometimes chosen for you; comfort and amenities aren't part of the equation. You must be tough and willing to sleep in, rough places. Level ground is unusual; smooth level terrain a luxury. I've spent some nights curled around rocks, or scooting back to a bed that I slid out of when a spot wasn't level.

One main reason to bivy out is to get inside an ultra-wary big-game animal's core area. Avoid sky and ridgelines, be silent, and especially don't set camp where air movement can carry your scent to your prey.

But what good is bivying out if you can't see, hear, or get to your hunting spot? Choose a bivy camp that will let you hear (I've spent many magical nights listening to nearby bugling elk), see (near a good vantage point), and access (get close in for a shot) game that you find.

136 SAVE YOUR STRENGTH

You have two plans of attack when it comes to a hunting camp, and when hard-core hunting is required, bivying can save you immense energy and effort.

With a non-bivy approach, you arise several hours before dawn, and climb two hours to your hunting area. You hunt the morning, then climb two hours back down to camp. You have lunch, check gear, and then climb two hours back up to hunt. After dark, you hike two hours back to camp. Sleep and repeat.

If you bivy out in your hunting area, it gets a lot easier. You awaken a few minutes before dawn, slip out and hunt. You come back to bivy camp and eat breakfast, and have a nap. If you need water, take a midday hike and get some. Hunt the evening, then relax at camp. Sleep and repeat.

The non-bivy includes eight hours of hiking per day; four of them in the dark. That exhausts even the toughest of hunters. Bivy hunting excludes some comforts of a big camp, but more than makes it up in saved time and effort.

137 BRING THE BIVY BASICS

Hardcore bivy hunting requires three or four items in addition to your standard gear. Here's how much weight it'll add.

TENT A bivy tent will add between 2 and 4 pounds (0.9–1.8 kg) to your setup. It's worth it when facing bad weather or creepy crawly critters such as mosquitoes, scorpions, and snakes.

SLEEPING BAG A good, superlight bag will weigh about 3 pounds (1.4 kg)— perhaps the most important weight you'll ever tote into the backcountry.

SLEEPING PAD Your pad shouldn't weigh more than 1 1/2 pounds (0.7 kg).

Top-end pads weigh half that. In cases where bulk is an issue, get a super-compact unit.

COOKSET If you want hot food on your trip, you'll need a cookset. Your superlight stove, pot, and fuel canister(s) shouldn't weigh more than 2 1/2 pounds (1.1 kg) at the most. Even with a cookset, your gear should weigh under 10 pounds (4.5 kg). Go minimal and it'll be half that. You'll have to carry extra water and food, but it's a small price to pay for the ability to go anywhere, sleep whenever darkness finds you, and hunt wildlife in all manner of remote places.

138 BUILD A BASE CAMP

Base camp should be welcoming. So, here's how to set up housekeeping.

CHOOSE LODGING Give priority to tent location. Set up on a smooth, level spot. Spread a tarp or ground-cloth underneath to keep wetness or stickers from finding their way through the floor and into your bedroom. Stake your tent down thoroughly.

PLACE THE FIREPIT Next, figure out where to place your firepit. You'll want it convenient to (but downwind from) tents and lean-tos. Build a ring of stones to surround your fire and help contain it. A few flat stones inside the ring make convenient places to keep food or coffee pots warm.

BUILD LEAN-TOS You need lean-tos in which to store gear. Keep them near to but out of the way of the main camp. In bad weather, a tarp over the camp or fire area protects from the elements.

GUARD WATER Convenient drinking water is key to a comfortable camp. Set

up camp near a nice spring, seep, or creek. Public lands often require campers to give water a fairly wide berth of 100 feet (30 m) or more. So know and abide by area regulations.

COLLECT FIREWOOD Build a good-sized pile of firewood complete with kindling. Stow it under a lean-to or cover it with a tarp. It'll be dry and ready when you need it.

STRETCH A CLOTHESLINE Put a finishing touch on your camp with a long taut line that will let you hang your wet clothes up to dry. In bad weather, hang it high above the firepit and under a stretched tarp.

ARRANGE SEATING Cut a few stumps or roll a couple of logs into position around the fire. Convenient, fireside seating is a lovely addition to any camp.

139 TIE THE KNOT

Knowing how to use ropes, cordage, or knots is an essential skill for the backcountry adventurer. You can tie a horse, throw a hitch on a pack, hang quarters, hoist food into a tree, stretch a high-line or tarp, pitch a lean-to, bind a splint, and lots more. Here are a few of the most useful, versatile backcountry knots—learn them well.

140 TWIRL UP A BOWLINE

The bowline has a thousand uses for every outdoorsman, from tying up your dog, to rigging lines on your boat, to hanging food in a tree to keep bears out of it. Anytime a non-slipping loop or knot is needed, the bowline excels. If you need to tie a knot in the middle of your best rope and untie it later, the bowline is your baby. Want to increase your knowledge of outdoor, survival, and emergency skills? The bowline is definitely a knot that you should have in your bag of tricks. Here's how it's done.

STEP 1 Turn a loop in your rope or string, working end crossing on top.

STEP 2 Thread the working end through the loop up from below, forming a second loop. This is the actual bowline loop. Now take the working end around the standing portion of the rope and back down through the original loop. (Think of the working end as a squirrel that pops out of a hole in a tree, runs around the tree, and pops back into his hole.) You can adjust the size of the bowline loop by feeding rope in or out from the standing portion of the rope.

STEP 3 Work the knot tight by pulling alternately on each strand where it enters the knot.

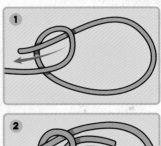

141

TIE A BUTTERFLY KNOT

Use this knot whenever you require a sturdy, yet easily removed loop in the middle of your rope.

STEP 1 Form a bight (or bend) in your rope, and twist it one full turn.

STEP 2 Take the end of the bight and circle it around the bottom of the twist and up through the center of the twist as shown.

STEP 3 Pull on the loop and both strands of the rope to work the knot tight.

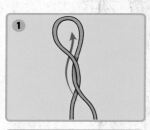
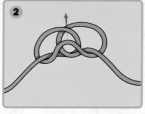
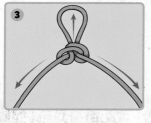

142 MAKE A ROPE TACKLE

Anytime you need to stretch a rope really tight, a rope tackle (also call a Dutchman knot) is the way to go.

STEP 1 Bring the ends of the rope that you're using together. Tie a loop (butterfly or bowline) in one end.

STEP 2 Thread the other end of the rope through the loop, then reverse directions with it.

STEP 3 Tie another butterfly loop back along this rope, making sure first that your other rope end will be able to reach it.

STEP 4 Thread that remaining rope end through the second loop. Your rope tackle is now set up and ready to use. Pull it as tight as you wish and tie off with a couple half hitches. Now you're ready to lift or tow a load.

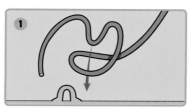
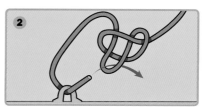
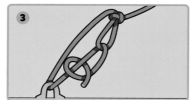

143 WHIP FINISH A ROPE END

The best way to protect the end of a rope from fraying is to "whip" it. Just make a bight in your whipping string, lay it on your rope, and cover with tight wraps. Then, tuck your working end through the bight, and pull on both ends to orient the cross under the middle of your wrap or "whip." Trim the ends flush.

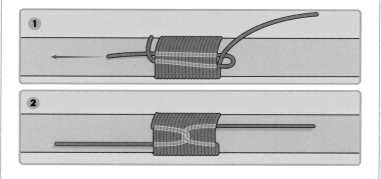

144 START A TOUGH FIRE

Getting a fire started isn't always easy, especially if conditions are humid, or you're at high altitude. Use these tips to prevail.

LOOK FOR DRY WOOD Damp wood is nearly impossible to start a fire with. Don't waste your energy. Instead, look for dry tinder and kindling. Look under downed logs, overhanging rocks, or thick evergreen canopy for pinecones, small dry twigs, and such. Another great source of dry kindling comes from the center of standing dead trees. Cut a dead tree down, cut out a section, and then split it to get to the dry heartwood.

FAN THE FLAMES Fire is reluctant to start at high altitude: Flames just gasp for air and collapse in defeat. Beat this problem by blowing gently on your new flame to provide additional oxygen. Once it gets going your fire will draw enough oxygen by itself, but until then you'll need to nurse it along.

STAY HIGH 'N DRY The toughest fire conditions are above 10,000 feet (3,000 m) and after days of rain and snow. Find or split dry tinder (feather sticks work great), slightly bigger dry kindling, and dry-as-possible firewood. Ignite the fine tinder first. Add small kindling; be careful not to snuff it out. Blow gently on the fire till it gains strength, and then add larger fuel. Tend carefully till it's a bona-fide backcountry blaze.

ARAM SAYS "Carry an aggressive-burning fire-starter like pitch pine, Vaseline-impregnated lint/cotton ball, or a tiny commercial fire-starting brick in your kit. Light it first, then use it to ignite your tinder."

145 CARVE A FEATHER STICK

Feather sticks are great for starting fires, especially in challenging conditions. Here's how to make them.

STEP 1 Find or split a dry stick about an inch in diameter.

STEP 2 Using a sharp knife, shave long fine curls down the length of the stick, leaving them attached at the bottom end.

STEP 3 Continue until you've converted most of your stick into shavings, all still attached. Set aside till you're ready to start a fire.

146 COLLECT PITCH PINE

One of the greatest fire starters in nature is pitch pine, commonly called fatwood. It ignites readily, burns hot and long, and can be found almost anywhere pine trees (especially pinyon) grow.

In a fit of pure curiosity, I once lit a good piece of fatwood, about 5 inches (12.5 cm) long and ½ inch (1.2 cm) wide, on fire and stuck one end in the ground. The pitch pine burned heartily for about 45 minutes before it finally burned out. When in need of a blaze, I'd sooner have a little piece of pitch pine than a whole armful of crumpled newspaper sheets.

Fatwood is usually located in the bottom section of dead pine trees, probably caused by an over-abundance of sap or "pitch" being present when the tree died. The sap saturates the wood in the stump, dries, and the result is a really good, super combustible kindling. Not all dead trees contain pitch-pine. In fact, you will probably need to spend some time hunting around to find some.

Once you locate a pitchy tree or stump, saw or chop out the fatwood. Split it into kindling sized pieces. Keep it hidden; don't show your buddies unless you want it all to disappear into their pockets and packs.

147 START A BOWDRILL FIRE

If you don't have matches, lighter, or firesteel, here's how to go primitive and start a fire with a bowdrill.

Tools and Materials

- A 3-foot (1 m) long, slightly bent stick for your bow
- A finger-thick stick 8 inches (20 cm) long for a spindle
- A length of string
- A ¾ x 1 ½ x 6 inch (2 x 6 x 15 cm) or longer fireboard
- A palm-sized stone, bone, or piece of wood with a divot in it that you can use for your socket

STEP 1 Gather materials (A). Your spindle and fireboard need to be dry and not too hard. Yucca or sotol stalks make good spindles. Cottonwood root makes a fine fireboard. Try cedar if none of the above are available in your area.

STEP 2 Whittle your spindle into a straight, round stick. Round the lower end, tapering it in to a long, blunt point.

STEP 3 String your bow (B) (paracord is ideal; bootlace a good second). You should struggle a bit when twisting your spindle into the string. It'll loosen when in use.

STEP 4 Carve a small hollow in the top of your fireboard, about ¾ inch (2 cm) from the edge. Use your spindle, socket,

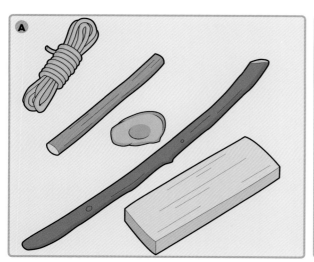

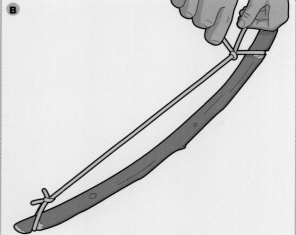

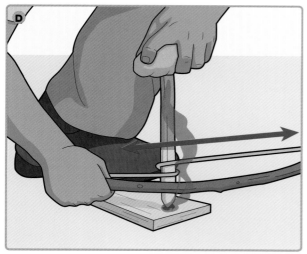

and bow (see steps 6 and 7) to deepen and shape your hole in preparation for starting your fire.

STEP 5 Carve a V-shaped notch into the fireboard's side, just reaching the center of your hole.

STEP 6 Lay your fireboard on a section of bark or even on a large leaf, anything that will safely catch your coal. Hold it with your foot. Twist your spindle into your bowstring and place it in your hole, socket on top. Brace everything using your left arm, leg, and knee.

STEP 7 Begin sawing or "bowing" gently with the full length of your bow. Be patient: this takes practice. Once you're

bowing smoothly, gradually speed up, and put pressure on the socket. Maintain a steady pace, saving energy for later.

STEP 8 When smoke begins curling from your fireboard, bow steadily faster and add more pressure. Keep it up until smoke pours from beneath your spindle. Pause, and hold everything in place. Watch the smoke: If it keeps rising for 10 to 15 seconds, you're good. If not, go back to bowing.

STEP 9 If smoke rises continuously when you're not bowing, gently remove the spindle. Carefully lift your fireboard away from the coal that's formed in your notch. Gently drop the coal into your tinder bundle and blow, softly at first, then harder and harder till your tinder bursts into flame.

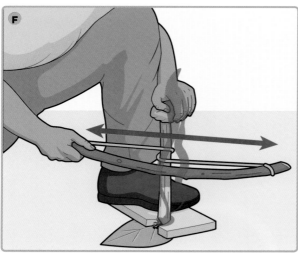

148 TRY USING YOUR HANDS

Many hard-core primitive technology folks prefer the hand-drill to a bow-drill for starting their fires. You give up some mechanical advantage, but your fire-starting set is far simpler and more compact. There's no bow, no socket, and no string—all you need is a long spindle and a fireboard.

The technique is very similar: Hold onto your fireboard with your foot and spin your spindle back and forth between your hands till smoke begins to curl. Get aggressive (this is a workout), spinning faster and using downward pressure. Your hands will travel down the spindle as you work. Just stop, rapidly relocate to the top, and continue. Repeat till smoke billows from under your spindle and you'll have a coal.

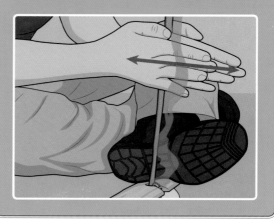

149 FIND THE PERFECT SITE

Choosing the right campsite can make or break your trip. Whether tonight's camp is a ten-day base camp location or an on-the-fly bivy setup, here's how to choose a good spot.

STAY SAFE Lightning is a serious safety concern. If nasty weather threatens, camp in a grove of healthy, consistent-height timber. Avoid tall trees and exposed ridges, meadows, or peaks. Flash flooding can put a damper on your trip, so always camp on high ground. Also, don't camp near standing dead trees. Falling timber can crush your trip—literally.

BEWARE BEARS Don't pitch your tent in any obvious hangouts. Avoid berry patches, bear trails, and salmon streams. Keep food, toothpaste, deodorant, or other tasty or smelly things several hundred yards (500 m) from camp.

KEEP COMFORTABLE Smooth ground is the best place to lay your weary body. Look for a clean, smooth, and ideally level place to pitch your tent. Water nearby, especially a potable high-country spring, adds comfort to any camp.

WARM UP What could be more comforting than a crackling campfire deep in the backcountry? Just make sure your fire stays contained and safe.

ENJOY THE ENVIRONMENT Watch the sun set over the peaks while you eat dinner. And have access to some activity such as fishing, climbing, or hunting. Set up near a great trout stream, trail, or big game spot.

150 RIG A TARP SHELTER

Shelter is paramount in any backcountry situation, especially for survival. It offers a dry place to store gear, firewood, and food, offers security, and protects you from the elements. A tarp can create an admirable shelter if used right.

MAKE A LEAN-TO An A-frame lean-to is one of the easiest shelters to make. Tie a smooth pole or stretch a rope tight between two trees (height depends on your tarp size). Throw your tarp over the pole or rope, and pull both sides out taut. Pile rocks along the edges to keep them tightly in place (A) or secure the edges using cordage and wooden stakes. Orient the lean-to so wind blows on the side, not the opening.

MAKE A DIAMOND This works well as a sleeping shelter with a fire for warmth or cooking at the front (B). First, point one corner of your tarp into the prevailing wind and anchor it down. Next, stretch the opposing corner and anchor it to a tree some 3 to 8 feet (1–2.4 m) above the ground. (Height depends on tarp size and how wide you want your shelter.) Stretch the two remaining corners out and anchor them. Pile rocks on the edges of your tarp to keep wind from finding its way into the back of the shelter. For more headroom, cut a pole and use it to raise the ceiling in the center.

GET CREATIVE Tarp shelter design is limited only by your imagination. Spread your tarp on the ground, lie down on one half, and pull the other half over you to keep out the rain. Stretch it high overhead for an awning or wrap it around poles for a tepee. Just keep it well anchored so the wind doesn't carry it away. If snow builds up, knock it off from the inside.

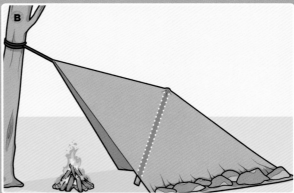

SKILLS

151 BUILD AN EMERGENCY SHELTER

Survival experts tout shelter as the first and most important requirement for survival. Construction techniques vary in different environments, but wits and ingenuity will enable you to adapt these basics to construct a good shelter.

FIND A GOOD SPOT The ideal location for an emergency shelter has plentiful building materials, as well as some preexisting structure to aid in the construction, such as a fairly sizeable overhanging rock or a large leaning deadfall log or tree. It will be sheltered from prevailing winds and located away from bottoms and low spots where cold air pools. Convenient water and firewood are icing on your survival cake.

FRAME IT OUT Lean some large sticks against your structure to frame your new home. Give yourself enough space to stretch out and store a little gear too, but keep interior dimensions small enough that your body heat will help warm your shelter.

FILL IT IN Lean more large sticks against your shelter to cover gaps. Take the time to fit them nicely into place.

COVER IT UP Face your entire shelter with large slabs of bark, evergreen boughs, smaller sticks, and so on. Work from the bottom up so that your shelter will shed water. Follow with duff, pine needles, leaves, and debris, till your shelter is waterproof.

KEEP DRY Install a floor of evergreen boughs or similar material to keep you and your gear dry and insulated.

AVOID BUGS In a rainforest or jungle type area, build your shelter on an elevated platform to protect yourself from insects—especially ticks—that roam the forest floor during the night.

Big Overhanging Rock	Deadfall Tree

152 MAKE A ROCK GROMMET

You can tie a rope or string to a tarp anywhere you wish using a rock grommet. Here's how.

STEP 1 Get a smooth rock about an inch (2.5 cm) across.

STEP 2 Place it on your tarp where you want to attach your cordage, and gather the tarp around the rock.

STEP 3 Using a clove hitch or slipknot, tie your cordage around the tarp-enshrouded rock as shown. You're good to go!

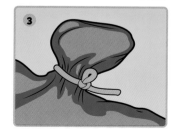

153 FIND WATER IN THE WILDERNESS

In the backcountry there are no faucets, and no cold bottles atop coolers. Drinking water has to be found and collected, and often purified as well. You need water, so listen up.

PLAN AHEAD Research reliable water sources in the area. Topo maps, Google Earth, local BLM (Bureau of Land Management), and NFS (National Forest Service) personnel can all provide valuable information.

KNOW YOUR SURROUNDINGS Most backcountry settings boast plentiful water sources, but in desert environments, water sources are few and far between, and hard to locate. On one hunt, my water source was at the base of a high ribbon cliff atop a 1,000-foot (300 m) tall escarpment. I accessed it from above via small steps carved in the sandstone hundreds of years earlier by thirsty Anasazi. If someone hadn't showed it to me, I'd never have known it was there.

LOOK FOR SIGNS If you're in dry country you'll need to know how to locate small seeps and tanks. The most obvious clues are vegetation and, to a lesser degree, animal and insect activity. Vegetation in the form of cottonwood trees, tamarack, willows, and such indicates water. Converging game or livestock trails, along with the consistent arrow-like flight of wild honeybees, can point to potential water sources. Sometimes, water can be found at the bottom of a ravine, wash, or at the base of a cliff in the form of a "hanging garden." There water seeps from under the cliff, watering a small but profuse marshy area that is suspended above its surroundings.

154 DRINK DEEP

My all-time favorite water is the kind that bursts from the ground or granite, flowing the most pure, clean water from natural aquifers deep within the Earth's belly. Try it sometime: Belly down near the source, lower your face into its limpid surface, and draw deeply. You might get a brain-freeze from the ice-cold mountain water, but it'll be one of the best drinks you ever experience.

Backcountry water emerging from sources deep underground will be pure and safe to drink. Snow banks and glacier melt should also be safe, though they may contain pollutants from the atmosphere. Stagnant, standing, or cloudy water should be purified. Don't drink untreated water from a series of springs or seeps that emerge and submerge repeatedly; follow the water to its original source, where it should be safe to drink without purification.

155 DISPOSE OF WASTE

Everybody does it. Yup, *everybody*. Unfortunately, (depending on your point of view) there are no potties in the backcountry. So what to do?

MAKE WATER The biggest concern when relieving yourself in the wilderness is water contamination. Most public lands require that you camp (and make waste) 200 feet (61 m) or further from a

lake, stream, or spring. So remain conscientious. Don't pee in or near water. You can irrigate a tree, make a golden waterfall over a cliff, or find a bathroom with a view. Just avoid water.

FERTILIZE THE WILDERNESS Typical protocol on public lands requires digging (and depositing in) a cat-hole. If you have a small shovel,

just wander away from camp and dig a 10-inch-deep (25 cm) hole, make your deposit, and bury that treasure for good. In the absence of a shovel a good backcountry trick is to pull a rock out of soft ground, set your "bear trap" in the resulting hole, and then replace the rock. Paperwork should go with your deposit—always buried thoroughly. Once again, don't deposit near water.

156 AVOID BAD-WATER BUGS

Most North American backcountry water is relatively safe. Though, if you are unused to it, you may experience a bit of a tummy-ache for a few days after drinking. However, some water is truly contaminated with Giardia (a nasty form of Cryptosporidium) or some other malignant invisible. Drinking it can render you seriously ill

so wisdom dictates treating all water that is not identifiably safe.

If you become seriously ill from drinking bad water, you should seek medical assistance. Some folks can recover unassisted from a dose of Crypto, or even Giardia, but if you or a group member gets really sick, dehydration from diarrhea and

vomiting will set in and you're gonna need help. Evacuate the sick member of your party (or yourself) ASAP

157 CATCH FISH BY HAND

Given the right kind of water, structure, and fish density, hand-fishing (often called noodling) is a great way to provide material for a big fish-feed. Here again, check local regulations before fishing.

GO SLOW Unlike our bear brothers who are adept at catching fish with lightning-like strikes of teeth and talons, you should move slow and steady. Fast movements alert fish that you're after them.

FIND HIDEY-HOLES When fish are disturbed they seek shelter under rocks, cutbanks, and so on. Find such spots that you can reach with your hands (you're probably going to spend most of your time in the water) and gently nudge fish toward them.

TICKLE THAT FISH Here comes the fun part. Sidle slowly up to a fish's hidey-hole and reach in. Slowly search for fish with your hands. When you find one, slowly and gently tickle your fingers up and down the length of its belly. This will lull the fish into a stupor. Continue tickling until you think the fish has relaxed, then grasp it firmly (ideally through the gills), and pull it out.

158 BUILD A FISH TRAP

A good fish trap will catch fish while you're hunting, doing chores, or even sleeping. Check local regulations (fish trapping is prohibited in many areas) before using a trap, unless you are in a true survival situation.

STEP 1 Gather 15 to 20 straight willows about 6 feet (2 m) long, and ½ inch (1.25 cm) in diameter at the tip. Also gather lots of fresh willow shoots about 4 feet (1.2 m) long.

STEP 2 Bind the willows at the tip with a shoot.

STEP 3 Twist or braid more shoots into a ring about 18 inches (45 cm) in diameter. Stick the butt ends of the willows through the ring equidistant apart. Weave more shoots through and around to solidify your joints.

STEP 4 Make the willows into a long, rigid cone by weaving shoots around them at 3 inch (7.5 cm) intervals. Start at the tip end. When gaps in the framework are larger than an inch (2.5 cm), add more sticks. Continue until you reach the large end, keeping the gaps about 1 inch (2.5 cm) wide.

STEP 5 Cut sticks about 14 inches (35 cm) long; fasten them to the large end of your cone so they form a funnel leading in. Weave them into place with shoots, keeping gaps an inch (2.5 cm) or less, and leaving the center of the funnel about 4 inches (10 cm) wide. Fish will be funneled into the cone, then unable to get out again.

STEP 6 Place your trap in a narrow spot in a fish-filled creek, ideally where underwater objects force the fish to travel through your trap. Anchor it in place with a few strategic rocks. Return when you're hungry.

159 SET A TROTLINE

A trotline, in all its variations, is simply a way to get more baited hooks in the water, resulting in more fish on the fire. Trotlines aren't legal everywhere, so check local regulations before setting one.

STEP 1 Scout out a fishy-looking hole with an anchor point (such as a tree or rock) on either side.

STEP 2 Lay out a section of cordage or rope that will be long enough to reach from anchor to anchor. Now, working at 2- to 4-foot (60–120 cm) intervals, attach a section of fishing line. Length is determined by desired bait depth.

STEP 3 Hook and bait each line. Add a sinker if there's a current through your fishing hole. Now stretch your rope

tightly from anchor to anchor. It's okay if the rope lies on or near the surface of the water.

STEP 4 Each baited hook should sink into the depths of your fishing hole. Observe your setup for a few minutes to see that everything is working, then come back a few hours later and collect your catch.

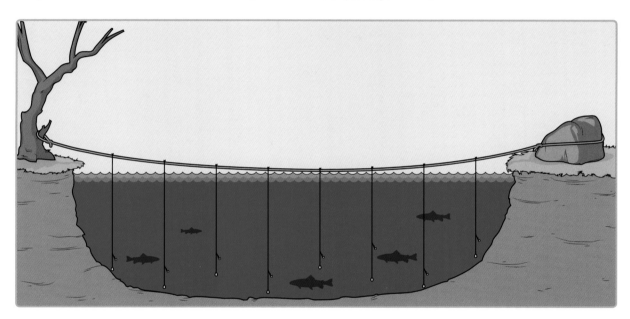

160 SNEAK AND PEEK FOR SPOOKY TROUT

Native, wild trout are spooky and hard to catch. Here's how to put some wild trout on the dinner menu.

SURVEY Watch a slow-moving trout stream from a distance. Pick out deep quiet spots with current leading in and an undercut bank or rock. Don't show yourself, cast your shadow across the water, or let your feet fall heavily.

RIG A ROD Set up a rod or willow pole with 6–8 feet (1.8–2.4 m) of line and a number 6 hook. If the current is rapid, add one split shot about 18 inches (45 cm) above the hook. Bait with a worm, grub, or grasshopper.

SNEAK A PEAK Carefully approach a fishing hole. Crawl on hands and knees or even your belly to avoid exposing yourself to fish. Peek through the grass at the bank's edge and drop your bait into the current just upstream of the hole. Let it drift naturally by the hole, then repeat. Vary your drift closer or further from the bank. If you're lucky, you'll get to watch a swirl of silver and pink as native wild trout take the bait

161 CLEAN YOUR CATCH

Here's a quick and easy way to clean a high-country trout.

STEP 1 Insert the point of your knife into the fish's vent. Cut along the fish's belly clear to the gills.

STEP 2 Insert your knife point just under the jawbone, push the point up and over the tongue, then down and out the opposite side as shown. Cut forward and out.

STEP 3 Insert one finger under the tongue and into the throat. Grasp the jawbone and head with your opposite hand. Pull out the tongue, gills, and innards toward the tail all together.

STEP 4 Push your thumbnail along the inside of the fish's backbone, removing the membranous blood-filled pocket located there.

STEP 5 Sever the trout's head and discard it along with the offal. Finally, rinse the cleaned fish thoroughly in fresh cold water.

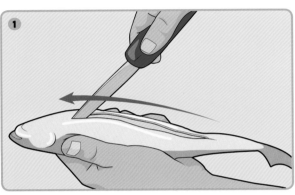

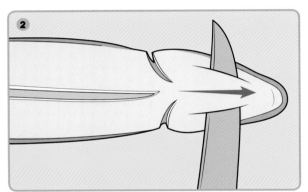

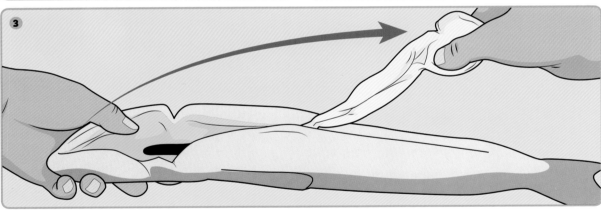

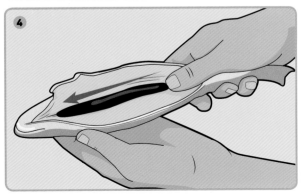

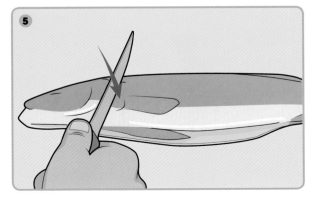

162 COOK CAVEMAN STYLE

So you've managed to spear, trap, noodle, or catch some fish. Good for you, especially if you're in an emergency survival situation. But how do you plan to cook your catch? You could grunt, swing your club around a couple times, and snarf them down raw . . . or not. Here's a great way to cook fish using only some hot coals.

FIRE UP THE COALS Get a fire going, preferably using hardwood. While it burns down to coals, clean your fish (don't skin or scale). Dig up some seasonings like salt and pepper, wild sage, or juniper berries. Season the inside

GET COOKING Once your fire has burned down to nice, gentle coals, set your fish on the coals, belly-up. The skin will toast and even burn, but will protect the meat inside. Watch carefully so that you don't overcook it.

EAT UP Remove your fish dinner from the coals and dig in. Discard the burnt skin, but save the bones. Fact is, the best nutrients in a trout are found in the bones. Using a green stick, slow-toast the bones over your coals for about 45 minutes. When they're done they crunch like savory crackers and taste wonderful. Don't forget to swing your

163 FIND CAMP IN THE DARK

When you're hunting, fishing, or even hiking the backcountry it's easy to end up miles from camp when night falls. Good navigation skills will take you home—usually.

MARK A WAYPOINT Carry a compact GPS unit in your pack and mark the camp's location on it. Just remember: Your waypoint will take you to camp in a straight line, which could lead you right over a cliff, into an impassable rock wall, or in to other wilderness dangers. Mark all significant obstacles (such as creek crossings and cliff trails) that you'd want to navigate to or through when making your way back.

USE LANDMARKS Choose landmarks near camp that will help you navigate back home. Ideally, they'll jut above their surroundings so they'll be visible against the night sky after dark. Memorize those landmarks and your camp's position relative to them.

PAY ATTENTION Wilderness wanderers have been finding their way home for centuries before GPS existed, and so can you. In fact, so should you. In a real survival situation, good woodsmanship skills will serve you far better than any electronic device. Pay attention to everything: Remember what the patch of timber near camp looks like, where to cross that creek, how all those mountains or meadows around camp are shaped. Try to take mental photos of the terrain you travel through. As you become familiar with your backcountry surroundings—like the rooms in your house at home—you'll be able to find your way around even in the dark of night.

WATCH YOUR BACKTRAIL Don't forget to look back. Terrain looks different when you see it from the opposite direction. So turn regularly and take a good look. That's what you'll see when returning to camp.

164 DON'T TRASH THE BACKCOUNTRY

Anyone willing to leave their trash in the wilderness is an idiot and a slob best suited to life on a chain gang. Finding some fool's empty pop bottle and potato chip bag discarded along a backcountry trail makes me angry enough to bite nails. If you're willing to pack it in, then you should also be determined to pack it out.

PACK IT IN, PACK IT OUT You'll see this sign posted near virtually every Forest Service trailhead, encouraging all travelers to remain responsible for themselves and all their trash. Follow their advice: Pack all unburnable trash out of the woods, and then dispose of it properly and safely.

CLEAN YOUR CAMP If you camp in a site that's commonly used (a visible firepit, stumps or logs to sit on, stack of firewood, and so on), clean the site thoroughly and leave it ready for its next visitor, complete with stacked firewood and kindling.

LEAVE NO TRACE Meant to minimize human impact on sensitive wilderness areas, "Leave No Trace" means erasing every sign that you were there. Clean up, remove fire rings, grind and scatter dead coals and ashes, and generally make like a criminal trying to hide evidence. A couple of backcountry storms later, no one will be able to tell that you were ever in the area.

165 CARE FOR YOUR HORSES

Your horses deserve all the water they want, and all the feed you can manage to give them. They work hard for you, so take care of them. A good horseman will see that his horses are fed and watered before he enjoys his own meal.

WATER YOUR MOUNT Horses need to drink at least once daily, and more often is better, especially if the weather is hot and your horses are working hard and losing fluids through sweating. Lead or ride them to water and give them plenty of time to tank up. Better yet, hobble or turn them loose to graze near water. They'll drink all they need.

FEED YOUR STEED A horse that's working hard should be allowed to graze for several hours each day, and be given a half-gallon of oats with molasses for extra protein. (If he's not working hard, you can eliminate the oats.) Horses usually have best friends within the band, so your best strategy is to keep one buddy tied while the other is hobbled or turned loose to graze. That way they're not likely to go walkabout; if they do, their tied-up buddy will let you know about it.

ARAM SAYS "Hang a small bell on each horse that's hobbled or turned loose to graze. The sound will help you keep track of their whereabouts, and find them should they go AWOL."

166 BEWARE BEARS

Wherever you go in North America, bears share the backcountry with you. Don't worry. That's part of the charm. Here's how to tell the difference between various bears and how to avoid being on their dinner menu.

BLACK BEAR The smallest of the bears ranges in color from midnight black up to blond. Cinnamon and chocolate are common color phases in certain regions, and are responsible for most of the "grizzly" sightings in areas where only black bears reside. Black bear tracks typically won't show claw marks—his claws are short and strong, and don't protrude as much as a grizzly's. Avoid trouble with *Ursus americanus* by keeping your camp clean and free of tasty, smelly things. If he attacks you, fight hard with any weapon available, 'cause he plans to eat you.

BROWN OR GRIZZLY BEAR Brothers in the same family, browns live in coastal areas and typically grow larger than the grizzly, due to more plentiful food sources. While the grizzly inhabits inland regions, his name coined by Lewis and Clark due to his grizzled, or silver-tip, hair color. Formally classified *Ursus arctos horribilis*, the name refers to the grizzly's "horrible" attitude. He's typically smaller and more aggressive, than brown bears. His long, dangerous claws leave visible marks ahead of their tracks. Avoid angering him by giving a wide berth—especially if he's near cubs or food. He often bluff attacks. If confronted, back away slowly, showing that you respect his territory. If he actually attacks you, get on your belly and play dead. If you're lucky, he'll eventually go away, leaving you only half-dead, instead of all the way dead.

POLAR BEAR *Ursus maritimus* is considered by many to be the largest and most dangerous of all North American bears. Few of us will experience the opportunity to fear Nanuq, but if you're one of the fortunate few, I'd suggest adopting the Inuit ways of prayer and respect. Nanuq will hunt you and eat you if he feels inclined, so rely on local ways to try to keep him away.

167 STEER CLEAR OF SNAKES

Folks worry a lot about bears in the backcountry, but your chances of encountering a venomous snake are far higher.

BE SMART Most bites are a result of alcohol and stupidity. Give snakes a wide berth and they'll go about their business.

KNOW THE LOCALS Research local snake species and populations. You're unlikely to run into a snake while hunting elk in the Rockies, but a desert Coues deer hunt is different.

WEAR ARMOR Where snake populations are high, consider donning snake boots or gaiters. The boots and gaiters will protect your feet and legs from unscrupulous slithering things.

GET HELP If a venomous snake bites someone, evacuate immediately. Keep the victim calm; a low pulse slows the spread of poison. Keep the bite lower than the heart for the same reason. Don't suck at it—your mouth is all mucous membrane, and venom will go right to your bloodstream.

KNOW VENOM Most venomous American snakes carry hemotoxin, which breaks down blood and tissue, causing swelling and pain. A few use neurotoxin, which attacks the central nervous system and brain, causing paralysis and respiratory arrest. Either way, get medical help fast.

> **ARAM SAYS** "Venom is precious to a snake. He may just strike defensively and save his venom for later. If you are bitten (heaven forbid) and the bite shows little to no reaction, that's likely what happened."

168 BE WOLF WARY

Although you're much more likely to be hit by lightning, your chances of suffering a wolf attack in North America are growing thanks to wolf reintroduction efforts. Several lethal wolf attacks have been documented in North America recently, including a 32-year-old woman in March 2010 in southwest Alaska and a 22-year-old man in November 2005 in Saskatchewan. During the 1800s (when wolves were common across the U.S.) wolf attacks were more frequent.

DON'T TEASE Don't use a predator call on wolves unless you're prepared to defend yourself and have a wolf tag. I know one man who, upon spying a pair of wolves, tried a few distress calls. The wolves charged like bats out of hell.

DON'T RUN Running will almost certainly trigger an attack. Wolves often make exploratory attacks to assess potential prey's response. Stand and defend yourself if necessary, but don't ever run.

DON'T UNDERESTIMATE The threat to your hunting privileges is far more likely than the threat to your life. But

should you face a wolf attack, prepare for a battle. Consider the following incident: In Ontario, Canada, in December 23, 1922, an old trapper mushed his sled dogs toward a nearby village to get his mail. Later that day, two Native Americans found his bones amid wolf tracks. They armed themselves with rifles and ammunition and took their dogsleds in pursuit of the wolves. The next day a search party found their bones amidst a pile of empty cartridges and dead wolves—16 in all. There were apparently still plenty of wolves to kill and devour the two brave souls.

169 WATCH OUT FOR BUGS

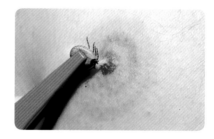

Ironically, smaller critters can be a bigger danger than bears, wolves, or lions. The greatest threat is to folks who are allergic, so foresight is your best protection. Carry all meds (Epi-pen, Benadryl, etc) to cope with an allergic reaction (or two) and teach members of your party how to help you should you get stung or bitten.

One of the most horrific, though remote, threats is an attack from Africanized or "killer" bees. If you encounter a bee swarm while in the south, give it a wide berth and stay very quiet. If you hear a sound like a World War II bomber going over, hunker down and hold entirely still till the black cloud of bees is gone.

Some of my least favorite critters-scorpions, spiders, and centipedes-can all be dangerous. If you venture into territory where some or all of these are common, you should sleep inside an insect-proof tent at night. Keep your gear inside as well and shake any footwear out thoroughly before you install your feet in them. I've found a scorpion inside my boot (with my foot) and it was a learning experience that I can't recommend.

If you spend time in tick-infested territory, you should give yourself some regular head-to-toe inspections. Carefully feel yourself over, paying special attention to armpits, groin, and nape-of-neck areas—anywhere short

hair or tender skin lives. If you find a tick embedded in your body, grasp it with a pair of tweezers or pliers and pull very slowly and gently till it relaxes and its head pulls out of your flesh. If you pull too hard or fast you'll break its head off inside your skin, which could result in an infection.

170 AVOID RUT RAGE

Every year folks are attacked by whitetail bucks, bull moose, and other rut-crazy critters. I'll add mama moose (protecting their baby calves) to this discussion, because avoidance tactics are the same.

BACK AWAY Unlike running from a predator (which will trigger an attack response), beating a rapid retreat may placate a rut-crazed buck or bull by giving him the impression that you're showing deference to his dominance.

GET TREED If there's a qualified tree nearby, climb out of your angry ungulate's reach. Get comfortable, 'cause he or she is likely to stand guard for a while. Once your bully wanders far away you can climb down and vacate the area.

DEFEND YOURSELF If you can't outrun or out-climb your pursuer, you'll have to resort to self-defense. Killing an animal without a tag or license can have serious legal consequences and, of course, killing a mama moose will leave a baby moose

171 FIGHT OFF A LION

Statistically, just over half of a mountain lion's human victims are dead upon impact. The lion hits them from behind, severs their spinal cord with their powerful jaws, and down they go. The other half see the lion coming and, if they respond correctly, survive the attack.

SHOOT THE STALKER If you see a lion hunting you, and you have a firearm, kill him. Any lion that's lost his fear of humans is a deadly threat to you and others. If you don't have a gun, well . . .

FIGHT FOR YOUR LIFE If a lion attacks you, he means to eat you, so fight like hell. Bluff him. Look as big and scary as you can and take the attack to him. Try to stay on your feet, get hold of a club, and beat him with it. If you go down, try to stab him repeatedly in the lungs and eyes with your knife. If you don't have a knife, gouge his eyes out with your thumb or fingers, or grab a rock and beat his brains out. The harder you fight the more likely he is to abandon the attack for easier prey.

172 BEWARE CARELESS COMPANIONS

Possibly the most dangerous thing you'll encounter in the woods is a careless hunting buddy. Every year people are accidentally shot by sloppy gun handlers, and some of them die. Don't be one of those folks.

SPEAK UP Don't hesitate to call someone out for careless behavior with a firearm. If they're allowing their firearm to point at folks, they need a comeuppance. Most guys will feel foolish enough after being admonished a time or two they'll pay attention to safety. If someone continues to wave their gun around, they need to be admonished sharply. I've personally been shot by accident so, a life-flight and five days in the hospital later, I know what I'm talking about.

KEEP EMPTY CHAMBERS Unless a shot is imminent, everyone should keep the chamber of their rifle clear, with very few exceptions . . . being hunted by a polar bear, maybe?

LEAVE IDIOTS HOME If someone refuses to handle their firearms safely, or insists on carrying a round in their rifle's chamber, leave 'em behind. There's absolutely no reason to compromise your safety or that of your party just because one person is stupid or careless.

173 ESCAPE A BIG CAT

A friend of mine who operates the local electric company hiked into a deep canyon to do a routine inspection. Afterward, he scouted up the canyon bottom looking for elk tracks. He saw a cougar suddenly appear in the brush—then another, and another.

Mountain lions are typically incredibly shy, avoiding all contact with humans. The fact that these cats were openly showing themselves to Shane concerned him. The three were obviously a mother lion with her two grown cubs—she'd likely weigh in at about 120 pounds (54 kg), the cubs 95 pounds (45 kg) or so each. Three hundred and ten pounds (141 kg) of potentially hungry mountain lion were shadowing Shane. He was not carrying a firearm.

Shane attempted to leave the canyon, but didn't get far. The cats rapidly began to close in on him. He climbed the nearest tree (which he described as just bigger than a Christmas tree) as high as he could, treed by three aggressive lions that were toying with him like a house cat with a mouse.

Fortunately, he was carrying a portable radio. He got a call through to some local guys who immediately grabbed rifles and headed to rescue him. While he waited for help to arrive he tried to encourage the cats to keep their distance.

"They didn't seem real hungry," he told me, "just intent on keeping me in that tree until they were hungry enough to come drag me out of it. I'd climb down from my tree, grab a rock, and throw it at them. They'd chase it, batting at it like a house cat plays with a ball. Then they'd come chase me back up the tree." He believed it was just a matter of time till they attacked him in earnest.

The rescuers arrived in time to prevent Shane from becoming cat food. As they approached his location they caught glimpses of the lions disappearing into the brush, but were unable to get a shot off. A very relieved Shane climbed out of his little tree to greet them.

Post Assessment

 DONE RIGHT

Shane survived an unusual and incredibly dangerous encounter. Had he not been carrying a radio, he'd have been eaten. Climbing the tree likely delayed a direct attack, as the cats probably felt they had him caught. Was throwing rocks at the lions a good idea? I don't know. Perhaps it kept them back till help arrived, but it had potential to rouse the cats to attack sooner.

DONE WRONG

The one big mistake Shane made was going into this territory with no firearm. A person can go afield thousands of times without encountering danger. (I've done it often.) But this occasion could have been lethal for Shane. If he'd carried a gun, a warning shot likely would have sent the cats on their way. If not, he'd have been prepared to defend himself.

174 MASTER SHOOTING POSITIONS

The three most important field positions for a hunter to learn are: prone, sitting, and offhand (standing), in that order. Master these, and you'll be prepared for every shot that comes your way.

A PRONE When used in conjunction with a support for your rifle (log, rock, pack), prone is the steadiest of all firing positions, and should be used whenever possible. Just lie down on the ground, legs spread, feet flat. Rest your rifle on your pack (or log, rock, or bipods) and wedge your left hand (southpaws reverse) between the rifle butt and the ground to adjust and support it. Both elbows should be planted firmly on the ground. Settle your cheek into the comb, relax, breathe, and squeeze the trigger.

B SITTING This is your next steadiest field position, especially if you can find support for your firearm; use it when you can't get a prone shot. Just plant your bottom firmly in the dirt, feet about shoulder width apart. Lock each elbow solidly onto each knee (wiggle this elbow/knee joint till you find a good lock—don't just balance bone-on-bone). Settle into a rest or cross-sticks if possible. Breathe and squeeze.

C OFFHAND OR STANDING When conditions prevent a prone or sitting shot, this is your fallback. Good accuracy is tough without good training and extensive practice. Correct offhand form has many variations, but for hunting purposes here's how. Set your feet about shoulder width apart, knees straight but not locked. Settle your rifle butt firmly into your shoulder, pulling rearward tension with your trigger hand. Grasp the forearm gently with your other hand, elbow tilted 45 degrees and below the hand. Relax into position. If your rifle points to one side, move your feet to bring it to bear. Relax, breathe, and squeeze the trigger. Once again, take advantage of any rest or support to steady your shot.

175 SHOOT WITH YOUR PACK ON

My brother stalked slowly through a thick copse of aspen, pack on his back and rifle in hand. The bull of a lifetime erupted from the forest in front of him, blasting along like a runaway locomotive. Joseph instinctively placed his crosshairs on its shoulder and made the finest shot of his life, dropping the bull to the forest floor. In a later hunt, a tremendous bull presented me a thread-the-needle shot through the timber. I raised my long rifle and made the shot, downing the biggest bull ever taken with a flintlock with one perfect shot through the heart and lungs. I, too, was wearing a pack.

Good shot chances occur in the blink of an eye, and can disappear just as quickly. Practice shooting while wearing your loaded pack. Shoot from different positions. Aiming while the shoulder strap fights for position with your rifle butt or stresses your archery form can be tough, so work the kinks out of that confrontation before the hunt. When the shot of a lifetime presents you'll make the shot, pack on your back, without even thinking about it.

176 TRAIN WITH YOUR RIFLE

Over two decades of guiding, the most common problem I've noticed among hunters was their inability to assume a quick and steady field position and acquire their target in their scope. In my opinion, more trophy animals have walked away unscathed and unknowing due to this lack of skill than all other factors combined.

Make several pre-hunt trips to the field to practice your field shooting positions. Move through the woods and ridges with your empty rifle at the ready. Pick out a target and find the best available field position. Rapidly assume the position, acquire the target in your crosshairs, get as steady as possible, and squeeze your trigger on a dry chamber. Make sure your crosshairs stay steady on the target through the click. Work your action immediately and click a steady follow-up shot. Move along, spot another target, and repeat.

For obvious reasons, exercise safety and treat all your targets as though you were really shooting at them—no unsafe backgrounds or farmer's cows as targets. Practice this exercise enough and when a shot at a critter presents itself, you'll automatically find and assume the best field position available, making the shot with ease and brining home dinner in one fell shot.

177 FIX A BOW ON THE FLY

Picture yourself on a deep backcountry elk hunt. A noisy bull stops broadside 30 yards (10 m) away. You draw your bow—but then, for some reason, it explodes in a maddening tangle of cables, cams, and strings. The bull exits the scene, but not to worry: you've still got five days of hunting left. Oh, wait—your bow is now completely out of commission.

CARRY A BOW-CARE KIT Assemble a small tool-kit for your bow, including Allen wrenches, thread-locking compound, and spare parts. Don't leave home without it.

GET RUGGED Backcountry archery equipment should be the toughest, most durable gear money can buy. Sights and rests are particularly vulnerable to damage, so get rugged.

CARE FOR CABLES AND CAMS One of the biggest disasters that can happen to a bow is derailed cables and string. It happens, though. (I know several hunters who have had small twigs get between cam and string or cable as they drew or let down their bow, resulting in the string or cable coming off.) You can travel a day out of the wilderness, another day into the city and an archery shop for repairs, and third day back into the wilderness. Or, you can try to re-string your bow in the backcountry. This is likely dangerous to your bow's health but, if it works, it could get you back in the game several days sooner.

PRESS IT INTO SHAPE You're going to need to compress your bow limbs before you can re-string it. This may not actually be possible on your model of bow without a proper bow press, but here's a tactic you can try. Find two solid bars and a 6 foot (2 m) length of paracord. Assemble your backcountry bow press as shown. Twist a stick into the paracord midway between cams until the limbs bend enough to reroute the string and cables. Get everything situated and then carefully untwist the paracord. Take a few test shots to make sure everything works and your sights are still on the money.

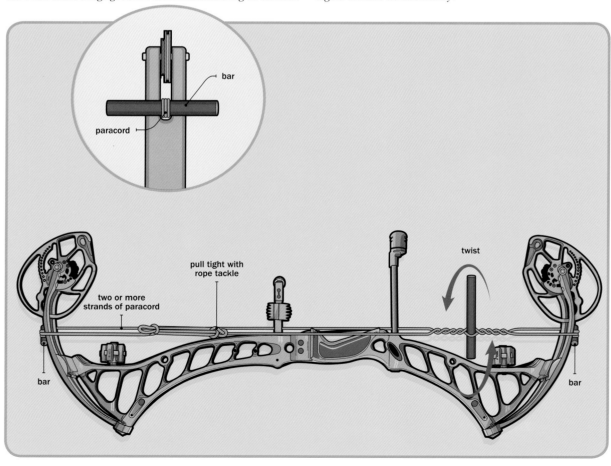

178 REPAIR A DROPPED RIFLE

Guns get dropped. Hunters fall on their rifles. Horses roll over them. When this happens in the backcountry you may have a problem on your hands.

PREPARE TO REPAIR Anyone hunting the backcountry should be prepared to resight a rifle after a fall. Carry about 20 extra rounds of ammo with you just in case.

CHECK ZERO Find a solid shooting position where you can take aim at some natural target, like a knothole on a dead tree or a spot on a rock. Take one or two careful shots. If you are hitting dead-on, great. If not, re-zero your scope.

DRIFT SIGHTS Not that long ago, every hunter used to know how to adjust iron sights. Not so anymore. If your front sight is bent, use the pliers on your multi-tool to straighten it. If either front or rear sight has been knocked off, use a punch and mallet to drift it back into alignment. (Use your multi-tool as an improvised punch, and a short heavy stick as a mallet.) Shoot to verify that you're back on zero.

PREVENT PROBLEMS If you are carrying your rifle strapped to your pack, you're going to want to shroud the scope and action in a lightweight foam pad in order to protect it should you happen to take a tumble. If you're hiking rifle-in-hand over treacherous terrain or footing, carry your gun in your downslope hand, so if your feet slip and you go down, your rifle will land on something soft (you).

179 USE YOUR SENSES

Wilderness animals are fully in touch with their senses. You should be too.

LOOK AND SEE I'm amazed at how people will pass through an area without remembering a thing about it. Don't just look at something and forget it. Learn to remember what the land you traversed through looks like.

USE YOUR EARS Many sounds in the woods go unnoticed by humans. Have you paid attention to squirrel chatter and birdcalls when hunting? Wild critters have their own languages and they listen to each other. Do the same.

SNIFF OUT GAME I've followed a sweet barnyard odor to herds of elk multiple times, and smelled rutting whitetails as well. Use scent on the wind (especially when hunting elk in thick timber) to help you find game.

FEEL THE WIND Be aware of air movement against your skin. Train yourself to pay attention, so that you always know what the wind is doing.

TASTE WILD GAME The best use of our sense of taste happens when we sink our teeth into that succulent mouthful of grilled tenderloin. The only way I've used taste while hunting is to check acorns to see if they're ripe and ready for wild critters to eat.

USE YOUR SIXTH SENSE Whether it's combined senses, past experiences, or instincts, trust your sixth sense. Does that storm building black against the horizon fill you with a strange sense of doom? Maybe it's time to leave the area or prep for a real tempest. Feeling inspired to hunt in a certain meadow? There may be wild elk there, just waiting for you. Feel like you're being watched? It's likely another predator—lion, bear, or man.

180 FIND A GOOD VANTAGE POINT

Often the hardest part about hunting in the backcountry is finding game. Good quality optics enable you to search vast areas of territory for animal movement.

LOOK IT OVER Find a vantage point that lets you study a large portion of your hunting area. This usually means getting above the surrounding terrain.

GET COMFORTABLE Find a comfy spot to set up. If you're sitting on a sharp rock and the sun is slow-cooking you, you won't glass effectively. Settle into a comfortable spot with a good seat, shade, and ideally, shelter from wind.

STAY STEADY Lock your elbows onto your knees or lie down over a big rock to steady your binocs while you glass.

Better yet, use a lightweight tripod to mount your field glasses or spotting scope. You'll find more game if your field of view is not dancing all over the countryside.

GLASS METHODICALLY Check out likely or nearby spots first. If you don't find game there, rapidly glass everything in sight for obvious animals. Next, methodically study the terrain one bit at a time, searching for hidden or hard-to-see animals. Once you spot a big buck or bull, plan a stalk and go get him.

181 HUNT A MIDDAY NAP

Stretched out in the midday sun, I dozed away exhaustion born of weeks of back-to-back guiding. Suddenly a stick cracked on the slope opposite a nearby wallow. My eyes opened and I glanced at my two bowhunters, one nearby, the other just behind a tree. They too, had heard the sound.

Short minutes later a magnificent six-by-seven bull followed twelve cow elk into the clearing around our wallow. We were hunting cows, and disappointment grew as we watched them circle the far side of the meadow and disappear. The bull was a different story. He left his cows and ambled between us and the wallow, dust puffing from beneath his feet a mere seven strides from my own. If only we'd had a bull tag.

The lesson: Don't head back to camp for your midday nap, unless you've got horses to feed or other chores to do. Instead, settle down for a rest near an elk wallow, game trail intersection or water hole. Big game animals often rise for an hour or two during midday to grab a snack or hunt up a drink. Find a comfortable spot to nap near a game magnet; if something shows, you'll be totally relaxed for the shot.

182 CAPE YOUR TROPHY

Caping an animal is a delicate process; you'll want to use a sharp knife and proceed carefully and slowly.

STEP 1 Make a circular cut around the animal just rearward of the crease behind the front shoulder. Make cuts from below the knee up the back of each front leg to join your circular cut.

STEP 2 Make a careful cut, beginning at the back edge of the skull where it joins the neck, all the way to your circular cut behind the shoulders. Stay perfectly in the dark line of hair that runs down the top of the neck. Cut from beneath to avoid cutting any hair.

STEP 3 Skin the cape forward all the way to the head. Work carefully to avoid scoring the skin.

STEP 4 Sever the head where the final vertebra meets the skull. At this point you can set the cape aside and finish the job later if necessary.

STEP 5 Facing off is the delicate part of the job, and should be done slowly and with extreme care. This method protects the cape the best, though it leaves a little extra fleshing work for the taxidermist. Begin with a "Y" cut that starts at the rear base of each antler and joins your back-of-the-neck cut in a— you guessed it— "Y" shape.

STEP 6 Skin the back of the skull, staying close to the bone rather than the skin. Sever each ear against the skull. Skin forward between the antlers.

STEP 7 Detach the skin from around the antler bases with a regular screwdriver or similar blunt tool. You will need to skin it away from the lower portion of the pedicle with your knife, but use the screwdriver to work the skin loose up around the burr (antler base).

STEP 8 Skin the cape forward, staying against the bone. Take extra care around the eyes (make sure you get all of the eyelids) and deep glands immediately in front of the eyes.

STEP 9 Next, you'll want to open the mouth wide enough that it's relatively easy for you to skin the gums away from both the upper and the lower jawbones. Carve the nose septum free with the cape; just continue to stay against bone.

STEP 10 Finish up the process of skinning from the back until you meet your mouth cuts and the cape comes free. Make sure your cape stays dry and as cold as possible so that the hair won't slip.

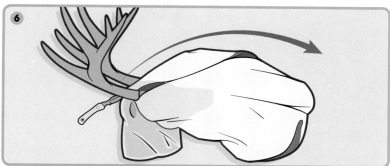

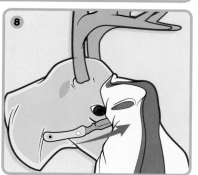

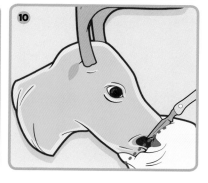

183

BRING WEED-FREE FEED

If you plan to carry some horse feed with you into the backcountry, know this: All public lands require you to use only certified weed-free feed. This will be mostly applicable to hay, because pellets, cubes, and grain usually don't contain viable weed seeds. Buy your hay from a reputable farm store—and make sure that it has been labeled "certified weed free".

On most backcountry trips, your horses will simply forage for fodder. There are typically no regulations restricting your steed from filling his belly, so let him eat up. (If any sensitive areas or plants are present, they should be listed at every trailhead.)

184 SKIN AND QUARTER GAME

If you've never processed an animal bigger than a deer, skinning and quartering an elk or moose in the backcountry (away from winches, tailgates, and tables) can seem like an insurmountable task. Here's the best way to process your meat in the backcountry. If done correctly, it's fairly quick; I can usually skin and quarter an elk alone in an hour or less.

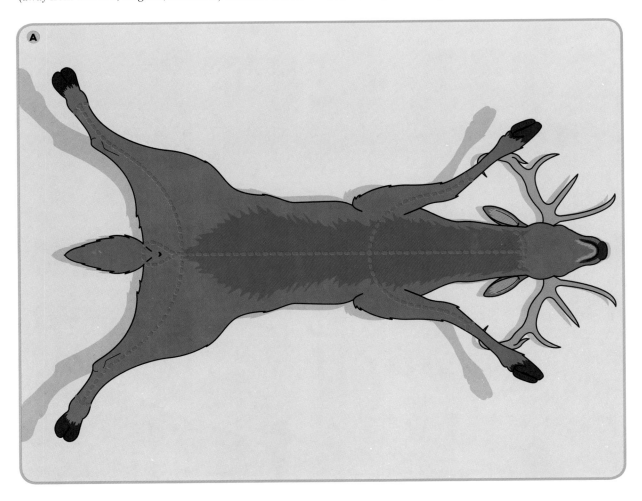

STEP 1 Make sure that your game is fully bled out. If you've shot him through the lungs or heart, then that will happen automatically. If not, cut his jugular just behind his jawbone, unless you plan to cape and shoulder mount the animal.

STEP 2 Make "rip" cuts (A). Circle the legs a little bit below the knee or hock. Then make a long rip cut from the jaw (or the sternum, if caping and mounting the animal) all the way back, ending with a teardrop shaped cut around the anus. Rip from your leg cuts up the back of each leg toward the centerline.

STEP 3 Skin the top half of the animal, keeping everything as clean as possible.

STEP 4 Detach the rear quarter from the carcass (B), removing as much meat with it as possible. Begin by making a cut from the hip bone or iliac crest, along the spine to the protuberance alongside the tail. Follow by lifting the leg high and cutting the meat away from the underside of the pelvis. Finish by severing the hip joint. Hang to cool.

STEP 5 Detach the front quarter from the rib cage. This quarter comes free much more easily because there is no joint. Carve as much meat free with the shoulder as possible. Hang to cool.

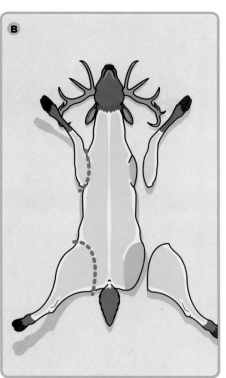

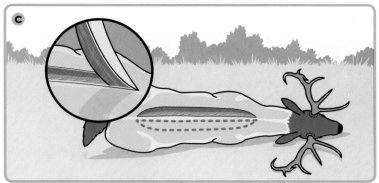

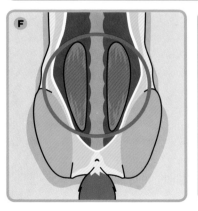

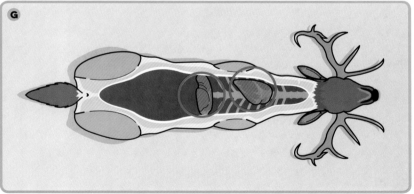

STEP 6 Carve the backstrap (my favorite piece of meat, by the way) free from the spine (C), taking your time to ensure that you do a nice clean job. Make your first cut along the spine from hip to neck. Follow up with a slice along the top of the ribs where they join with the spine. This cut should meet your first cut at right angles all along the rib/spine joint, freeing up the backstrap. Hang it up to cool (D) after this step is complete.

STEP 7 Trim away all leftover meat on the neck and ribs. Toss the trimmings in a meat sack and hang to cool (E).

STEP 8 Roll the carcass over and repeat the entire process on the other half of the animal.

STEP 9 Open a large flap into the abdominal cavity. Reach in and carefully remove the tenderloins that sit under either side of the rearward

portion of spine (F). These are incredibly tender and tasty, so treat them with care. Set aside to cool. Next, take the liver, exercising care not to cut the bile sack. Afterward, you can reach forward into the chest cavity and collect the heart. (G)

STEP 10 Okay, now all of the hard work is done. Once all your meat cools, seal it securely in game bags to keep birds, flies, and hornets away.

185 BE A BACKCOUNTRY MEAT PACKER

Wild meat has no chemicals, hormones, antibiotics, or other unpleasantness. It behooves us to take care of our harvest.

COOL IT QUICK Skinning and cooling game rapidly are key to quality, mild-tasting meat. Don't waste. Get the skin off and the quarters hung to air. In a pinch, put meat (wrapped in a garbage bag) in a cold stream, lake, or spring.

KEEP IT CLEAN Keep dirt, leaves, bark, hair, and gunk (especially stomach or gut matter) away from your meat.

LET IT GLAZE When hung out to cool, meat will naturally form a dry protective surface, which is called a skin, crust, or glaze. Let this happen when possible to help your meat stay fresh and clean.

KEEP IT COLD Make sure that your meat remains in a cool, shaded spot until you're ready to pack everything out of the wilderness. Ideally, it'll never get above 42˚F (5˚ C). If the weather gets hot during the day, keep the bagged meat submerged in cold water.

186 HORSEPACK YOUR MEAT

Horses or mules make packing big loads of meat easy. They can also carry heavy loads quickly out of the backcountry, so they make early season hunts (when temps are high and meat can spoil fast) possible.

If your horse has never carried meat before, teach him that it's okay. Approach the carcass with him and let him investigate it. Keep your attitude casual to show him there's nothing to be concerned about. If he's nervous, smear a handful of blood over his nose and slightly into his nostrils.

When he can smell it, he'll get used to it more quickly.

You'll need to balance the load, just like any other cargo; luckily, big game animals conveniently have two matching sides. Configure your loads to include matching parts and pieces on either side. For instance, load up a front quarter, scrap meat, backstrap, and tenderloin from one side of your harvest on one side of your pack animal, and then put the same pieces from the opposite side on the other side of your packhorse. They should balance perfectly.

187 TRY THESE TRICKS

Here are a few tips that will make your meat-packing life easier.

KEEP 'EM CLEAN Line your panniers with contractor trash bags to keep them clean from blood and gore.

HANG 'EM RIGHT Hang the quarters from your sawbucks using a clean set of horse hobbles. Buckle them around the bone above the joint, with the middle portion of the hobbles around the sawbuck.

PUT THE BACK IN FRONT If you're loading all four quarters on one horse, put the rear quarters (heavier) on the front sawbucks and the front quarters on the rear sawbucks. If you're loading just one set of quarters, hang them from the front sawbucks.

LEAVE BONES BEHIND If your horse needs to carry a lot of meat over a long distance, bone it out to reduce weight.

188 BACKPACK YOUR MEAT

You've made a good hunt. There's blood on the ground and meat in the tree—a lot of it, in fact. And you're gonna have to pack it out yourself.

GET YOUR MINDSET If the only way you've got to get your meat out of the backcountry is your backpack, you've got your work cut out for you. Here's the key: Work efficiently, but don't rush. The biggest mistake you can make at this point is to get in a hurry and strain a tendon, ligament, or joint. Do that and someone may have to pack you out of the wilderness.

LIGHTEN UP Your best strategy is to bone out all the meat to eliminate a lot of unnecessary weight. Then, divide the meat into loads. Your physique and level of fitness will dictate how much you should carry. Don't be a hero, but carry as much as you can. I usually manage a little over 100 pounds (45 kg) per load. You might do more or less.

BAG AND GO Before stuffing meat into your backpack, line it with a contractor-grade trash bag, to keep both the meat and your pack clean. Stuff your load in, tie off the bag, and cinch your compression straps down on the load. Shuttle your meat one load at a time to camp or the trailhead. It'll take dogged grit and determination to get through this; hang in there. When all the meat is safely in the truck, you can be proud of a job well done.

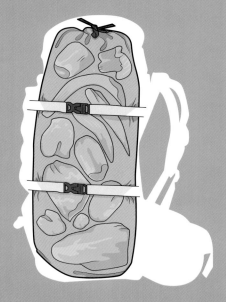

189 CARE FOR YOUR CAPE

Occasionally, we are fortunate enough to harvest a truly noteworthy animal. Honoring that animal with a shoulder or European mount creates a trophy that'll transport us to a special time and place every time we look at it. Keeping your cape in good condition for that mount can be tough. Here are some techniques that will help.

CLEAN IT UP Spread your cape out quickly after caping it off. Wipe away any dirt and debris. Trim off meat or fat.

SALT IT DOWN If weather is cold—50˚F (10˚C) or below—this step is unnecessary, but it can't hurt. If it's warm out, salt is the only way you'll preserve your trophy from spoiling and hair slippage. Spread the cape out and sprinkle non-iodized salt liberally over the flesh side, rubbing handfuls into the lips, nose, eyes, and ears. Repeat several times during the next 36 hours.

DRAIN AND DRY Once the salt has had a chance to work, it'll bring "water" to the surface. Spread the cape over a bush or on an incline where the moisture can run off. Try to keep as much salt on the hide as possible. Once the cape is thoroughly salted and becoming stiff and dry, fold it tightly, flesh sides together. Roll it into a tight bundle, face in the middle. Keep it as cool as possible until you deliver it to your taxidermist or drop it in your freezer at home.

190 GET SOME ALL-AMERICAN IVORY

Years ago, I lay in my wilderness camp listening to a bull bugling throughout the night, tempting me into a game of tag-the-elk. Finally, dawn broke cold, fog hanging above the high-country wilderness. I stalked those haunting bugles as they drew me deeper and deeper into the timber.

Eventually we met and I won the game, placing my tag on his mist-wet 5x6 antlers. As I opened his mouth to check out his ivories I was overjoyed to discover a one-of-a-kind trophy: double ivories, nestled comfortably against each other on each side of his mouth—a bull with four ivories. I'd never seen that before, nor have I seen it (or spoken to anyone who has ever seen it) since.

In my opinion, elk ivories are a quintessential symbol of wildness, freedom, and high-lonesome territory mystique. They aren't true ivory, but they do possess a mysterious beauty all their own and they are readily fashioned into pendants, buttons, jewelry, and so forth. Native Americans prized them for decorating their buckskin shirts, dresses, and accoutrements. Folks used to believe that bulls made their piercing bugle by blowing across the ivories (which is of course not true, by the way), hence the nickname "bugle teeth." Both cows and bulls possess them.

You can remove the ivories by carefully cutting around them with the point of your knife. Work around and around, separating the tooth root from its surrounding tissue. Crank on it with your fingers occasionally. You should never use pliers to extract the ivories—you'll scar the tooth. Be patient, and sooner or later it'll come free. Repeat on the other side.

191 CHOOSE YOUR TROPHY STYLE

Before packing your trophy out of the backcountry you'll want to lighten it up as much as possible, either by cleaning the skull off for a European mount, or cutting the skull plate out for a shoulder mount.

The European style mount entails cleaning the skull down to the bone and bleaching it nice and white. The mount, dark antlers contrasting nicely with the white bone, is then mounted on the wall. To prep your skull for a Euro trophy (and lighten it up for the trip to the trailhead) follow the directions for facing a cape off (see item 182).

Once the skin is removed, you can use your knife to detach the lower jaw. Whittle and discard all meat, fat, and eyeballs from the skull. Skin the upper palate free from the bone. Use a wire or stick to stir the brains, then shake and flush them out till the brain cavity is clean. Set the clean skull in the sun to dry.

For a skull plate, begin with the caped-off skull propped securely on its nose. Make your first cut (you'll need a good saw for this) beginning at the rear edge of the skull, several inches rearward of the antler bases. Cut toward the bottom edge of the eye sockets. Be careful to keep your cut straight and level. Keep cutting until you reach the eye.

Next, start a second cut at the top of the skull several inches (about 15 cm) in front of the antler bases. This cut should go right through the back edge of the eye sockets and intersect your first cut at right angles. Shake any remaining brains free of the skull plate.

Finally, trim away leftover fat, meat, and tissue. Set in the sun to dry. (This method also works good for simple skull-plate mounts: just saw the skull out through hair, skin, and all. Trim it up later and fasten it to the wall.)

192

TRY TENDER-LOIN

One of the finest trophies to be had in the backcountry is tenderloin grilled over a smoky fire. In fact, many hunters traditionally honor an animal by eating the tenderloins or heart while in the wilderness. Just roll it in salt and pepper, and grill or skewer it over your campfire. You'll never taste anything like it.

SURVIVAL

PERHAPS THE MOST INFLUENTIAL

backcountry experience I ever had occurred when I was thirteen. A local rancher invited my brother Joseph and I to accompany him into the desert to gather cattle. It was a dream come true for me—before it became the scariest experience of my life. We were miles into a ragged canyon maze and had picked up about a dozen cattle. The rancher told me to stay with the cows and push them toward the trailhead. Too embarrassed to admit that I'd no idea where that was, I agreed. He recognized my fears, I think; before riding off with Joseph to find more cattle he said, "Just foller the cows. They know where they're going!"

I follered the cows. Then the desert canyon seemed to close in on me, and the sky seemed to whisper, "You'll never find your way out." I realized I'd made a huge mistake, following the rancher with no regard to where we were going. Eventually he and my brother showed up along with more cows, and I let my winded cattle stop and wait. The rancher mumbled a phrase like, "Never seen cows get there so fast," and I made a resolution to pay attention to where I was going, every time.

So far I've focused on thriving in the backcountry, not survival. But, unfortunately, stuff happens. People get lost, chewed on by bears or lions, caught in storms or avalanches, or struck by lightning. People die. But don't let that stop you. Let it inspire you to prepare for whatever worst-case scenario you encounter. That's what this chapter is about—keeping alive in a disaster. Just remember: Pay attention to where you're going.

193 BE A FIELD MEDIC

The backcountry can be a beautiful place, but ultimately you're still in the wilderness, and it can be dangerous there, especially if you or a

INJURY OR ILLNESS	IT NEEDS A BAND-AID	MONITOR IT AND CARRY ON
CUTS, ABRASIONS, AND BLISTERS	Toughen up (see item 194)	If small but deep cut, suture if possible
MINOR SPRAINS	——	Wrap in Ace bandage or medical tape
DENTAL DAMAGE	——	Chipped tooth (see item 213)
DISLOCATIONS	——	Small dislocations (fingers, toes) (see item 204)
BROKEN BONES OR SPINAL INJURIES	——	Fingers and toes if reduced (see items 205–206)
HEAD INJURY	——	If victim is unconscious less than one minute with no signs of concussion
GUNSHOT	——	——
IMPACT (FALL, KICKED BY OR THROWN FROM HORSE)	——	Watch carefully for signs of internal injury (see item 210)
SLIVER OR THORN	If it's little, yank and move on	If it's big, dig it out and watch for infection (see items 194 & 196)
FEVER, COLD, OR COUGH	——	If mild head cold or fever (see item 211)
STOMACH FLU OR FOOD POISONING	——	Keep hydrated and monitor (see items 207–208)
INFECTION AND BLOOD POISONING (SEPTICEMIA)	——	If it's minor, keep it clean; treat with antibiotics
ABDOMINAL PAIN	——	Short term (see item 208)
BURNS	——	1st degree (see item 198)
ILLNESS FROM IMPROPERLY TREATED DRINKING WATER	——	If illness passes quickly
HEAT ILLNESS	——	Mild heat exhaustion (see item 229–231)
COLD ILLNESS	——	Mild hypothermia (see items 221–224)
ALTITUDE ILLNESS	——	Persistent headache (see items 199–200)
TESTICULAR TORSION	——	If successfully reduced (see item 215)
UNUSUAL VAGINAL BLEEDING	——	——

companion are hurt. Take a look over this chart to get an idea of
how to handle various injuries or emergencies in the field.

SEE A DOCTOR IN A DAY OR TWO	NON-EMERGENCY EVACUATION	GET EMERGENCY EVACUATION
If infection develops	If an injury needs more than just a suture (see item 195)	If bleeding can't be stopped (see item 197)
⸺	⸺	⸺
Minor toothache	Severe toothache, teeth or jaw broken	⸺
Small dislocations (fingers, toes)	Large dislocations (shoulder)	Hip dislocation
Ribs; fingers or toes if you can't reduce them	Arms, collarbones, hands	Femur, hips, spine, neck, multiple ribs
If victim has signs of concussion	If victim is unconscious more than a minute, shows signs of reduced consciousness level	If victim doesn't regain full consciousness, or if visible distortion of head
⸺	⸺	Get them out NOW
⸺	If you suspect internal injury	Evident internal injury; shock; poor peripheral circulation; distended abdomen
If infection develops	If large enough that removal isn't practical	If impaled by large object
⸺	Persistent fever of 103°F (39°C) or higher; could be HAPE (see item 202) or pneumonia	Don't wait until this is necessary; over 104°F (40°C); may be poison or heat stroke
⸺	If victim can't keep any fluids down or becomes badly dehydrated	⸺
Check in as soon as you get home	If infection shows red line extending up limb (septicemia; see item 239)	If red line from septicemia reaches armpit or groin
Intermittent	Persistent (see item 209)	If pain is unbearable get them out NOW—this could be dangerous
⸺	2nd and 3rd degree (if able to travel)	3rd degree (if unable to travel); 4th degree
If illness doesn't pass (see item 156)	If victim becomes dehydrated	⸺
⸺	Advanced heat exhaustion	Heat stroke—get them out NOW
Mild frostbite	Advanced frostbite	Severe hypothermia (patient semi- or fully unconscious)
⸺	Signs of HAPE or HACE (see items 201–202)	Advanced HAPE or HACE
⸺	⸺	If unable to reduce
Moderate (see item 217)	Heavy	Heavy; severe pain and cramping (possible ectopic pregnancy)

194 CARE FOR A CUT

The most common backcountry injury is probably a cut—often self-inflicted. Cuts range from minor things that barely bleed to gaping wounds that can drain the life out of us. They are inflicted by a myriad of weapons and circumstances, from a mesquite thorn to the teeth of your least favorite mule to your own knife. Here's how to treat them.

Ⓐ SMALL PARTIAL CUT Don't worry about any small cuts, they're practically inevitable. Just wash thoroughly and keep the area clean. Bandage if you wish. The only threat here is infection. The cut let you know if it becomes infected, with redness, swelling, and tenderness.

Ⓑ SMALL FULL CUT A cut that goes clear through the skin is a little more serious, because it won't heal as quickly and is likely to scar if left unsewn. Clean thoroughly and close with butterfly bandage, steri-strips, or sutures. Monitor for infection.

Ⓒ LARGE CUTS OR GASHES These wounds will usually bleed significantly. Apply pressure to the wound and elevate it above the heart until the bleeding subsides, then irrigate and clean thoroughly. Bandage with sterile dressings, and then get this person to a doc for treatment.

195 HANDLE SEVERE BLEEDING

If you or a companion suffers an injury that severs a vessel, act fast: This is life threatening. Arterial bleeding pulses or spurts from the wound every time the heart beats. Venous bleeding is smooth and fast.

Your first priority is to stop the bleeding. If possible, apply pressure with a sterile dressing; if not, use anything clean, bulky, and absorbent. Elevate the wound above the heart. If you have a clotting agent such as QuickClot, use it. If more bleeding control is needed, use a pressure point above the wound. For an arm, it's where you can feel a pulse inside just below the armpit; for a leg, it's near the groin, where the leg meets the torso. Find the pulse and cut it off with firm direct pressure. Get a medevac fast.

For severe blood loss, a tourniquet can be used on a limb. Only use one if absolutely necessary; use can often result in the loss of the limb. Tighten a wide, broad band around the patient's limb just above the wound until blood flow stops. Leave it on only as long as necessary.

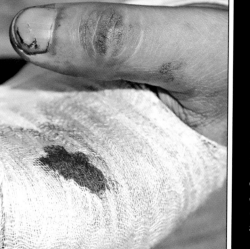

196 CLEAN A WOUND RIGHT

Correct wound cleaning promotes healing, reduces scarring, and helps prevent infection.

Once bleeding is stemmed, you should irrigate the wound thoroughly. First scrub around the wound and pick or brush any dirt or debris away. Then wash with a high-pressure stream of pure water. If you don't have a syringe you can improvise with a plastic bag: Poke a pinhole in one corner and squeeze the water out in a stiff stream. Use plenty of water, and avoid breathing or coughing on the wound, or adding contamination in any other way.

Large dirty wounds, injuries made by animals, or wounds with any tendons, ligaments, or bones exposed are incredibly tough to get completely clean. Get the wound as clean as you can, but don't try to close this wound. Just pack or cover it with sterile dressings and get the patient to a doctor.

197 KNOW WHEN TO GO

Some cuts and scrapes you can tough out; other hurts will need some professional care. If it's serious enough, you should never hesitate to get an injured companion to medical care.

Evacuate anyone who has a wound that can't be closed in the field, or who has any sort of infected wound that doesn't improve within 12 to 24 hours.

You should *rapidly* evacuate anyone who has a wound that is heavily contaminated, was caused by an animal bite, or if it shows signs of serious infection. Likewise, get the victim to help quickly if they have suffered any serious trauma involving an open joint space, damage to tendons or ligaments, deep facial injury, or any sort of crushing or impaling injury.

198 TREAT A BURN

Burns can be excruciating. Serious burns are not common in the backcountry, but minor burns are. Should you or a member of your party experience a serious burn, here's what to do.

COOL IT Immediately cool the burn with cool water. If you don't, tissue damage (cooking) will continue for a surprising amount of time.

EVALUATE DAMAGE Burns are divided into three basic categories. Superficial or "first degree" burns have red, swollen, painful skin. Rarely serious, this person should be fit to stay in the backcountry. In the case of partial-thickness or "second degree" burns, the victim will develop blisters over the burned area; these can manifest immediately, but sometimes show up an hour or more after the burn is cooled. If the surface area of the burn is extensive, evacuation is advised. Full-thickness or "third degree" is the bad one. The skin is not sensitive to touch, has no blisters, and is pale or charred. Get help immediately.

TREAT THE BURN Gently wash the area with tepid water and mild soap. If blisters have burst, clean away the skin (don't break any blisters, though). Spread a thin layer of antibiotic ointment over the burn and cover with clean gauze or clothing. For a full-thickness burn, cover it with a clean, dry cloth or gauze. Elevate the burn and use ibuprofen to control pain and swelling. Keep the patient warm and well hydrated.

199 PREVENT MOUNTAIN SICKNESS

Altitude sickness can strike without warning, attacking even experienced high-country adventurers who've never had an issue before. Here are some helpful preventative practices recommended by Buck Tilton in his excellent little book, *Backcountry First Aid*.

TAKE IT SLOW Above 10,000 feet (3,000 m), only ascend 1,000 to 1,500 feet (300–500 m) higher each night. This'll give you a chance to acclimatize. You can climb high during the day, but sleep low at night.

KEEP IN SHAPE Exercise lightly every day.

DRINK UP Drink plenty of water. Doesn't prevent mountain sickness, but is important for general health.

DINE RIGHT Eat plenty of carbohydrate-rich, low-fat foods. Above 16,000 feet (4,877 m), a diet of at least 70% carbs is recommended.

STAY HEALTHY Avoid alcohol and sedatives.

TALK TO A DOC Consult your physician about the use of acetazolamide to prevent AMS, nifedipine to prevent HAPE, and dexamethasone to prevent AMS and HACE.

200 AVOID ALTITUDE SICKNESS

The higher in elevation you travel, the less oxygen is available to your heaving lungs and pounding heart. If you go too high, too fast, you can possibly become life-threateningly ill. Altitude sickness is divided into two categories: mild and severe.

Flatlanders who travel to an elevation of 10,000 feet (3,000 m) or higher can experience headaches, nausea, fatigue, difficulty sleeping, loss of appetite, shortness of breath when active, and lassitude—which is also termed "Acute Mountain Sickness," or AMS—though mountain sickness is not uncommon at even lower elevations. The best treatment is to not go up until symptoms go down. Stay hydrated and well fed, and exercise lightly. Once your symptoms reduce or disappear, you can resume the ascent. If symptoms don't stop inside two days, descend 2,000 feet (600 m) or more. Usually they will resolve.

201 HANDLE HACE

High-altitude cerebral edema (HACE) is a severe and life-threatening form of mountain sickness. Edema builds in the spinal column and brain cavity, essentially squeezing all things cerebral. Decisive action is needed to keep the patient alive.

SYMPTOMS The first sign of HACE is often ataxia (loss of coordination). An ataxic person cannot stand still with their feet together and eyes closed, nor can they walk in a straight line. Accompanying symptoms include a severe headache unrelieved by rest and medication, personality changes (altitude sickness causes attitude sickness), even seizures or coma.

TREATMENT Get this person to lower elevation—fast. In addition to descending, the best treatment is supplemental oxygen. The drug dexamethasone (sold as Decadron) can be included in treatment, if prescribed by a physician.

202 SAVE YOUR LUNGS

High-altitude pulmonary edema (HAPE) is another serious illness that can manifest in thin air. Fluid builds in the lungs and chest, eventually killing the victim, similar to bad pneumonia. HAPE can be deadly. Get this person out of the high country, pronto.

SYMPTOMS HAPE typically manifests with chest pain, constant shortness of breath, very rapid heartbeat, and productive cough. Signs and symptoms of mild mountain sickness (headache, lethargy, and nausea) will often be present as well.

TREATMENT As with a HACE victim, get them to lower elevations as soon as possible. Give supplemental oxygen as well, if it's available. The drug nifedipine (sold as Procardia) can be administered if prescribed by a doctor.

203 BE VIGILANT

The backcountry is an ideal setting for broken bones and dislocated joints to occur. Whether you're climbing rocks, stalking through deadfall, riding a horse, or crossing a rushing creek, the potential for injury is there. You can reduce the risk with common sense and good judgment, but prepare to deal with it when it comes your way. The best offense is defense, so know how to react in emergency situations.

204 RESET A DISLOCATION

Some dislocations can be "reduced," or straightened, in the field. Some can't. Simply put, a joint is dislocated when the ends of the bones in the joint do not line up. If you decide to try to reduce a dislocation, you'll need to work quickly; the longer since the injury occurred, the harder it will be to reduce. Stay calm, and encourage the victim to relax, especially in the injured joint area. Pull gentle traction in-line, trying to move the joint into normal alignment. Don't use force. Some increase in pain may occur, but if dramatic pain occurs, cease your efforts.

TOES OR FINGERS Common, typically easy to reduce. Bend the digit, pull on the end, and gently press the joint into place. Splint loosely to its neighbor (A).

WRISTS Reduction for wrists is typically simple, but fractures are usually present. Splint well (B) and get to a doc. The same procedure goes for ankles as well.

LEGS Use gentle traction to pull the leg straight (C), splint securely, and carry the patient—he's not likely to walk.

KNEES Kneecaps are usually easy to reduce. Gently pull traction and straighten the leg, massaging the patella (kneecap) into place in the process (D).

SHOULDERS A very common dislocation that can often be reduced. Lay the victim down, grip their arm at the elbow, and apply traction in-line with the arm, then out and away from the body, ending with the arm raised to the square (E).

HIP This one is very painful and difficult to reduce. Get a helicopter for this person.

JAWS Oral dislocations are typically reducible. Wrap your thumbs with clean cloth or gauze, stick them in the mouth, and press down and forward on the back molars (F).

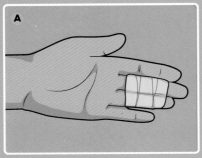
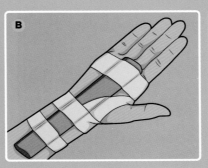
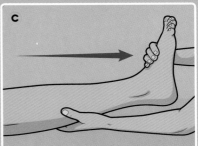

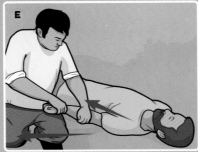
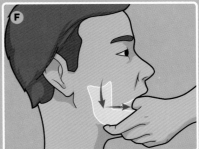

205 TAKE CARE OF A BREAK

Breaks can range in severity from simple fractures to terrible compound breaks with bones protruding from the flesh. All are painful; some are truly excruciating. Some proud owners of broken bones can stay in the backcountry, but most need evacuation.

ASSESS WITH LAF You can assess less obvious injuries (no broken bones sticking out) by following the LAF system. "Look": Remove clothing and get a good visual of the injured area, checking for discoloration, swelling, guarding, and discrepancies with the uninjured side. "Ask": "Do you think it's broken?" and "How bad does it hurt?" "Feel": Gently touch the damaged area, checking for point tenderness.

FIX SIMPLE BREAKS If the injury appears to be a simple break, but is misaligned, try to "reduce," or straighten, the break. Apply gentle in-line traction on the limb until muscles relax and you're able to gently

realign and reset the limb. Don't use force; stop if pain increases.

EVACUATE OPEN FRACTURES If bones protrude from the skin, get an airlift on the way ASAP. If it's going to be more than four or five hours till help arrives, you'll need to gently clean the bone and the wound, and then apply traction until the bone goes back under the skin—the bone will live longer there. Bandage the wound, apply a splint, and evacuate urgently.

SPLINT AND SUPPORT Broken limbs should be splinted in a natural, comfortable position. Be sure to keep the break immobilized, as well as the joints above and below the break.

USE PAIN MEDS The victim is going to be really ready for a painkilling drug. Give it to them. Apply ice if it's available and elevate the injury to help prevent swelling.

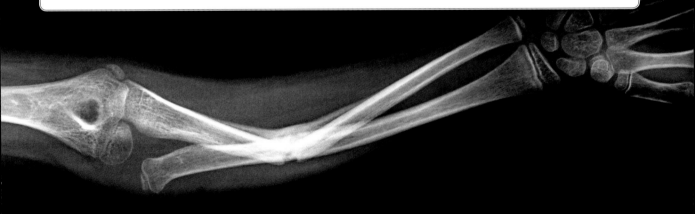

206 MAKE A BREAK FOR IT

If you break an arm or a toe, maybe you're gruff enough to tough it out, but these breaks? Don't even think about it. Get help and get out fast—these breaks require special attention and immediate evacuation.

FLAIL CHEST Multiple broken ribs carry a distinct risk of a punctured lung and possible death.

BROKEN PELVIS Internal bleeding is a common complication.

FEMUR FRACTURE Considered the most painful break that a human can experience, a femur needs a traction splint and a gentle evacuation.

HIP FRACTURE Similar to a femur break. Ouch!

BACK OR NECK INJURY These can have serious long-term implications. Gently stabilize the head and neck to avoid further injury, and get the victim to medical care quickly.

SKULL INJURY Without immediate medical care, this person will probably die. Protect the injury as best you can and evacuate very gently but rapidly.

207 SURVIVE FOOD POISONING

Food poisoning is bad enough when you're within close range of your own luxurious porcelain throne. Food and water poisoning can cause dehydration, a potential killer when you're in the wilderness. Keep these signs in mind to avoid putting yourself in danger and don't ever be afraid to call it quits when your life is at stake.

AVOID FOODBORNE ILLNESS If you've watched enough reality-TV survival shows, you'll have noticed that many of the contestants fail to stay in the game because they drink bad water. They experience diarrhea and vomit in volcanic proportions, which if left unchecked cause serious dehydration.

Food poisoning can result in the same symptoms. Either of these can become life threatening.

DEAL WITH DEHYDRATION Frequent vomiting and diarrhea (especially) will lead to dehydration. Someone who is dehydrated can experience thirst, dry mouth, and dizziness, and pass dark yellow urine. You need to be aggressive to keep yourself or whoever is in trouble hydrated. Mix a teaspoon (5.75 g) of salt and eight teaspoons (34 g) of sugar into one liter of water, and sip this mixture constantly—drink at the rate of about a quarter-liter per hour, along with all the water you can tolerate. Rice, grains, bananas, and potatoes are okay to eat.

Avoid consuming dairy products, coffee, and alcohol. Over-the-counter meds such as Imodium are effective to help control diarrhea.

EVACUATE YOURSELF If you're still in trouble—vomiting, fighting the backdoor trot, and in pain—after 24 to 72 hours (depending on severity) you should evacuate, especially if you can't keep hydrated. Get yourself or your patient to a doctor where fluids and electrolytes can be given intravenously.

208 QUIT BELLYACHING

You probably don't need to flee the backcountry at the slightest sign of an ailment. Here are some tips to help you decide if you should tough it out or seek assistance.

TREAT A BELLYACHE Abdominal illnesses are among the hardest to diagnose and treat because it's impossible to see what's going on in there. The trouble could come from camp food, a raging case of appendicitis, bad water, or a stomach flu. We simply have to do our best to read

symptoms, care for the patient, and, should it become necessary, evacuate in time.

ADDRESS NON-EVAC SYMPTOMS A person suffering from a 24-hour stomach flu or a bad hot dog can usually stay in the backcountry. Vomiting and diarrhea are not life-threatening, unless they result in severe dehydration. Keep this person hydrated, comfortable, and monitored. Most of the time they'll recover without complications.

209 EVALUATE AND EVACUATE

As we've already covered, some stomach pain can be treated in the backcountry with very little trouble. However, you should immediately hunt up a doctor if the abdominal pain is accompanied by any of the following problems. Evacuate as gently as possible, with the patient in the position of greatest comfort. Avoid anything by mouth except small sips of water.

What to Look For

- Signs or symptoms of shock

- Pain persisting longer than 12–24 hours

- Localized pain, especially if the pain involves guarding (protecting the area), abdominal tenderness, rigidity, or distension

- Blood found in vomit (looks like coffee grounds), feces (looks like black tar), or urine (reddish)

- Vomiting and/or diarrhea persisting for more than 24 to 72 hours, especially if dehydration occurs

- A prolonged fever above 102°F (39°C)

- Signs or symptoms of pregnancy

- Pain that increases with jarring (footfalls)

210 ADDRESS INTERNAL INJURY

If you're out in the wilderness and experience abdominal pain or bleeding from places that shouldn't be bleeding, it's better to be safe than sorry and head to the hospital. Here are some signs to watch for.

ABDOMINAL INJURIES Picture yourself climbing a short but steep, recently rained-on section of cliff toward a perfect vantage point. Suddenly, your feet shoot out from under you and you're falling. It's only a little distance, but your left side crashes into a basketball-sized rock. You sit up, but something feels terribly wrong. An hour later you're experiencing symptoms of shock and your abdomen is becoming slightly distended, causing you to hold or "guard" your abdomen. You don't know it yet, but you've ruptured your spleen; if you don't get to a hospital, you'll be dead within a few hours.

INTERNAL INJURY Typically caused by blunt trauma, internal injuries can be life-threatening. Assessing the problem is difficult at best. Monitor potential victims (after falling, being thrown from a horse, getting kicked by a mule, and so on) carefully for signs of shock, distended belly, abdominal pain, rigidity, and guarding. Watch for blood in vomit (looks like coffee grounds), stool (resembles black tar), or urine (red or pink color). Anyone bleeding internally needs a helicopter ride to the nearest hospital.

IMPALEMENT This is serious stuff and it will require an immediate airlift. One bit of medical protocol: if possible, don't remove the impaled object. Removing it may result in accelerated bleeding and earlier death. Just try to gently secure the impaled object in place with bandaging and get a life-flight posthaste.

211 TAME AN EARACHE

A bad earache will easily reduce the friendliest person to an imitation of a grumpy grizzly bear. They hurt, badly.

In Buck Tilton's immortal words, "Don't poke anything in your ear smaller than your elbow." If a bug or other small object is stuck in your ear, flush it out with water or alcohol.

Earaches can also be a common side effect of head colds, especially if you're changing your altitude—and thus the surrounding air pressure—regularly. If your ear begins to hurt, don't wait till the pain gets bad; apply homeopathic drops into the canal (I've had superb luck with Hyland's) or fresh-squeezed onion juice, followed by a small wad of cotton or tissue.

212 DON'T BE AN EYESORE

I ducked under a low-hanging limb, intently scanning the mule deer terrain unfolding before me. Seconds later I heard a pained grunt from my brother behind me and turned to see him holding his eye. I frantically peeled the angry red eye open and looked for damage. To my great relief (and his even greater relief), a good gouge showed inside the lid, but the eyeball was untouched. There's always plenty of potential for an eye injury in the wilderness, so exercise care, and take eye injuries seriously—everyone wants to continue enjoying their eyesight.

BLACK EYE Shiners aren't usually serious unless the injury also scratches or cuts the eye itself, or causes changes in vision. If that's the case, get the person to a doctor. An airlift isn't necessary, but a sense of urgency is.

FOREIGN OBJECTS Examine the affected eye carefully. If you find a small object loose in the eye, try to flush it out or fish it out with a corner of tissue or clean cloth. If the object is lodged in or has penetrated the eye (especially if it's large), protect the area and the object and get to a doc.

EYE INFECTIONS An eye that's itchy, swollen, and red is likely infected, especially if colorful pus or discharge is present. Flush the eye with clean water and apply antibiotic ointment multiple times a day. If the eye doesn't clear up within a couple days, make your way to a doctor for an exam.

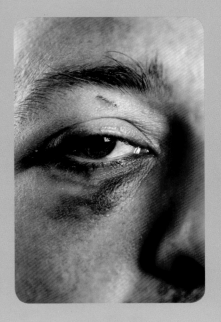

213 EVADE THE TOOTH FAIRY

Dentists are uncommon in wilderness settings. Legend tells of a cowboy who was working in the backcountry when he developed a terrible toothache. After several days of agony he decided to make the long ride to town to have his tooth pulled. While en route the pain became more than he could bear, so he drew his pistol, jammed the muzzle against his offending tooth, and blew the bad tooth out the side of his cheek. I never did hear if he felt better afterward, nor do I recommend the procedure.

FIX A LOST FILLING Clove oil eases the pain of a missing filling. Plug the hole with wax, sugarless gum or, ideally, stuff called Cavit that's made for the purpose. This should keep you somewhat comfortable till your trip is over and you can see a dentist.

REPLACE A LOST TOOTH If a tooth gets knocked out, immediately rinse it thoroughly (don't scrub it), and stick it back in the socket. It may "take." If you can't get it back in, hang on to it so the dentist can look at it.

RELIEVE A BROKEN TOOTH Broken teeth are agonizing, especially with exposed pulp. Place a small bit of aspirin right on the pulp. It'll burn, but it also cauterizes the tooth and decreases pain. Don't put aspirin on gums; it'll burn the tissue. Take painkillers and get to a dentist.

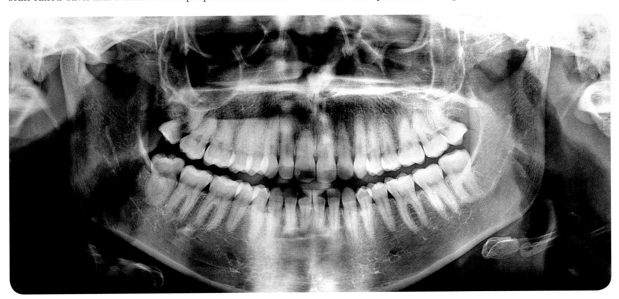

214 ASSIST A CHOKING VICTIM

The most common thing for folks to choke on is food—and it can happen in the backcountry just like anywhere else. Treatment is the same regardless.

As long as the person can speak or cough, let them try to rid themselves of the obstruction. If they go silent, that is the time to take steps to help them clear their airway.

Wrap your arms around whoever is choking from behind. Then, clasp your fists together, thumbs pointed toward the abdomen. Pull inward and upward with quick, forceful motions just above the navel until the object is expelled. If you are alone and choking, you can also perform abdominal thrusts on yourself, or over a nearby object.

215 TREAT SERIOUS MALE TRAUMA

Just face it: Rawhide tough and bull strong as you might picture your backcountry self to be, you're susceptible to some rather undignified human frailties. Here are some of the least dignified.

EPIDIDYMITIS Even the name is unappealing. Inflammation of the epididymis (the testicular duct) is characterized by a red, swollen, painful scrotum, and sometimes accompanied by fever. Temporary relief can be accomplished with support (such as a jockstrap or triangular bandage), cool compresses, and rest. Antibiotics are recommended. This poor feller needs to see a doc.

TESTICULAR TORSION Sounds awful, doesn't it? This happens when one of the testicles rotates within the scrotum. Pain may come suddenly or slowly. The scrotum will become red and swollen, and pain is acute. Lack of blood supply means rapid death for the testicle, usually within a few hours. Typically, testes will rotate inwardly, so attempt to return the testis back to normal position by gently lifting and rotating the testicle in an outward direction. If that doesn't work, try rotating two turns back in the opposite direction. If you're successful, relief will be immediate and blessed. If you can't reduce the twist, give some pain meds, rig some support, and evacuate as rapidly as possible.

216 DON'T MIX BEARS AND BLOOD

Some years ago a group of survival students and their instructors slumbered peacefully in a primitive wickiup near where I live. A big black bear nosed his way around the shelter, then suddenly shouldered his way through the blanket-covered door to the inside. Picking his way through the sleepers, he grabbed one of the students and dragged her out the door. Surprised students and instructors boiled out into the night, spooking the bear away. The fortunate young lady was unharmed; the bear's teeth had been diverted by her sleeping bag. The woman was menstruating.

Now, I don't subscribe to the idea that bears are attracted to menstruating women on a reproductive level. But it's a fact that bears are attracted to blood, and to the scent of blood. Therefore wisdom dictates that if you're a woman in the backcountry and the moon is right, you should take some extra precautions. Bathe regularly, and keep feminine hygiene products (either scented or used) far from where you're sleeping. And keep a dog, horse, fellow camper, or firearm handy. The animal can warn you of unwanted visitors, your fellow camper can bludgeon the bear as he drags your sleepy self out of the tent, and a gun can, well, give ol' bruin a necessary attitude adjustment.

217 DEAL WITH FEMALE ISSUES

Several specific maladies can plague the backcountry huntress or adventuress. Unfamiliar activities, unusual exertion over extended periods, and less sanitary conditions can trigger changes or problems not usually experienced.

IRREGULARITY It's common for women to experience altered menstrual cycles when they're adventuring in the backcountry. Not to worry—it's likely a simple result of different conditions and levels of exertion. However, any abnormal bleeding coupled with unusual abdominal pain is grounds for evacuation.

POSSIBLE PREGNANCY Abdominal pain and vaginal bleeding together with possible pregnancy indicate potential ectopic pregnancy, miscarriage, or other complications. A rapid evacuation is in order.

INFECTION Redness, itching, and discomfort in the vaginal area indicate an infection. Milder cases can be effectively treated in the backcountry with daily washing and exposing the affected area to direct sunlight for 30 minutes per day. Severe cases merit a trip to the doctor for treatment.

URINARY TRACT INFECTION UTIs cause discomfort, burning, and increased frequency of urination. The patient may experience lower abdominal pain or a lack of energy. Blood and or pus may show up in the urine. Treat this unhappy malady (which can happen to men as well) with some aggressive hydrating and washing the perineal area daily. Avoid consuming sugar, caffeine, alcohol, and spicy foods. Evacuate and get medical care if the subject's condition doesn't improve, or if they begin to experience pain in the kidney region.

218 BECOME A HORSE MECHANIC

Horses are typically pretty problem-free, so long as they're fed, watered, and cared for. They can drink brackish water, eat tough old grass, and sleep tied to a tree in a snowstorm. They'll still cheerfully pack you around the backcountry.

DEAL WITH A LOST SHOE A common problem horses experience in the wilderness is a thrown, lost, or tossed shoe. Your four-footed friend won't have long before his hoof wears down and chips, and he gets too sore-footed to carry a load. The best temporary fix is an Easy-Boot—a rubber shoe that buckles over the hoof. These are notorious for falling off, never to be seen again, so fit it tightly and latch it securely. It's a good idea to wire the latch down—that way it can't pop open until you want it to.

DOCTOR A SORE BACK Another malady experienced by hardworking horses is a sore back (similar to how your shoulders feel after carrying a heavy pack for hours). These sore spots can become open sores if you aren't attentive. Check your horse's back when you unsaddle, looking for "dry spots"—places where the pressure from your saddle or packsaddle prevents the skin from circulating sweat, and where sores can develop. If your horse becomes real tender, change up your pad, or saddle, or both.

TREAT A CINCH SORE Similar to saddle sores, cinch sores are more common. The cinch, combined with lots of sweat, rubs in the armpit region; the hair gets rubbed out, and the skin rubbed raw. These sores aren't debilitating unless severe, but they're really sensitive. Prevent cinch sores with a quality mohair or neoprene cinch (keep it clean) and get your horse "hardened" (in shape) before using him extensively. Should a sore develop, keep it soft with salve, and ride with your cinch a little looser and more rearward than usual.

219 BE A MEDIC TO YOUR MOUNT

Second to the injury or death of a human friend, a lethal wreck for a horse is tragic. It's rare, but it does happen; there's really no way to get an emergency evac for a horse, let alone a rescue helicopter. Here are some worst-case scenarios and how best to respond.

BROKEN LEG A leg injury is almost always lethal for a horse—nearly 99 percent. A broken leg can't be splinted or cast effectively, especially not when you're in the backcountry. Sadly, the best thing to do is to fill him with oats, love him up a bunch, and put a merciful bullet in his brain. Then, if you're like me, you'll go have a good cry.

PUNCTURED ABDOMEN If a horse is stuck by a sharp branch or gored by a mad cow, your most important course of action is to keep those insides inside. If any organs are exposed, first be very sure they're clean, and then use clean hands to put them back. (You may have to lie the horse down on his side and tie him in place first to do this.) If you have some proper suture equipment in your medical supplies, and you can stitch up the various layers of belly lining, muscle, and skin, sew him up. If not, wrap his torso with clean material, then ease him to a vet.

220 SEW YOUR HORSE UP

I trotted to the back of my trailer and opened the gate. As I unloaded my horses out of the trailer, I noticed a lot of blood splattered along one side. A couple of my steeds had gotten in a tiff, and one had banged her cheek into an aluminum strut, tearing a long gash in her face. If the gash went left untreated it would gape widely and heal slowly, leaving an ugly scar, so I grabbed my suture kit. It was a simple task to stitch her up, wash her off, and get on the trail.

STEP 1 Clean and irrigate the wound thoroughly. Apply some antibiotic powder or ointment to the wound. Most horses and some dogs will allow you to sew them up without anesthetic. If they fight, you'll have to make the call: Is the wound bad enough to warrant hog-tying them to repair it, or should you abandon the idea and let it heal without stitches?

STEP 2 Using a curved suture needle, make a stitch by piercing down through the skin on one side and then up through the skin on the opposite side of the wound. Pay attention; these holes will pull together and heal in that position, so get 'em straight. If the wound forms a corner, take your first stitches at the corner, pulling the flap into position before sewing the rest.

STEP 3 Tie the stitch off with a surgeon's knot, followed by three or four overhand knots, alternating to form multiple square knots atop each other. Trim both ends of the suture to about $^3/_8$ inch (1 cm).

STEP 4 Repeat, making a stitch every quarter-inch (6 mm) or so, until the wound is nicely closed. Wash it clean, and try to convince your horse that you still love him.

> **ARAM SAYS** "A surgeon's knot is actually a pretty simple one: It's just a double-wrapped overhand knot. If you tie it right, it'll keep tension for you."

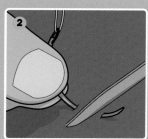
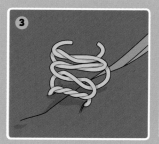
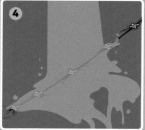

221
SPOT THE SIGNS OF HYPOTHERMIA

Hypothermia is the danger you are most likely to encounter in the backcountry. It stalks the wilderness adventurer like a silent spectre, reaching cold fingers toward anyone who grows careless. Hypothermia can occur at surprisingly warm temps—even a 60˚F (16˚C), rainy, windy day can prove deadly.

Hypothermia is divided into three stages, ranging from just getting started to almost dead. Mild, or stage one, is characterized by mildly impaired ability and motor function and shivering. Lots of us have been mildly hypothermic, and will be again. Stage two, or moderate, is when hypothermia really rears its head: You shiver uncontrollably and violently (your body's attempt to warm your core before it's too late). You'll be afflicted by "umbles" (grumbles, stumbles, mumbles, and fumbles) and performing even simple tasks (such as starting a fire) will become incredibly difficult. Severe, or stage three, brings muscular rigidity, stupor, and coma, and respiration and heart rate decrease until they're both undetectable.

222
COME IN FROM THE COLD

Hypothermia can be deadly, but if it's noticed and treated quickly, a victim stands a good chance of recovery.

TREAT MILD AND MODERATE The bottom line here is simple: get warm. If someone is experiencing either mild or moderate hypothermia, get them out of any damp or wet clothing and into dry clothing. Move to a warm spot out of the wind and hydrate the patient, ideally with a lukewarm sweet drink. Simple carbohydrates provide energy as well. The person can shiver, talk, and eat—encourage them to do just that. Give them hot water bottles or chemical heat packs for their hands and feet, and encourage them to snuggle

TREAT SEVERE CHILL A severely hypothermic person needs to be handled and treated gently. They may still be semiconscious, or they may have progressed to the point that their heartbeat and breathing are imperceptible, and they've stopped shivering. If needed, give rescue breaths for ten minutes before moving them. Get their clothing off and build a cocoon around and under them with warm insulation. Wrap hot water bottles or heat packs in fabric and place them over their heart, in their armpits, and at their groin, in that order. Complete the cocoon with a wind and vapor barrier. Only their mouth and nose should be uncovered. Do not try to force food or drink into them.

223 CARE FOR FROSTBITE

Severe frostbite is an introduction to a frigid hell. Frostbite prefers small bits—extremities such as fingers, toes, ears, and nose—but can claim entire feet and hands, attack cheekbones and chins, and generally wreak serious permanent havoc on unprotected body parts. Frostbite danger increases as the temperature decreases. Giving proper treatment can reduce the extent of permanent damage, but frostbitten areas are very susceptible to cold, and they will refreeze readily; don't let that happen.

Partial-thickness frostbite is characterized by pale, numb skin that is movable, or skin that will take and hold a dent (kind of like cold dough), and is treated with warm skin—in other words, hold your frostbitten ear or nose with a warm hand, or stick your frozen fingers in an armpit or against your stomach. Don't rub the skin or place it near heat greater than 108˚F (42˚C). Drink lots of water and take aspirin or ibuprofen for pain.

In a full-thickness frostbite case, the skin is numb, pale, and hard. This person is in real trouble, especially if the injury encompasses their feet or hands. Evacuation is in order, and may be easier to do before extremities are thawed. Agony accompanies thawing,

so hiking out on frozen feet may be better, less painful, or faster than being carried out after thawing, particularly if there's danger of refreezing.

To thaw full-thickness frostbite, immerse the injury in a water bath at 105 to 108˚F (41–42˚C)—no hotter than

that. Warm for half an hour or longer, until you're very sure that the injury is completely thawed out. Pain will be extreme, so send some aspirin (ideally) or ibuprofen down the hatch before warming begins. Hydrate and evacuate the victim.

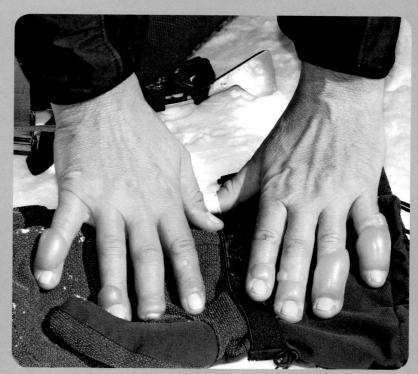

224 ESCAPE THE TRENCHES

The name "trenchfoot" was coined by soldiers who spent days on end hunkered down in the cold, wet trenches of Europe. They wore wet boots and socks for days without a change, and their feet essentially began to rot.

Also known as "immersion foot," non-freezing cold injuries (the proper name) can happen to feet or hands alike. It's caused by prolonged exposure to cold and wet. Nothing freezes, but tissue becomes pale or mottled, and painful. Prevention is simple: Keep your feet dry, change socks regularly, and don't let your extremities get cold.

Get affected areas dry and warm, and keep them that way. Hydrate and take aspirin or ibuprofen for pain.

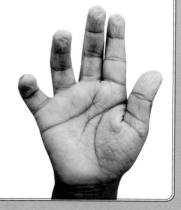

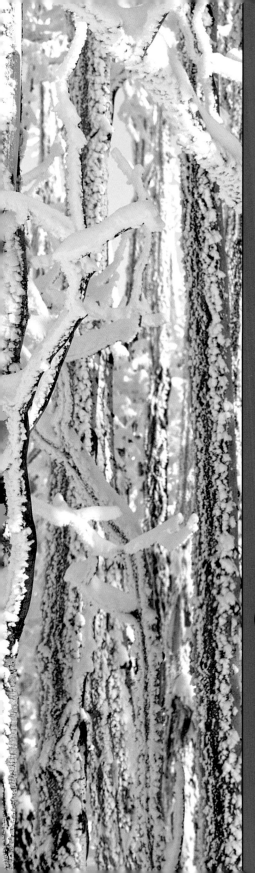

225 AVOID HYPOTHERMIA

Condensation from my breath left icicles on my mustache as a frigid wind whipped snow through the air, so thick at times that I couldn't see the cattle in front of me. I was 50 miles (80 km) from town and riding on the thin edge of danger.

While gathering cattle on a remote range, a cold norther blew in, whipping through the coulees and leaving 6 inches (15 cm) of snow on the ground in the first hour. Not fully familiar with the area, I struggled to maintain a sense of direction as visibility fell to nothing. Steam rose from the cattle ahead of me as snow melted on their backs, rising as vapor whipped away by the wind.

Blowing snow built up, covering me in white from hat to spur. The cows broke for desert timber, trying to escape the storm in the shelter of the trees. I galloped to head them off, my horse jumping a wash almost hidden by snow. I turned the herd back toward the cabin and corrals, but the trail was buried by drifting snow. The cows seemed to know their way, but after their attempted runaway I doubted them. My horse was content with our route, though, so I trusted the animals to find the cabin through the storm.

Fear washed over me in waves; night was coming on and I was growing very cold. If we didn't find the cabin, I'd have to abandon the cattle and seek shelter. I had no sleeping bag or tent, but I was wearing a coat and chaps and had a lighter in my pocket. I'd need a fire big enough to stay warm—or at least alive—through the night.

Darkness fell, the cattle moving well through the pinyon and juniper forest. They suddenly stacked up ahead of me, breaking to both sides as I urged them on. Then, I saw the gate. Relief surged over me: I was at the cabin pasture. I spurred forward, opened the gate, then charged through the trees for my errant cows. I hadn't come this far to have them escape now. I pushed them through the gate and stepped stiffly from my weary horse to shut it behind them. It was six degrees below zero (-21 °C).

Post Assessment

 DONE RIGHT

My strongest move was keeping my head, even though I was in a tough situation. If I'd panicked and left the cattle to search for the cabin, I likely would have ended up totally disoriented and waiting out the frigid, stormy night under some overhanging tree. I did also have a lighter in my pocket, so I probably would have been okay—but even then it wouldn't have been fun.

DONE WRONG

I should have just followed my own policy and carried a compass and GPS with me. My footwear wasn't properly up to the task, either—my leather cowboy boots became wet from snow melting on them, and then they froze, leaving my feet in danger of frostbite, as well as further contributing to my overall hypothermic condition.

226 DISMOUNT IN AN EMERGENCY

Most times, the safest place to be is seated on your horse. But in some cases you need to abandon ship, fast. If you can't, you might be crushed, trampled, or even slammed into something much harder than yourself.

BAIL OUT When your horse falls (I mean completely down), there's real danger of getting your leg jammed under him and possibly broken. Be aware and ready to reflexively throw yourself off your horse and out of harm's way should he fall.

WATCH YOUR HEAD Some horses will mischievously walk under low-hanging limbs to try to drag their rider off. These rascals can usually be circumvented. Some evil steeds will run out of control into thick brush or timber. If you see a low limb headed your way, bail off

before impact unless you're trick-rider enough to stand in the saddle, leap over the limb as your runaway goes under it, and land back in the saddle.

DON'T GET REARED OVER The very worst habit that a horse can develop is rearing over backward to dump a rider. It's highly dangerous and can leave a green or unlucky rider crushed on the ground. Get off this horse and stay off.

AVOID CLIFFHANGERS If you're in dangerous terrain that has cliff trails with big drop-offs, don't take a skittish steed. They might get worked up at the wrong time and dance off a cliff; I've seen it happen. Even with a good, smart horse, there are times to dismount and walk that section of hairline cliff trail instead.

227 LIVE THROUGH A FLASH FLOOD

Unbelievable violence characterizes flash flooding in narrow desert canyons. Heavy rains in arid desert canyon country can build a wave of runoff water within minutes. When the wave is bottled into a raging torrent fighting to get through a narrow canyon, nothing can withstand it. Trees are torn free and flung downstream, huge boulders roll underwater, and new shapes are chiseled from the earth.

WATCH THE WEATHER Beware of rain where you are, but also rain that may be falling upstream from your position. Flash floods can travel far beyond the actual storm. If there's even a remote chance of a flood, consider relocating.

CLIMB FOR SAFETY The only safe haven is high above the canyon floor. Try to find a high bench—preferably one with an exit from the canyon—and wait it out. The flood could be gone in hours, or it could hold you hostage for days. If you're in the canyon bottom and you feel a wave of cool humid air accompanied by a rumble like the sound of a freight train, you have just moments to climb to safety. Run for any elevation you can, and get as high as you can. Don't waste time—your life depends on quick thinking and fast action.

CLING ON If the worst happens and you find yourself swept away in a flash flood, keep your wits about you. Keep your feet pointed downstream to protect you from obstacles. Make every effort to get hold of something—a root, tree,

rock, or cliff ledge—that you can hang onto and keep your head above water. Ideally, you'll be able to climb up and out of the flood's grasp. You may have to hang on for hours or even more than a day until the flood subsides. Don't give up; people do survive flash floods in this manner.

228 DON'T GET THUNDERSTRUCK

Does it happen? Yup, though it's rare—but I know two people who got splashed, and two who were struck directly. Both splash victims were mostly unscathed. One of those directly hit died; the other blames his baldness on the lightning.

Lightning typically splashes electricity around when it strikes. These splashes can cause substantial damage (burns, temporary nervous disorders, and so on), but are rarely fatal. One of the splash victims I know was washing dishes when her house was struck. A blue ball of lightning came down the wall to the sink, jumping up the spray left by her hands as she leaped back. It knocked her flat on the floor, but left her otherwise unharmed.

A direct strike, meanwhile, can really mess you up. It can burn, cook, or scorch you. Worse yet, it's likely to stop your breathing and maybe your heart. On a positive note, strike victims who receive CPR immediately after they are struck

have a high rate of survival. Rescue breathing and chest compressions help keep oxygen flowing to vital organs until the heart and lungs begin to work again—there's often nothing really wrong with them; they just got stunned by an overdose of electricity.

A rapid response is critical: The victim will have only minutes to live if their heart or breathing has been stopped. Assess the victim (or victims) quickly to determine if they're breathing and they have a pulse. If one or the other of these is missing, administer appropriate CPR; if at all possible, get a defibrillator on the way. A lightning strike victim's heart may restart on its own or it may need some help. Secondary treatment should include caring for burns and any other injuries, followed by evacuation. Serious complications can develop later, so get the victim out of the backcountry and to a hospital ASAP.

229 PREVENT HEAT ILLNESS

When hunting or adventuring in a hot environment, heat illness is a constant threat. Know these signs, and how to treat them.

RISK FACTORS	PREVENTION PRACTICES
Hot weather (obviously)	Rest in shade frequently
High humidity	Eat salty snacks to maintain a healthy sodium level in your body
Unused to heat	Allow yourself time to acclimatize to hot environments
Being overweight	Be physically fit
Caffeine, alcohol, some drugs	Avoid alcohol, caffeine, and risk-increasing drugs (i.e. antihistamines)
Youth or old age	Wear cool clothing and a hat
Dehydration (the biggest factor)	Hydrate conscientiously; keep urine clear and moderately copious

230 HANDLE HEAT

The mid-afternoon air temperature was 104°F (40°C) and it had been several hours since I'd had a drink. I was working cattle and too proud to admit that I was in trouble. We finished the job and I headed home. When I walked into my house, I stuck a thermometer in my mouth. It registered 103.5°F (39.7°C), almost as hot as the air. Two basic stages of heat illness exist—heat exhaustion and heat stroke. I was hovering along the border.

HEAT EXHAUSTION Many people mistakenly call this "heat stroke." (See below for that.) Heat exhaustion signs and symptoms are thirst, sweating, pale or flushed skin, headache, and perhaps nausea or vomiting. Urine will be dark yellow and infrequent. Exhaustion typically results from working and sweating hard, causing you to lose salts and become dehydrated. Core temperature may be a bit elevated. Treatment is simple: Rest and hydrate. Eat salty snacks and drink frequently. You should be back to normal within a day.

HEAT STROKE A person with heat stroke is beginning to die. Their core temperature is so high that their internal organs—including the brain—are cooking. Overexertion and/or severe dehydration are the common causes, building core temperatures to 105°F (40.5°C) and higher. Skin is typically hot, red, and sometimes dry. Rapid respiration and heart rate will accompany a headache. Advanced heatstroke causes personality changes and disorientation. Aggressive cooling is the only chance for survival. Remove their clothing, drench them with water, and fan them to speed cooling. Massage limbs to stimulate circulation. Focus your cooling efforts on the head and neck. Apply cold packs to neck, groin, armpits, and limbs. Give cool water, if the person is able to drink it. Do not give fever-fighting drugs. Rapid evacuation is important for anyone who has experienced an altered mental state.

231 TREAT THE TRICK KILLER

It's hot out, so you carry plenty of water and hydrate often. All is well at first, but eventually you start to feel weak and light-headed. You press on, drinking more water to cope with the heat. A headache comes on and you feel especially nauseous. Anxiety follows and you feel incredibly irritated and are somehow disoriented—were you going up or down? You swallow another big drink. Then, you're overtaken by a seizure, and collapse comatose on the ground.

You did everything right, except for one thing, which ultimately killed you: You neglected to replace salt lost to sweating and drank too much water. This led to hyponatremia—dangerously low sodium levels in your blood.

Individuals who are suffering from hyponatremia will manifest symptoms very similar to those that go with heat exhaustion, with one big difference. Their urine will be clear and copious, instead of yellow and infrequent, and they will not be thirsty.

Prevention is very easy: Regularly snack on salty foods. That's all you need. Treatment is just as simple, too—take rest in the shade and slowly eat salty snacks and foods. Don't drink fluids for a while. Once your body reestablishes a proper sodium balance, you'll become thirsty again, you'll urinate less, and the problem will be solved. However, anyone who has already experienced an altered mental state still needs to be evacuated and see a doctor ASAP.

After a successful week of high-country wilderness elk hunting, I loaded my horses and headed out. A mile of dangerous cliff trail ran between my hunting area and the trailhead—most of it too narrow to turn a horse around, let alone a whole pack train.

This was early October; the moose rut was still in session. There was no way around the enraged moose and I couldn't turn my pack train back. My only course of action was to bluff the bull into turning back down the trail.

I gathered my courage, hoping Eli was big enough to keep his footing if the bull charged. If not, we'd tumble down the near-vertical scree slope below.

The moose raised his massive head, red eyes rolling in their sockets. Saliva drooled from his mouth.

At the last minute the bull decided we were more than he wanted to tackle. He spun around on the cliff trail and headed out.

Halfway down the trail, my horse, a big mustang named Eli, snorted and stopped dead in his tracks.

Ahead of us was a scattered mess of backpacks, hikers, and pack goats. "What happened?" I asked.

"A bull moose charged us," said the nearest hiker, perched on a rock. The hikers pointed him out, behind a pine tree some 40 yards (37 m) away—right on the trail.

I spurred my horses into a high trot, waving my arms and shouting like a madman.

I watched with relief as the bull trotted down the trail ahead of us and disappeared into the forest. That was too close.

233 DOCTOR AN ANIMAL BITE

If you're the unfortunate victim of a large animal attack in the backcountry you've got a big problem: infection. Lions, bears, coyotes, wolves, and so on all have bacteria in their mouth that is foreign to humans and will quickly cause bites to become septic.

BLEED IT OUT If you have a real bleeder, you need to stop the flow. But flowing blood will help cleanse wounds, so let more minor wounds—especially puncture wounds—seep blood for a while. You can even encourage the bleeding with gentle squeezing or pressure around the puncture.

CLEAN THE WOUND Irrigate all cuts, punctures, and abrasions—anywhere the skin is broken—with plenty of clean water. Pick or scrub away debris. Puncture wounds are very difficult to get clean, so give particular attention to them. Use all the water pressure you can to forcefully irrigate everything.

CATCH SOME RAYS Sunshine is one of nature's best disinfectants. After you clean your wounds, pat them dry with a clean cloth and allow direct sunlight to shine into the wounds for 30 minutes before you bandage them.

MEDICATE YOURSELF You'll be in considerable pain, so swallow some ibuprofen. More importantly, dig out your emergency stash of broad-spectrum oral antibiotics from your kit (see item 013) and take them. Preventing infection is your primary objective at this point.

SEW UP If you're desperate and tough enough, you can sew your own wounds closed (see item 220). I've sewn myself up on two different occasions.

EVACUATE The realistic alternative to sewing: get yourself to a doc who can stitch you back together and keep infection at bay while you heal.

234 SURVIVE A SCORPION STING

I lay in my blankets on the ground, sleeping peacefully. Suddenly, a brilliant burning pain pierced my brain. Then I realized the pain was originating from my left calf. I hunted the critter down and crushed him—it was a scorpion, over 3 inches (7.6 cm) long.

TREAT THE PAIN Most scorpions found in the U.S. don't deliver a dangerous sting. It does sting, burn, and throb like getting hit by a killer bee from hell, but it'll eventually go away. There is one antidote that will effectively quell the sting permanently, if applied within a few minutes—it's called Purr-fectly Herbal Bite & Sting Salve, available online. It's good for any kind of bite or sting, but I've found it incredibly effective at neutralizing scorpion stings.

AVOID SERIOUS DANGER Of more than 70 subspecies of scorpions in North America, only one is truly dangerous. The Arizona bark scorpion looks rather similar to several other North American scorpions, including the common hairy scorpion. One obvious difference is that the Arizona bark scorpion has long, slender pincers; other similar varieties have slightly fatter pincers. If you're stung by one of these little devils, get to a doctor. The sting will bring salivation, sweating, strong anxiety, gastrointestinal upset, and (the deadly one) respiratory distress. Immediate evacuation is in order.

BE WARY WORLDWIDE Other areas of the world, in particular Africa, boast much higher populations of various deadly scorpions—including one little bugger that can—shudder—shoot its venom almost a yard (1 m).

235 AVOID EIGHT-LEGGED ENEMIES

There are two common venomous spiders in North America: the black widow and the brown recluse. A bite from either is a serious issue, and is grounds for evacuation. If possible, kill the spider and bring it with you for identification.

BLACK WIDOW Bites are typically painless for the first few minutes; they may even go unnoticed. Redness and pain will show up at the bite site, accompanied by very painful muscle cramping in the back and abdomen. Headache, vomiting, chills, and sweating are common. Take a painkiller and get to a doc.

BROWN RECLUSE Bites produce a painful blister with a bull's-eye appearance within a few hours. In time, the bite will assume the look of a cigarette burn. Fever, chills, and weakness are typical side effects. The venom will then continue to eat at the flesh surrounding the bite (necrosis), so get to a doctor for help halting the damage.

236 SURVIVE THE JAWS OF DEATH

(As told by South Cox, traditional bowmaker and backcountry expert.)
Two friends and I backpacked about 7 miles (11 km) into the Northern California wilderness to hunt bears and deer. On the fourth day, we rose early to cross a canyon and set up an ambush for a band of bucks. I'd seen them regularly crossing a saddle on a far ridge, so my two hunting partners and I spread out on the ridge, hoping one of us would get a shot.

Late in the morning, I spotted a bear busily feeding ahead of me. I'd seen plenty on this trip—this one was the fiftieth in three-and-a-half days. I had a bear tag in my pocket, so I went into stalk mode and closed the distance to 30 yards (27 m). Spotting two cubs nearby, I relaxed, laying my bow on the ground and unzipping my pack to dig out my camera.

The sow must have heard me digging in my pack, because she stood on a rock to see better—then she spotted me and charged. I thought she was bluffing; I yelled and waved my arms till she was about 20 yards (18 m) away and closing fast. I ran. Twenty yards (18 m) later she crashed into me, knocking me down. My mind was incredibly clear—I went through a protection checklist: curl into a ball on my knees, hands locked behind my neck to protect it, elbows in tight so she couldn't get hold of my arms. I felt no pain, just tremendous pressure with each bite, then blood flowing.

The bear never growled, but her breath was terrible. She stopped biting and was silent. I felt like I was tipping over, so I shifted to steady myself. Instantly she was upon me again with renewed ferocity. I held still and let her chew. She let up, and I stayed motionless. After a while she finally left. I cautiously stood, looked around, and shouted for my friends. Fortunately one was an EMT, and he began patching me up. The other one, a distance runner, took off to call a helicopter. I had 19 nasty puncture wounds from the bear's teeth, and numerous abrasions and scratches from her claws.

A few weeks later I returned, almost filling my bear tag. The rush of adrenaline and fear I felt at coming within 20 yards (18 m) of another bear was indescribable. I didn't get a shot, but I did face down my fears.

Post Assessment

DONE RIGHT

South faced a rare kind of black bear attack: The sow attacked for defense, not for food. This was more typical of grizzly or brown bear behavior. South responded properly once she had him, demonstrating submission. If he had fought back (the usual recommended defense to black bear attacks; they often intend to eat you) she would have kept attacking. He would have been hurt even worse or killed.

DONE WRONG

South was slightly cavalier, setting aside his bow (his only weapon) in the presence of a sow with cubs, to get his camera. I asked him how it might have gone had he stood his ground instead of running. "I've wondered that so many times—quite possibly she was bluffing, and would have stopped at the last moment. Who knows?" A can of bear spray is also good backup in bear-filled territory.

237 GET YOUR BEARINGS

An experienced backwoodsman friend of mine says that he's never been lost . . . but he sure has been confused a few times. Here are a few ways to help you get your bearings.

GAZE UP AT THE STARS In the northern hemisphere, there's one star that faithfully maintains its position in the night sky—the North Star. How do you pick out one star from the millions of shiners rotating above? It's simple: the North Star is the bright one that's pointed to by the front edge of the big dipper. Should you find yourself traveling in the southern hemisphere, the Southern Cross performs the same noble task—a heavenly guide to backcountry travelers.

READ THE SUNRISE The sun and moon always come up in the east, and set in the west, every time. Unless the poles switch in an apocalyptic flip, it's going to stay that way.

STUDY YOUR SURROUNDINGS If you look around you can find clues pointing the way. In some environments, moss grows heavily on the northern sides of tree trunks. Do the prevailing winds blow from the southwest? Check out trees and grass; bent and fatigued by the wind, they'll all be leaning toward the northeast. In plenty of places south and west slopes are relatively open and grassy, while the north and east slopes are covered with dense timber or brush.

REMEMBER LANDMARKS Memorize some distant landmarks. Is there a recognizable peak in the north? What about that lake far to the west? Check out that long northeast to southwest valley—it must stretch to 50 miles (80 km) or better. Commit various features to memory, and just one glimpse of them will help orient you.

238 SIGNAL FOR HELP

So you're deep in the wilderness and you need help—you're lost, hurt, or trapped by heavy snow. You used up the battery on your sat-phone telling your sweetie all about the elk you killed, and now you can't call for help. What do you do?

SHOOT THREE SHOTS A trio of evenly spaced gunshots means "I need help." Now, three-shot strings occur naturally during hunting seasons, so if you're trying to summon help you should fire three shots, wait 60 seconds, fire three more, wait another minute, and fire three more. It's unmistakable to anyone who hears. (Firing signal shots with your bow is considered ineffective.)

BURN A SIGNAL FIRE A campfire is visible for many miles during the dark of night, and by day a fire builds a column of smoke that can be seen from a great distance. Kindle your blaze on a high point or in a big meadow so it's readily seen. Make sure fuel is readily to hand—you may need to keep your fire burning for several days. By day, burn green boughs on top of your flame to create heavy smoke, especially if you hear a plane or helicopter. By night, burn dry wood that feeds a big, bright flame.

WRITE A NOTE Find a meadow or park and write a huge note in it, using whatever materials you have: dark rocks on light dirt, green branches over yellow grass, or similar items. If there's any snow on the ground you can tromp a message into the white canvas simply by trudging out the letters. The universal distress message is S.O.S. Draw attention to your note with a signal fire, or a bright tarp or coat hung up in a visible location—any aircraft flying over the area should spot it and read your note.

LEAVE A LIGHT ON Display a lighted headlamp (preferably on strobe setting) in a visible place at night. If rescuers are searching for you, they'll see it and come looking.

239 STAY PUT OR HIKE OUT

There may come a time when your very survival (or that of a friend) depends on this choice. Life or death can be determined in one moment of lucidity or stupidity. Exercise wisdom.

STAY AND PRAY You've broken your leg on a backcountry solo hunt, and are barely able to crawl to water and back. Fortunately, you got the break straightened and splinted. Your best bet is to stay put, keep a signal fire going, and pray that you're found quickly.

Alternatively, let's say you're on your way out of a desert wilderness when you're suddenly cut off from the trailhead by a roaring flash flood. It's your birthday tomorrow, and you're really looking forward to cake and ice cream. Should you attempt to cross the flash flood and continue on to the trailhead? It may look doable—the water can't be more than chest-deep—but don't try it or you'll drown. Stay put and wait for the flood to recede; it'll end up being one of your most memorable birthdays.

GATHER COURAGE AND GO You're on a late-season elk hunt when you take a fall, badly spraining your ankle. It's a modest hike back to the trailhead, but the weather is really turning cold, and snow threatens. It's time to build a crutch, collect your courage, and shrug into your pack. This trip out will be the hardest thing you've ever done, but if you want to stay alive you've got to do it.

Another scenario: Your hunting buddy cut himself while quartering an elk several days ago, and the wound is getting really angry and red. Infection is setting in and your friend is feverish and weak. There's a red streak running from the wound to just above his elbow. But you haven't shot your elk yet—should you stay and continue hunting, or get your buddy to the hospital? This is a no-brainer: Get your friend out before blood poisoning (septicemia) kills him. Carry as much of his gear as you can, and stash the rest. Offer them a shoulder and encouraging words, and don't stop till you're in the emergency room.

240 BUILD A CRUTCH

Sprain an ankle or bust a leg in the backcountry, and you'll discover how scarce clinics and medical supply stores are in the wilderness. Here are two ways to build a crutch in the woods.

CUT A FORKED STICK The fastest wilderness crutch is simply a forked stick cut to shape (A). Use paracord to lash a shirt or socks into the fork so it doesn't bite into your armpit.

BUILD A "T" If you have time and tools you can fashion a more sophisticated crutch by attaching a cross-member atop a nice straight stick (B). Pad it nicely, and this will be a much more comfortable crutch than the forked kind.

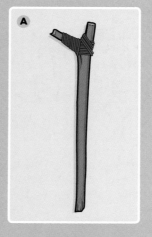

241 FIND A LOST BUDDY

My wife, brother, and I had packed about 17 miles (27 km) into the wilderness after elk. Hunting had been tough, so Joseph made a forced march into the next canyon to scout for elk. We expected him back shortly after dark, but he didn't show. Eventually we decided to turn in, setting my alarm for 2:00 a.m. If he hadn't returned by then we'd go searching. Finally at 1:00 a.m. the tent zipper whistled and he slipped into his sleeping bag. He'd found elk just at dusk some 7 miles (11 km) away, and it had taken him hours of hiking through the night to get back to camp.

DON'T PANIC If Trina and I had just panicked and immediately gone off looking for Joseph, we'd have spent the night stumbling around in the woods, endangering ourselves, and likely getting lost in the darkness. Instead, we trusted my brother's skill to get him back safely, resting in case we had to mount a search.

PLAN AHEAD Talk with your party about how to deal with missing people: If someone doesn't return, will you mount a search within hours? Or will you wait, giving the person time to surmount whatever obstacles impede their return trip to camp? Planning ahead will eliminate confusion.

KEEP IN TOUCH Communicate with everyone in your party, so you'll know where to start looking should anyone fail to return.

STAY SAFE The worst occurrence in a missing person situation is yet another person going missing. Ensure searchers stay safe and don't get lost themselves.

GET INTO THEIR MIND To find a missing person, think the way they would. Are they likely to stay put and wait for help or will they go looking for something familiar? Are they calm, or likely to panic? Will they head to high ground, build a signal fire, blow a whistle, or shoot a firearm?

LOOK OUT One or more searchers should climb to a high vantage point and keep a lookout for a signal fire or plume of smoke, and listen for the sounds of gunshots.

CALL PROFESSIONALS If you aren't able to turn up your missing buddy within a short time, call or send for Search and Rescue.

242 PULL THROUGH PANIC

In any kind of disaster, panic can be your worst enemy. Keep a clear head and calm attitude, and you'll greatly improve your chance of survival.

STOP AND BREATHE Disaster usually strikes suddenly. Most folks' natural reaction is to panic. Stop reacting, stop the danger, if still present, and take a few slow, deep breaths. It'll help clear your head and calm the adrenaline. Repeat whenever you feel yourself starting to lose control.

ASSESS AND PLAN Stay mentally ahead of events. Take time to assess the cause and extent of the problem, and how to handle it. If you're lost, sit down while you assess and plan. Going on may just get you more lost.

BUILD A FIRE If you're scared and fighting panic, a fire can transform the entire situation. Build one. Now you have friendly source of warmth, something to watch as you plan, a way to heat food and water, and a way to signal for help.

243 SURVIVE AN AVALANCHE

This book focuses mainly on hunting and adventuring in the backcountry when deep snow is not present. Unless you're hunting the abominable snowman, you're not likely to take a tumble in an avalanche with your rifle in hand. You'll more likely be cross-country skiing or snowshoeing. However it happens, here's what to do.

WEATHER THE RIDE Staying alive while rolling downhill in a tangled morass of snow is the first step. If the slide is small enough, try "swimming" to the side and to safety. If you're buried in moving snow, protect your face with your arms and hands to keep it from getting into your airway and smothering you. As the avalanche slows, work to open and keep a breathing space, however small, around your face.

STAY CALM Once the snow stops moving, the next priority is to stay alive—and if possible, dig out. Avalanche snow can be extremely rigid once it stops; your whole body may be held in a "cast" of snow. That's why it's so important to create a breathing space before it stops moving.

SPIT AND DIG You'll likely be completely disoriented by your tumbling ride in the avalanche—you might not even know which way is up. Muster enough saliva for a slow spit, and then watch which way gravity takes it. That'll tell you which way is down (and up). Start digging upward. Even if you are only moving a spoonful of snow at a time, the work will still help to keep you warm, and it'll be your best chance for survival.

CARRY A BEACON If you are going to be heading out into avalanche territory, it's only smart to strap on an avalanche beacon. Should the worst occur, this life-saving device will help rescuers find you under the snow. Time is of the essence in a case like this, so give them every chance you can to find you and get you out in time.

244
BUILD A DUFF BED

Long before we had sleeping bags stuffed with European goose down or warm-when-wet synthetic fill, hunters and adventurers still kept warm at night. Here's a way to sleep cozy and warm (well, sort of) using only materials found in nature.

BREAK WIND The first requirement for staying warm (especially if you're motionless and asleep) is no wind. Moving air carries heat from the surface of your skin. Try looking for a sheltered place with as little air movement as possible. It could be a rock overhang, the lee of a big log or blowdown, or even a thick patch of underbrush.

MAKE A BED Clear a spot to sleep, ideally finding or building 18-inch (45-cm) walls or barriers around your nest. Logs, sticks, gear, rocks, and more can be utilized to build your walls.

GATHER INSULATION Collect dry "duff"—leaves, grasses, soft bark, moss, and the like—and fill your bed as fully as you can, the deeper the warmer.

SNUGGLE IN Lie down on your duff bed so you have plenty of insulation between you and the ground. Now pull more of the duff over yourself, covering up everything nicely, and tucking duff around your head and neck. Be sure that you get enough insulation around your feet to keep them warm. If you have a poncho, blanket, or tarp you can spread it over your duff bed to protect against wind and moisture. Only your face should be exposed. Sleep tight!

245 SLEEP INSIDE A FRESH HIDE

Drifting through the timber like a wraith of smoke (I'm making this part up, but knowing him I think that's exactly how he'd move) my friend closed the distance on a herd of elk, several bulls among them bugling intermittently. He held a long muzzleloading rifle in hand, powderhorn slung over his shoulder. A bull showed briefly through the timber and my friend put a round lead ball through his lungs. Drawing his knife to begin the quartering process he glanced at the western horizon—darkness was falling fast, and he was far from camp in unfamiliar territory.

This particular friend was raised by one of the most backcountry-savvy hunters I know—a present-day mountain man for sure. My friend knows the ways of the wilderness and he had no qualms about spending a night away from camp, rather than attempting to stumble his way back through the darkness. So he completed his skinning and quartering chores, rolled up in the fresh hide, and slumbered the night away.

246 CRAWL INTO A CARCASS

Legend tells us of a buffalo hunter who got caught on the open plains in a deadly blizzard. Death would claim him if he didn't find shelter fast, so he pulled the innards out of a big buffalo that he'd just killed, and crawled into the warm body cavity. Three days later, after the blizzard had blown through on its way toward Mexico, his buddies went off in search, and found him trapped inside the frozen buffalo carcass. He was alive, so they chopped him out and warmed him up. I reckon that you could curl up inside any large carcass—buffalo, cattle, or horse—if you were desperate enough. Just make sure that you can get out before it freezes solid through.

247 SLEEP LIKE A HOBO

Should you find yourself in immediate need of shelter, just climb into a contractor grade trash bag, and pull another over your head and torso, cutting a 6-inch (15-cm) hole to breathe through. If you can find dry insulation—clothing, duff, newspaper—pull it inside and distribute it around you. Lie down on something to insulate you from the ground (such as a saddle pad, piled leaves, or evergreen boughs), and get some rest.

248 BE A BACKCOUNTRY PHARMACIST

Some of the best backcountry medicine can be found simply by looking around. Plants and herbs good for treating injuries and ailments, and filling hungry bellies, grow in almost every wilderness setting. Take some time to not only get familiar with the terrain you'll be visiting on your backcountry adventure, but the plants that grow in that area, and you'll have everything that grows at your disposal.

249 USE SOME YARROW

This super-common plant, *Achillea millefolium*, grows all over the American West, from below the ponderosa belt to the timberline. Its cheery white flowers, fern-like leaves, and angular stem brewed into a tea are great for colds, flu, and fever. It's helpful in stanching bleeding, and beneficial for inner ailments such as hemorrhoids, urinary problems, diarrhea, excessive menstrual bleeding, and epididymitis. Rubbed onto the skin, yarrow acts as a mosquito repellent.

250 PICK A PLANTAIN

Plantago major is a common weed found around the world, in grass, lawns, along stream banks, and in pastures. Best when fresh, plantain shines for bite or abrasion treatment. Just pick a leaf, chew it into a bolus, and pack it onto the wound. It's great for taking the sting out of a mosquito bite, or soothing a bee or hornet sting, and is also reputed to be effective on snakebites. Like many herbs it's beneficial for treating cough, bellyache, irritated innards, and so on when taken as a tea, tincture, or decoction. As a side benefit, the small leaves of young plants make a tasty edible green.

251 MULTITASK WITH MULLEIN

Also known as *Verbascum thapsus*, this tall, stately plant is typically found in the lower ponderosa belt in the west, and untended ground elsewhere. Mullein has many uses for a backcountry traveler, most humorously as a substitute toilet paper. The large velvety leaves come with a natural floral design and provide a comfy and effective wipe. The leaves and flowers are effective at treating pain and aiding relaxed sleep when crushed and steeped in sweetened water and sipped throughout the day. (Don't use the seeds.) The dried leaves have been used for centuries to treat a bad cough—just roll your own, or smoke them in a pipe. Exercise moderation; too much can be an irritant.

252 WIELD A WILLOW

The *Salix* genus is an essential first aid plant for a wilderness buff. There are scads of willow varieties, but uses and benefits are virtually the same. The twigs and bark of young or new growth plants are strongest, and when steeped into a tea (or simply chewed slowly) are great for reducing inflammation in joints and membranes, as well as reducing pain or headache. Willow is also a good antiseptic for infections and wounds when slow-boiled into a strong poultice or wash.

253 TRY STINGING NETTLE

Known as *Urtica*, this infamous plant has gotten a bad reputation, but it's actually one of the good guys. It's edible: Gather the small young leaves, roll them up between your fingers to neutralize the spines, and eat them fresh, cook them like spinach, or add to soups. As a medicinal plant, stinging nettle is best used as a tea to treat mild internal bleeding (capillary bleeding from coughing or vomiting, excessive menstruation, nosebleeds), to help recover from the aftereffects of a severe cough, and as a spring tonic. It also promotes bone healing when taken internally.

254 EAT BEAR ROOT

Ligusticum porter, also known as osha or "bear root," is a high-elevation, extremely effective herb. The problem is, osha can be easily confused with water hemlock, which is deadly poisonous. Two distinct differences let you know which plant you're dealing with. Osha roots are rather hairy, and have a brown covering, like a thin bark; hemlock roots are usually smooth, "naked," and light-colored. Osha root smells much like celery, but positively overpowering, while hemlock roots are relatively scentless. Don't harvest or use osha unless you're absolutely positive that you can identify the right plant, otherwise you might kill rather than cure yourself or your patient.

Osha is highly effective at treating sore throats and bronchial inflammation. Simply chew a grape-sized piece of the root; it'll soothe and anesthetize almost immediately. It's great for treating viral infections, lowers blood pressure, and helps relieve the symptoms of altitude sickness. It's one of my all-time favorite herbs (because it works so well) and perhaps because its counterfeit is so dangerous.

255 PICK THESE PLANTS (TO EAT)

These plants are found over most of America, some worldwide. I've included them because they're all readily identifiable, and because they provide a lot of nutrition—enough to keep you alive in a survival scenario.

A COMMON CATTAIL These plants are edible top to bottom. Dig the roots, peel and eat them raw, sliced and dried, or ground into flour. In the spring pull the young shoots and peel the outer leaves away. Eat the tender yellow-gold inner part. They're also good boiled or sautéed. Later in the season, you can bake with the flowers, or dry them for later use. Cattail down can be stripped and used as padding for pillows and insulation.

B PRICKLY PEAR Prickly pear plants are widespread across dry territory. They're a bit hazardous to work with due to their tiny, evil little spines, but the purple fruit that grows atop the pads is tasty and nutritious, and even the pads themselves, skinned and roasted or boiled, provide both food and moisture.

C DANDELION If you're lucky you might even find these in your yard. Eat the young, tender leaves (preferably from a plant that lives predominantly in shade) raw, or in soups or sautés. Pop the yellow blossom in your mouth for a colorful treat, or add them to pancakes like blueberries. Dig the root and roast, dry, and grind it for a coffee substitute.

D BULL THISTLE Thistles (though not delicious) can still provide nutrition. Eat the very young leaves as a salad. Peel the stem and eat the pithy inner core raw or cooked. Dig the roots and crown and boil them with seasoning for a pleasant meal.

E ACORNS These have long been a main source of nutrition for different indigenous peoples around the globe. Gather them as they ripen, or wild critters will eat your share. White oak acorns are more palatable than those from red oaks, but both are edible. Crack the shells off and boil the kernels in water for 45 minutes, changing the water a couple of times to get rid of bitter tannins. Grind into a flour or meal and eat fresh, or dry for later use.

F WATERCRESS Widespread across much of the world, this is ideal cooked like spinach, used in soups, sprinkled on salads and side dishes, and also eaten as a fresh streamside snack. It grows submerged (fully or partially) in and along streams and springs, and has a nice peppery bite, making it the perfect backcountry spice. It's also rich in vitamins and said to increase wit. It does have a superficial resemblance to water hemlock (which is very poisonous), so study up before eating it.

256 BARK UP THE RIGHT TREE

When hunger really sets in, nasty foods begin to taste good. Take tree bark, for example: No one searches out bark as a delicacy, but in desperate times it's a viable source of nutrition. Eat the "tender" inner cambium layer, not the rough, scaly outer bark. Lots of tree varieties have edible bark, including cottonwood, pine, aspen, birch, willow, maple, tamarack, and more. You can eat the bark raw, or shred, boil, and serve under dandelion greens and insect parts, or grind it into flour and serve as gruel for breakfast.

257 SNACK ON BUGS

When things get really tough, accept any food that nature offers—with gratitude. It might be tree bark, stinging nettle, termites, or horseflesh. It may taste terrible, but you'll live.

BE AN ANTEATER Termites and ants are caloric feasts. Just think of the torn-up logs you've passed in the backcountry, where a hungry bear has turned a rotten log to kindling in a search for termites. They must be good to warrant that much effort. Shuffle them in a hot skillet for six or seven minutes before eating. Bon appetit!

GULP DOWN GRASSHOPPERS Wait, those aren't candy bars? Grasshoppers are very common in dry backcountry meadows. Use a shirt or big hat to toss over them, then reach under to secure your prize. (Hint: they move slower during cool mornings and evenings.) To clean them, twist their heads one quarter turn and then pull them off. The entrails—where most of the parasites live—will come out with the head. Discard the head, guts, and legs. Eat them raw or, for more protection from parasites, cook thoroughly.

BLACKLIST SOME BUGS There are a few bugs you should never eat. I'm not enough of an expert to list them all (after all, I do prefer deer, elk, or moose meat), but a good general rule to follow is: if the bug is brightly colored, don't eat it— it's likely toxic.

258 EAT YOUR HORSE

When desperation reaches a climactic point, you may have to eat your horse—especially if he's injured, or likely to starve to death himself. You might find yourself snowed into the high country with no food, no way out, and freezing amid head-high snowdrifts.

As a kid, I knew an old cowboy who (according to legend) had been in a terrible backcountry horse wreck. While riding a green-broke horse through a very narrow slot canyon, the horse blew up and then reared over backward. With no way to escape, the cowboy was caught under the horse, both his legs broken. He shot the horse, straightened and splinted his legs the best he could, and lived on horse meat until he healed up enough to hobble back to town.

This may sound brutal—especially to horse lovers—but should you find yourself in this situation, take advantage of everything your horse has to offer. Eat the meat, of course, and make jerky with the meat that you can't immediately consume. Stretch the skin for a shelter, or cut it into rawhide strips, which are useful for a myriad of tasks. Braid the mane and tail hair into cordage, snares, or other tools. Harvest the back sinew to use for sewing, cordage, or floss. Use the bones for tools. You get the picture.

259 PRAY FOR HELP

It's a simple piece of advice, and one that you're welcome to disregard, should you choose to. But I can tell you this much: Having someone to talk to—even if you don't believe He exists—can be a tremendous relief when you're alone, struggling for your life in the backcountry. And if He does hear you (I'm convinced of it), then perhaps He will send a little help your way.

I'm a religious man, to be sure. Perhaps that's partially due to my time spent in the wilderness, where evidence of God (to my way of thinking) is abundant. God Bless.

260 CARVE A FISHHOOK

Fishhooks don't have to be metal and have eyes. Here's how to make your own all-natural hook in the backcountry.

STEP 1 Find a strong hardwood stick or twig that's about 2 to 3 inches (5–7.5 cm) long. Whittle it down till it's about $^1/_8$ inch (3 mm) in diameter. Carve a point on each end; final length should be just over an inch (2.5 cm). You can use bone or antler to make a stronger hook, but be warned: it's harder to work.

STEP 2 Carve a very shallow "V" groove around the center of the hook. Tie your line around this groove. Add a little sticky pine sap to help hold it in place.

STEP 3 Hold your hook parallel to the line and slide on a fat worm, grasshopper, or grub. Go fishing. When a fish eats your bait, the hook will turn sideways, catching the fish.

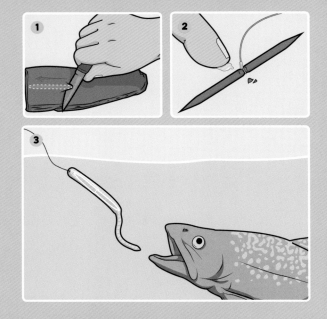

261 KNAP A STONE KNIFE

Should you find yourself in a survival situation without a knife, you can quickly fashion a usable cutting edge with only a suitable chunk of flint (or similar stone such as chert, jasper, chalcedony, or obsidian) and a hammerstone.

FIND SOME FLINT Many areas of the world have usable rock. Look for a piece that's clean—meaning free of fractures and coarse granular areas. It'll need a good platform, or ledge, to break flakes from (A).

GO TOOL SHOPPING Find a good hammerstone. Search along dry creeks and riverbeds for a round or oval tight-grained stone about the size of a big lemon (B).

GET HAMMERED Nestle the flint in the dirt so flakes don't shoot away when you strike. Take a few practice swings with the hammerstone; don't hit it yet. Once you have the swing and angle down (C), take a confident crack at the flint and follow through. You should knock a flake off your flint. Set it aside and clean up the edges of your platform with small strokes and rubbing motions with the hammerstone. Repeat. With practice you'll make good usable blades.

UPBRAID THE EDGES Handle your flakes to learn how they fit in your hands. Then, use your hammerstone to "upbraid" or rub away sharp edges that might contact your skin, so you don't cut yourself when using your new knife.

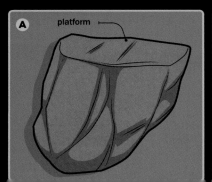

platform

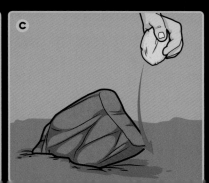

262 SMOKE SOME JERKY

Modern jerky-making methods won't work if you're in the backcountry (unless you have a dehydrator that plugs into a current bush), but people have been preserving meat for centuries without electricity or forced air. Here's how to make your own wilderness jerky.

BUILD A RACK Use straight green sticks to fashion a drying rack that will hold all the meat you want to dry. Make sure it's sturdy—having your meat-laden rack collapse into the dirt would be a real bummer.

SLICE YOUR MEAT Cut all your meat into strips no thicker than ¼ inch (6 mm). If you have salt, sprinkle it (and any other desired seasoning) on both sides of the meat.

HANG IT ALL Set your rack in position (you won't be able to move it once it's loaded) and suspend all your meat strips on the rack.

SMOKE IT Build and then maintain a smoky fire under or downwind of the meat. You shouldn't cook the meat, but a constant cloud of smoke will infuse your jerky with flavor and, more importantly, keep the majority of the flies and hornets off the meat.

STORE YOUR JERKY Once your jerky is good and dry (it should break when bent), pull the strips off your rack and store them in a dry, shady location. Eat it for snacks, use it in soups and stews, or pound it into pemmican.

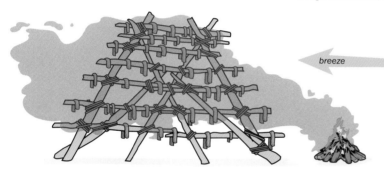

breeze

263 UNHOOK YOURSELF

One of the most memorable backcountry moments that you can experience is the one where you sink a fishhook solidly into your own hide. Not only does it hurt, it also efficiently strips you of all dignity. Now, you can limp your way to the trailhead and a doctor who will numb you and remove the offending hook, or you can toughen up, get it out yourself, and keep fishing. Here's how.

STEP 1 Cut the line off the hook. Tie a loop in a length of string, and place it around the bend of the hook.

STEP 2 Grasp the string firmly with one hand. Use one finger from the other hand to carefully and firmly press the offending hook straight down to loosen the barb. Hold it firmly.

STEP 3 Jerk the hook out. Scream. Tie the hook back on your line and go fishing to help yourself feel better.

Make sure the wound bleeds to cleanse itself, and keep a bit of antibiotic ointment on it to prevent infection.

ARAM SAYS "If the hook is really big, or if the point has broken (or is close to) the surface of your skin, this method may serve better: Simply push the point of the hook out through the skin, snip off the barb with your multi-tool, and back the hook out."

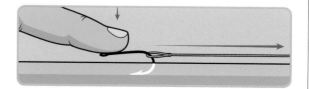

264 TIE IT ALL TOGETHER

If there's one single skill that I have used more often than any other, it's knot tying. Whether I'm pitching my tent at the end of a daylong journey, hanging up elk quarters on a tree or frame after a kill, loading up a backpack or a pack horse before heading on down the trail, or splinting a broken leg or arm, I'm constantly tying knots. If you want to truly do well in the backcountry yourself, learning the ropes is a crucial skill for you to have. Thus, taking the time to teach a few more of the knots that I use the most seems like a pretty good way for me to wrap things up—or to tie it all together.

265 SECURE A SLIPKNOT

The slipknot is probably my most-used knot. It's quick, easy, and above all, dependable. Once tied and jerked tight, though, it's really hard to untie. In critical usage, tie an overhand knot in the working end to prevent the knot from slipping. Here are two ways to tie it.

A DROP OVER Turn a loop in your rope, and then pull a bight of the standing part through. Drop over your tie-to object, and pull tight.

B TIE AROUND Wrap the working end of your rope around a tree trunk, or whatever you want to tie to. Then tie an overhand knot in the working end around the standing part of your rope. Pull tight.

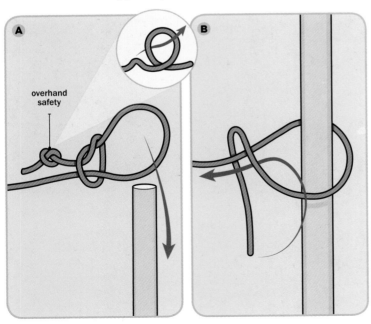

266 MAKE A BLOOD KNOT

This knot is dedicated to leather. It can make a decorative yet strong joint, or "tie," between two small straps or laces.

STEP 1 Pull all your straps nice and tight first—you can't tighten this knot once it's formed.

STEP 2 Make a careful cut along the center of the top strap, about the same length as the strap itself is wide. Stick the lower strap through this cut and pull it tight.

STEP 3 Make a second cut in the second strap (now on top). Stick the first strap through this cut and pull it tight. Smooth and pound the blood knot down until it looks firm and comfy. All done!

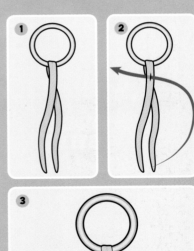

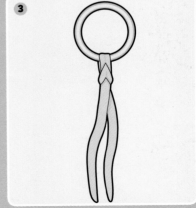

267 LEARN THE PRUSIK KNOT

This is a friction knot—it's one of my least-used, but most important knots. Use it for climbing a rope, tightening tent guy lines, or any task where you need a moveable gripping knot. When grasped, it slides along the standing rope, but if you pull on the ends it holds firm till Hades freezes over.

A GO CLIMBING Take a 6- to 8-foot (1.8- to 2.4-m) piece of small rope and then double it. Wrap the bight around any standing rope (that you want to climb) twice, tucking the double ends through the bight loop each time. Smooth out the wraps and pull tight. Tie the doubled ends together, forming a loop that you can stick your foot through. Repeat with another small rope. Now you can climb your standing rope by lifting one foot while pushing the prusik knot up the rope. Stand on that foot, and raise the other foot and knot. Slowly but surely you'll reach the top.

B TIE A TENT ROPE Wrap the working end of your tent rope around your stake, and then tie a prusik around the standing part by making two wraps below, crossing your working end back across itself, then two more wraps above, going under the crossing part and toward the other wraps as shown. Tighten your knot and then scoot it toward the tent, pulling all the slack out of the standing part. Presto!

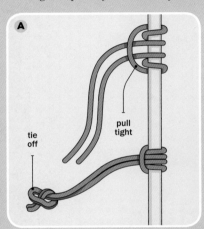

A
tie off
pull tight

B

268 TIE A SHEET BEND

This knot is fantastic for attaching two different-sized ropes end-to-end (A). It's simple, easy to tie, and is considered one of the most essential of all knots. If the rope sizes are drastically different, tie a double sheet bend (B) for more security. Always tie the knot so that both free ends are on the same side of the finished knot. If you don't, it's called a "left hand sheet bend," and might work loose.

Form a bend in the biggest diameter rope. Then, put one end of the other rope through the loop formed by the bend, around both strands of the bend, and tuck it back under itself, making sure that both ends finish up on the same side of the knot. To fashion a double sheet bend, simply take an extra wrap around the bend and under itself, finishing up the knot the same way.

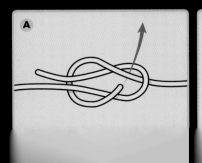

A

B

GO FORTH AND CONQUER

Last October, I needed a little bit of peace and solitude. There were a few days left in Utah's general deer season, so I saddled a horse and a pack horse, tossed sleeping bag, spotting scope, food, and whatnot into the panniers, and swung aboard.

As I rode a few hours into the desert I relaxed, worldly cares falling away with every footfall. I unsaddled on a tiny bench, took up my rifle and climbed a rocky peak. Just before dark ten muley bucks emerged from the slope below me, and I made meat of the biggest. After skinning, quartering, and hanging him to cool, I hiked on through the darkness to my little camp. I tended to my horses, brewed water for a Mountain House meal over a tiny cedar fire, and stretched my bed out on a small tarp. After my dinner, I relaxed in my sleeping bag, watching all the stars blink sleepily in the desert sky above. Life was good.

The backcountry can be a scary place, especially if you're alone. But most men and some women I know have a basic need to take risks, face dangers, and conquer some tough experiences. Emerging from a tough wilderness trip usually leaves us with a faint sense of relief, a strong sense of triumph, and a distant longing to return.

I remember topping out on a high-country ridge in Idaho some years back. I was scouting new country for a future elk hunt, and as I sat there on my horse and looked over that territory, a complete sense of intimidation came over me. I stared across a huge canyon, a couple of miles wide and thousands of feet deep. Ominous clouds loomed over me like huge drunken bodyguards, and thunder grumbled off in the distance. I studied that country for a while—it looked elk rich—then turned my horse and rode down the rain-wet trail toward the trailhead. I returned in September, bow in hand, and that time, that big, intimidating country welcomed me with sunshiny days, frosty nights, and bugling bulls. That time it felt like coming home.

Now, it's time for you to venture forth. You've read this book, hopefully learning enough backcountry wisdom to keep you alive. Take it with you, if you like; I'd rather see it dog-eared and rain-spattered instead of gathering dust on your bookshelf.

The point I'm trying to make is this: Go. Get the gear, practice the skills, then take the plunge. Regardless of whether you're hiking a ridge in Arkansas, canoeing deep in the Boundary Waters, or hunting way up in the Rocky Mountains, the backcountry will feed you with its bounty, cradle you against its rocky breast, and chew you up and spit you out, all in one trip. It'll also feed your soul. You will emerge a stronger, better person, thirsting to return.

You shouldn't simply try to conquer the backcountry—the wilderness will be a far better ally than adversary. Instead, work to conquer your own fears, problems, and insufficiencies. Climb that high peak, cross that running creek, and follow that distant bugle. You'll always end up finding a great deal more than you ever hoped for.

INDEX

A

abdomen, punctured, in horses, 219
abdominal injuries, 210
abdominal pain, 193, 208, 209
acorns, 255
Acute Mountain Sickness (AMS), 200
Africanized bees, 169
airlifts. *See* evacuation
alcohol, 031
altitude, enduring, 005
altitude sickness, 199, 200, 201, 202
animal bites, 233
animals. *See* hunting; *specific animals*
ants, eating, 257
archery. See bows
autumn, dressing for, 046
avalanches, surviving, 243

B

back sores, in horses, 218
backcountry, defining, 001
backpacks. See packs
backtrail, watching, 102, 163
bacon, frying, 029
bait, fishing, 083
balaclavas, 047
barefoot shoes, 052
bark, edible, 256
barrel, keeping clean and dry, 134
base camp, 138
beacons, avalanche, 243
beanies, 047
bear root, 254
bear spray, 071
bearings, getting, 237
bears
    attacks by, 236
    avoiding, 073, 149
    and blood, 216
    preparing protection against, 071, 072
    types of, 166
bees, 169
bells, 069

beverages, 031
bird hunting, 076
bit, inserting in horse's mouth, 113
bites
    animal, 233
    spider, 235
bivy sacks, 019
bivy tents, 137
bivying out, 135, 136, 137
black bears, 166, 236
black eyes, 212
Black Widow spider bites, 235
blades. *See also* knives
    choosing, 032
    sharpening, 033
    stone, making, 261
blanket gun cases, 067
bleeding, severe, 195
blisters, 131, 193
BLM land, 129
blood knots, 266
blood poisoning, 193, 239
blowing, by horses, 127
bomber hats, 047
bones, broken, 193, 205, 206
boots
    breaking in, 051, 131
    choosing, 052
    for horses, 065, 107, 218
bowdrill, starting fire with, 147
bowline knots, 140
bows
    carrying, 133
    hunting with, 075
    repairing, 177
    shooting from horseback, 125
    types of, 126
breakaways, 117
breaking in boots, 051, 131
breaks, 193, 205, 206
breast collars, 068
bridles, 068, 113
broken bones, 193, 205, 206
broken legs, in horses, 219
broken teeth, 213
brown bears, 166

Brown Recluse spider bites, 235
bucks, rut-crazy, 170
bugs
    dangerous, 169
    eating, 257
bull thistle, 255
bulls, rut-crazy, 170
burns, treating, 198
bushwhacking, 095
butterfly knots, 141

C

cameras, 056, 057
campfire cooking, 029, 162
camps
    base, 138
    bivy, 135, 137
    cleaning, 164
    emergency shelters, 151
    finding good site for, 149
    finding in dark, 163
    hunting, 136
    outfitted, 006
    tarp shelters, 150
canteens, 011, 028, 061
cape, caring for, 189
caping animals, 182
carcasses, crawling into, 246
carelessness, with firearms, 172.
    See also safety
cattails, 255
centipedes, 169
charging electronic devices, 057
children, taking into backcountry, 018
chlorine, purifying water with, 030
choking, dealing with, 214
cinch sores, in horses, 218
cleaning
    camps, 164
    fish, 161
    gear, 089
    wounds, 196
clotheslines, in camp, 138
clothing

choosing, 044
dressing for season, 046
footwear, 051, 052, 131
gloves, 048
hats, 049
head coverings, 047
layering, 053
long johns, 045
wild rag, 054
clove hitch, 038
coals, cooking fish over, 162
colors, on topo maps, 098
compasses, 011, 041, 085
contour lines, on topo maps, 097
contractor-grade trash bags (CTBs),
050, 065, 079, 247
cooking. *See also* meals
campfire, 029
fish, 162
cooksets, 011, 137
cordage, 037, 061, 065. *See also* knots
coues deer, hunting, 074
cough, severe, 193
creeks, crossing, 101, 130
crutches, building, 240
curry combs, 065
cuts, caring for, 193, 194

dandelion, 255
deer, hunting, 074
dehydration, 207
diamond hitch, throwing, 115
diamond tarp shelters, 150
direction, sense of, 039
dislocations, reducing, 193, 204
dismounting horses, 226
distances, on topo maps, 099
do it yourself trips, 006
dogs, bringing to backcountry, 070
drinks, 031. See also water
drop camps, 006
duck hunting, 076
duff bed, building, 244

earaches, 211
Easyboots, 065, 107, 218
edible plants, 255, 256
electronic devices, charging, 057
elk, hunting, 074
elk ivories, 190
emergencies. *See also* evacuation;
specific emergency situations
med kits for, 013
signaling distress during, 014
emergency shelters, 151, 245, 246, 247
epididymitis, 215
European mount, 189, 191
evacuation
breaks necessitating, 205, 206
in cases of dehydration, 207
in cases of emergency, 197
evaluating need for, 209
for internal injuries, 210
external frame packs, 010
eye injuries, 212

fall, dressing for, 046
fatwood, 146
fear
facing, 004
handling in horses, 106
feather sticks, 145
feces, disposing of, 155
federal wilderness areas, 129
federal wildlife refuges, 129
feed, for horses, 165, 183
feet, protecting, 131. See also boots
fever, 193, 209, 239
fillings, lost, 213
fire starters, 011, 036, 061, 144, 145, 146
firearms
carelessness with, 172
carrying methods, 133
carrying on horseback, 124

drops and falls with, 178
hunting gear, 074
keeping barrel clean and dry, 134
muzzleloaders, 077
protecting against bears with, 071, 072
saddle scabbards, 066, 068, 086, 124
safety, 080, 172
shooting positions, 174
shooting with pack on, 175
signaling for help with, 238
training with, 176
wool blanket gun cases, 067
firepits, 138
fires
signal, 238
starting, 144, 147, 148
firewood, 138, 144
first aid, 002, 013, 193. *See also specific
injuries or illnesses*
fishhooks
carving, 260
removing from flesh, 263
fishing
bait for, 083
cleaning catch, 161
cooking catch, 162
general discussion, 081
by hand, 157
kits for, 082
traps for, 158
trotlines, setting, 159
trout, 160
fishing line, 084
fitness, importance of, 005
flash flooding, 227
flint knives, making, 261
fly-tents, 019
food. See meals
food poisoning, 193, 207
footwear, 051, 052, 131
Forest Service land, 129
frostbite, 223
full-service outfitters, 006
full-thickness frostbite, 223

INDEX

G

game. *See* hunting
game bags, 079
gear. *See also specific gear*
  absolutely essential, 061, 092
  basic, 011
  bivy hunting, 137
  fishing, 082
  for horsepacking, 065
  hunting, 074
  packhorse, 069
  repairing, 088
  saddle horse, 068
  storing, 089
gloves, 048
Google Earth, 103
GPS units, 039
Graham, Matt, 059
grasshoppers, eating, 257
grit, showing, 132
grizzly bears, 166
group trips, 017
grouse, hunting, 076
gun cases, wool blanket, 067
gun safety, 080, 172. *See also* firearms
gunshot wounds, 193

H

halters, 069, 112
hand-drill, starting fire with, 148
hand-fishing, 157
handheld radios, 055
hatchets, 032, 065
hats, 047, 049
hay, weed free, 183
head colds, 193, 211
head coverings, 047
head injuries, 193
headlamps, 011, 035, 092
heat illness, 229, 230
help, signaling for, 238
herbs. *See* medicinal plants; *specific herbs*

herd, importance to horses, 107
hide, sleeping inside fresh, 245
High-Altitude Cerebral Edema (HACE),
  201, 202
hiking boots, 052
hiking out, decision-making about, 239
hobbles, 068, 069, 111
hooves, caring for, 107
horsepacking. *See also* horses
  bushwhacking, 095
  choosing good mount, 064
  diamond hitch, throwing, 115
  food, carrying, 026
  gear for, 065
  general discussion, 062
  leading horses, 118
  leadrope, handling, 119
  loading up, 116
  meat, carrying, 186, 187
  mess kit for, 027
  options for, 063
  real experiences with, 042
  rules of, 114
  saddling, 110
  setup for horses, 069
  stringing horses, 117
  travel speed, estimating, 094
horses. *See also* horsepacking
  allowing to blow, 127
  bridles, putting on, 113
  bushwhacking with, 095
  caring for, 107, 165, 218, 219, 220
  carrying rifles on, 124
  choosing good, 064
  creeks, crossing with, 101
  dismounting, 226
  eating, 258
  fear in, handling, 106
  feed for, 165, 183
  halters, putting on, 112
  handling, gaining skills in, 002
  hobbling, 111
  inexperienced, danger of using, 043
  lethal injuries to, 219
  obstacles, overcoming, 128
  riding, 121, 122, 128

saddle scabbards, 066, 068, 086, 124
saddling, 109, 110
shooting from horseback, 125
staking, 120
hot spots, on feet, 051, 131, 132
human waste, disposing of, 155
hunting
  in backcountry, 078
  backpacking meat, 188
  bird, 076
  bowhunting, 075
  camps for, 135, 136, 137
  cape, caring for, 189
  caping animals, 182
  dogs, taking along when, 070
  elk ivories, 190
  gear for, 074
  horsepacking meat, 186, 187
  meat, handling, 079, 184, 185
  midday napping while, 181
  with muzzleloaders, 077
  shooting positions, 174
  skinning and quartering game, 184
  trophies, 182, 189, 190, 191, 192
  vantage point, finding, 180
hunting sneakers, 052
hydration, importance of, 132, 207
hyponatremia, 231
hypothermia, 221, 222, 225

I

illnesses, assessing, 193. *See also specific*
  illnesses
immersion foot, 224
impact injuries, 193
impalement, 193, 210
infections, dealing with, 193, 212, 217
injuries. *See also specific injuries; wounds*
  assessing, 193
  defending against, 203
internal, 210
insects
  dangerous, 169
  eating, 257

insulated hiking boots, 052
internal frame packs, 010
internal injuries, 210
iodine, purifying water with, 030
ivories, elk, 190

J

jerky, making, 262
jumper cables, 090

K

key, stashing under vehicle, 090
killer bees, 169
knives
  absolutely essential, 061
  choosing, 032
  machetes, 034
  for processing meat after hunt, 079
  sharpening, 033
  stone, making, 261
knots
  blood, 266
  bowline, 140
  butterfly, 141
  clove hitch, 038
  general discussion, 139, 264
  prusik, 267
  rope tackle, 142
  sheet bend, 268
  slipknot, 265

L

LAF system, assessing broken bones
  with, 205
landmarks, navigating by, 163, 237
landscape, reading, 100
layering clothing, 053
leading packhorses, 118
leadrope, 069, 119
lean-tos, 138, 150

legs, broken, in horses, 219
life-flights. See evacuation
lighters, 092
lightning, 105, 108, 228
long johns, 045
lost persons, 241

M

machetes, 034
maps, 011, 040, 041, 096, 097, 098, 099
meals
  campfire cooking, 029
  mess kit, 027
  planning, 023, 025, 026
  supplementing, 024
meat
  backpacking, 188
  handling after hunt, 079, 184, 185
  horsepacking, 186, 187
  jerky, making, 262
medicinal plants, 248, 249, 250, 251,
  252, 253, 254
medicine, packing, 013
menstruation, 216, 217
midday napping, while hunting, 181
mild hypothermia, 221, 222
minimalists, 059, 061
missing people, 241
mittens, 048
moderate hypothermia, 221, 222
moisture ratings, sleeping bags, 021
monuments, national, 129
moose
  avoiding angry, 170
  confrontation with, 232
  hunting, 074
mountain lions, 171, 173
mountain sickness, 199, 200, 201, 202
mule deer, hunting, 074
mullein, 251
multi-tools, 060, 092
muzzleloaders, 077

N

Nanuq (polar bears), 073, 166
napping, while hunting, 181
national monuments, 129
national parks, 129
navigation
  back to camp, 163
  bearings, getting, 237
  compasses, 011, 041, 085
  gaining skills in, 002
  GPS units, 039
  maps, 011, 040, 041, 096, 097,
    098, 099
non-freezing cold injuries, 224
noodling, 157
North Star, 237
nosebags, 065
notes, taking, 058

O

offhand shooting position, 174
osha, 254
outfitters
  full-service, 006
  horsepack, 063

P

pack boots, 052
pack rope, 069
packhorses. See also horses
  bushwhacking with, 095
  choosing good mount, 064
  diamond hitch, throwing, 115
  food, carrying on, 026
  gear for working with, 065
  general discussion, 062
  leading, 118
  leadrope, handling, 119
  loading up, 116
  meat, carrying, 186, 187
  mess kit for, 027

INDEX

options for, 063
real experiences with, 042
rules of horsepacking, 114
saddling, 110
setup for, 069
stringing, 117
travel speed, estimating, 094
packs
adjusting, 012, 132
basic items to pack, 011
choosing, 008
comparing options, 009
doggy, 070
features of, 007
food, carrying in, 025
frame types, 010
loading, 015
meat, carrying, 188
mess kit for, 027
shooting with pack on, 175
packsaddle pads, 069
packsaddles, 069
pain
abdominal, 193, 208, 209
fixing, 132
foot, 131
panic, dealing with, 242
panniers, 069
parks, national, 129
partial-thickness frostbite, 223
pee, disposing of, 155
pitch pine, 146
planning backcountry trips, 093
plantain, 250
plants
edible, 255, 256
medicinal, 248, 249, 250, 251,
252, 253, 254
poisonous snakes, 167
polar bears, 073, 166
praying, 259
pregnancy, 217
prickly pear, 255
primitive survival, 059
prone shooting position, 174
pronghorn antelope, hunting, 074
prusik knots, 267

punctured abdomen, in horses, 219
purifying water, 011, 030

Q

quartering game, 184

R

radios, 055
rainstorms, 105
reducing dislocations, 193, 204
reins, handling, 121
repair kit, 087
repairs
to bows, 177
to gear, 088
riding horses, 121, 122, 128
rifle scabbards, 066, 068, 086, 124.
See also firearms
rock grommets, 152
rope tackle, 142
ropes. See also cordage; knots
uses for, 037
whip finishing, 143
route, planning, 093
rut-crazy animals, 170

S

saddle bags, 068
saddle horses. See also horses
choosing, 064
setup for, 068
saddle pads, 068
saddle scabbards, 066, 068, 086, 124
saddles, 068
saddling horses, 109, 110
safety
with firearms, 080, 172
when camping, 149
when horseback riding, 122
salt
consuming, 207, 229, 230, 231

preserving cape with, 189
Satellite Personal Trackers (SPOTs), 014
sat-phones, 014
saws, 065
scabbards, saddle, 066, 068, 086, 124
scale
handheld, 065
on topo maps, 099
scarves, 054
scorpions, 169, 234
season, dressing for, 046
seating, in camp, 138
senses, using, 179
septicemia, 193, 239
severe hypothermia, 221, 222
sharpening blades, 033
sheet bend, 268
shelter. See also tents
choosing, 019
creating with tarp, 150
emergency, 151, 245, 246, 247
proper gear for, 020
shoes. See also boots
choosing, 052
for horses, 107, 218
shooting. See also firearms; hunting
from horseback, 125
with pack on, 175
positions for, 174
shots, signaling for help with, 238
shoulder mount, 189, 191
signaling for help, 238
silk scarves, 054
sitting shooting position, 174
skills. See also specific skills
backcountry, necessary, 002
practicing, 003
skinning game, 184
skull plates, 191
sleeping bags, 011, 020, 021, 137
sleeping pads, 011, 022, 137
slings, for firearms, 133
slipknots, 265
slivers, dealing with, 193
snacks, 025, 026, 132, 231
snakes, 167
snowstorms, 105

socks, 051, 052, 131
sodium levels, maintaining, 231
solo trips
  preparing for, 004
  tips for, 016
sores, on horses, 218
space blankets, 061
speed, estimating travel, 094
spiders, 169, 235
spine injuries, 193
splashes, lightning, 228
sprains, caring for, 193
spring, dressing for, 046
spurs, 123
staking horses, 120
standing shooting position, 174
stars, navigating by, 237
staying put, decision-making about, 239
steel canteens, 011, 028, 061
stinging nettle, 253
stitches, for horses, 220
stomach flu, 193, 208
stomach pain, 208, 209
stone knives, making, 261
storage, gear, 089
storms
  lightning, 108
  watching out for, 104
  weathering, 105
strapping firearms on, 133
streams, crossing, 101, 130
stringing packhorses, 117
summer, dressing for, 046
sunrise, navigating by, 237
survival. *See also specific survival situations*
  gear for, stashing in vehicle, 090
  keeping wits in situations of, 003
  primitive, 059
sutures, for horses, 220

tarp shelters, 150
tarps, 019, 065, 069

tea, 031
teeth, problems with, 193, 213
temperature ratings, sleeping bags, 021
tenderloin, 192
tent pack, 011
tents, 019, 020, 137
termites, eating, 257
testicular torsion, 215
thistles, 255
thorns, dealing with, 193
ticks, 169
tires, preparing for trouble with, 090
tooth problems, 193, 213
topographical (topo) maps, 040, 041, 096, 097, 098, 099
toughing it out, 132
trailhead etiquette, 091
training
  with firearms, 176
  before solo trips, 004
  for survival situations, 003
traps, fish, 158
trash, packing out, 164
trash bags, 050, 065, 079, 247
travel speed, estimating, 094
trenchfoot, 224
trips, planning, 093
trophies, 182, 189, 190, 191, 192
trotlines, setting, 159
trout, fishing for, 160

urinary tract infection (UTIs), 217
urine, disposing of, 155

vaginal infections, 217
vantage point, finding, 180
vehicle, preparing for expeditions, 090
venomous snakes, 167
vitamin drink mixes, 031

walkie-talkies, 055
walking sticks, cutting, 101, 130
waste, human, 155
water
  in base camp, 138
  boiling, 029, 030
  contaminated, 156
  crossing, 101, 130
  finding, 153
  for horses, 165
  purifying, 011, 030
  sources of, 154
water hemlock, 254
water poisoning, 207
watercress, 255
waypoint, marking, 163
weed-free horse feed, 183
weight, sleeping bag, 021
whip finishing ropes, 143
wild rag, 054
wilderness, defining, 001
wilderness areas, federal, 129
wildlife refuges, 129
willow, 252
windstorms, 105
winter, dressing for, 046
wire, 065
wits, keeping in survival situations, 003
wolves, 168
wool, 044, 045
wool blanket gun cases, 067
wool socks, 052
wounds
  from animal bites, 233
  cleaning, 196
  cuts, 194
  gunshot, 193
  need for evacuation, 197
  severe bleeding, 195

yarrow, 249

PHOTOGRAPHY CREDITS

All photos courtesy of *Aram von Benedikt* unless otherwise noted.

Backcountry: 011 (5. pot, spork); *Backcountry Access*: 243; *Denver Bryan*: 018, 091, 110, 11, 133; *Buck Knives*: 032 (1. Fixed-Blade Buck "Fishing" Knife, 4. Superlight Buck Skeleton Knife, 5. Superlight Folder by Buck); *Cabela*: 079 (sharpener); *Cavallo Horse & Rider*: 065 (G. easyboots); *Pat Clayton*: 081; *Cliff Gardiner & John Keller*: 067, 145; *Garmin*: 039; *Goal Zero*: 057; *Google Earth*: 103; *Gränsfors Bruk*: 032 (6. Hatchet); *John Hafner*: 014, 041, 048, 056, 061, 062, 070, 075, pg. 82, 093, 131, 176, 181, 199; *Kleen Kanteen*: 011 (7. canteen); *Loews*: 079 (gamebag); *MSR*: 011 (5. stove); *Morakniv*: 032 (3. Lightweight Mora Knife); *Mountain Hardware*: 011 (1. tent, 10. sleeping bag); *Outfitters Supply*: 065 (C. scale); *Portable Aqua*: 011 (water purification) *Priceton Tec*: 035; *Robinsons Equestrian*: 065 (H. curry comb); *Shutterstock*: title page, intro (Backcountry toolkit background), ch. 1 GEAR (background), 001–004, 006, 009 (shoeprint, backpack), 010, 011 (2. backpack, 4. map/compass, 8. headlamp), 013, 016, 017, 019, 022, 023, 027, 029–031, 034, 036, 049, 050 (Backcountry toolkit background), 051, 054 (Backcountry toolkit background), 055, 058, 059, 065 (A. hatchet, B. saw, F. cordage, E. wire, I. tarp, J. trash bags), 072–074, 076, 079 (knives, trash bags), 080, 082, 085, 087, 088, ch. 2 SKILLS (background), 092, 094, 104, 106, 122. 123, 127, 129, 132, 134, 144, 146, 150, 154, 156, 157, 160, 162–171, 173, 178, ch. 3 SURVIVAL (background), 193–196, 198, 203, 205–207, 209, 211–213, 215–218, 221, 223, 224, 227, 228, 231, 233–235, 237–239, 241, 243 (waterfall), 244–246, 249–254, 255 (all photos), 256–259, pp. 212–213, index (background), pp. 220–221; *Jeffrey B. Banke/Shutterstock*: 161; *Slumberjack*: 021 (A. green sleeping bag); *Trail Max*: 065 (D. nosebags); *Therm-A-Rest*: 011 (3. sleep pad), 021 (B. orange sleeping bag); *USGS*: 040, 096; *Ultimate Survival Technologies Brands*: 011 (9. lighter); *Woolpower*: 045

ABOUT THE AUTHOR

Aram von Benedikt grew up in southern Utah, running wild through the desert canyons and high mountains that form the region. Horses, cattle, guns, bows, and ropes were his early teachers, in conjunction with several thousand books that replaced a TV in his home. He studied one winter at Brigham Young University, then chose to return to the School of the Wilderness to further his education. He owned and operated his own small outfitting business in Utah for ten years, before working as wildlife manager for a 386,000-acre low-fence ranch in West Texas for two years. After experiencing an epiphany that raising his kids and being self-sufficient was more important than money, he moved home to Utah to do just that. He now resides in his hometown with his wife, Trina, and five young children, in a log house that he built with his own hands.

Aram has hunted and guided from Arizona to Montana, and for everything from javelina to moose. He's hunted extensively with rifle, traditional muzzleloader, and bow, among other things harvesting a Henry Mountains Bison with a longbow, and the largest bull elk ever killed (402 gross) with a Flintlock rifle. He builds his own saddles, bows, arrows, longrifles, and buckskins, and trains his own horses. He fell into the outdoor writing profession accidentally, when an editor got the impression that he had "authentic" experience and ability, and enough skill with the English language to make himself understood—sort of. It's now competing with his kids and beef cows for attention.

ABOUT THE MAGAZINE

Since it was founded in 1898, *Outdoor Life* magazine has provided backcountry hunting and fishing hints, survival tips, wilderness skills, gear reports, and other essential information for hands-on outdoor enthusiasts. Each issue delivers the best advice in sportsmanship as well as thrilling true-life tales, detailed gear reviews, insider hunting, shooting, and fishing hints, and much more to nearly 1 million readers. Its survival-themed Web site also covers disaster preparedness and the skills you need to thrive anywhere from the backcountry to the urban jungles.

A NOTE TO READERS

ACKNOWLEDGMENTS

I'd like to thank Mariah Bear, Allister Fein, Ian Cannon, and the rest of the crew at Weldon Owen for their tireless encouragement, help, and support. I want to thank editors Andrew McKean, Alex Robinson, Natalie Krebs, and John Taranto for believing in me, and going the extra mile to prove it. I owe thanks to my brother, Joseph von Benedikt, for dragging me into the writing profession on his coattails, as well as for the gems of literary advice he's handed me along the way. He's the real professional.

Most of all I want to thank my lovely wife Trina, who has had to pull a lot of my slack (bucking hay, feeding cattle, processing meat, raising kids and so on) while I've been chained to this keyboard. In addition, anytime I found myself wandering about, searching for something to write that I couldn't find, she'd invariably come up with the perfect solution. She patiently put up with my grumpy attitude, dropped everything to take a photo that I needed badly, and fed me when I was hungry. And, no, you can't borrow her while you're writing your own book.

I dedicate this book to my children—may you experience the depth and magnificence of the backcountry as I have, and may it teach you to work hard, have integrity, and find joy.

Lastly, I need to thank those who have taught me about the backcountry: the mountain men who've mentored me, the horses who have carried me, the wildlife that has fed me, and the deep wilderness itself that has nurtured me.

OutdoorLife

CHIEF EXECUTIVE OFFICER Eric Zinczenko
VP, PUBLISHING DIRECTOR Gregory D. Gatto
EDITORIAL DIRECTOR Anthony Licata
EDITOR-IN-CHIEF Andrew McKean
MANAGING EDITOR Jean McKenna
SENIOR DEPUTY EDITOR John B. Snow
DEPUTY EDITOR Gerry Bethge
ASSISTANT MANAGING EDITOR Margaret M. Nussey
ASSISTANT EDITOR Natalie Krebs
SENIOR ADMINISTRATIVE ASSISTANT Maribel Martin
DESIGN DIRECTOR Sean Johnston
ART DIRECTOR Brian Struble

ASSOCIATE ART DIRECTORS Russ Smith & James A. Walsh
PHOTOGRAPHY DIRECTOR John Toolan
PHOTO EDITOR Justin Appenzeller
PRODUCTION MANAGER Judith Weber
DIGITAL DIRECTOR Nate Matthews
ONLINE CONTENT EDITOR Alex Robinson

2 Park Avenue
New York, NY 10016
www.outdoorlife.com